2012

# The Jewish Press in the Third Reich

This study throws light for the first time on a neglected but very important aspect of Jewish life in the Third Reich, the Jewish Press. This term does not refer to the significant number of Jews involved in the German media up to the Second World War but to the 65 newspapers and magazines published by 53 publishing houses with a specific German-Jewish readership in mind. These publications appeared until the end of 1938 and allow a valuable insight into the situation of the German Jews under the Nazi regime. They movingly document the efforts of the Jews to cope with the increasing precariousness of their existence in Germany and to find solutions to the growing problems of survival. In the 1930s, more than ever before, the press became an important platform for debate, encouragement, information, warnings about the latest anti-Jewish measures and, last but not least, entertainment. It therefore assumed a vital function within the Jewish community. At the same time, however, as Jewish life became more and more restricted due to anti-Jewish policies, pressure on the Jewish press in the form of ever heavier censorship increased and made its task more and more difficult until the Nazis put an end to it altogether, thus depriving the Jewish community of a vital link with the outside world and signalling the end of Jewish life in pre-war Germany.

**Herbert Freeden**, author and journalist, lives in Jerusalem.

**William Templer** is a professional translator and teaches in the Department of English Philology at Cyril and Methodius University, Veliko Turnovo, Bulgaria.

# The Jewish Press in the Third Reich

## By Herbert Freeden

*Translated by William Templer*

**BERG**
*Providence / Oxford*

Published in 1993 by

**Berg Publishers, Inc.**

Editorial offices:
165 Taber Avenue, Providence, RI 02906, U.S.A.
150 Cowley Road, Oxford, OX4 1JJ, UK

**Library of Congress Cataloging-in-Publication Data**
Freeden, Herbert, 1909–
    [Jüdische Presse im Dritten Reich, English]
    The Jewish press in the Third Reich / by Herbert Freeden :
translated by William Templer.
        p.  cm.
    Translation of: Die jüdische Presse im Dritten Reich.
    Includes bibliographical references and index.
    ISBN 0-85496-686-2
    1. Jewish newspapers—Germany—History—20th century.
    2. Jewish periodicals—Germany—History—20th century.  3. Jews—
Germany—History—1933–1945.  4. Germany—Ethnic relations.  I.
Title.
PN5650.F713    1992
073'.089924—dc20                                    92–5743
                                                      CIP


A CIP catalogue record of this book is available from the British Library.
ISBN 0-85496-686-2

Printed in the United States at E.B. Edwards Brothers, Ann Arbor, MI.

Lost post in the war of liberation ...
I fought
Without any hope of victory,
I knew I'd never return home
In one piece.

HEINRICH HEINE

# Contents

# Tables

# Preface

M y intention here has not been to write a monograph about individual Jewish papers in Germany, not even within a specific period (1933–1939). Rather, I have endeavored to explore the web of interconnections between these papers and periodicals and to describe, over and beyond the purely journalistic elements, the ways in which the problematic nature of Jewish existence during that era manifested itself in the disputes and debates of the time.

Each of the topics dealt with here – *Deutschtum* and Judaism, assimilation and Zionism, Palestine and the diaspora, Orthodoxy vs. religious liberalism, European or Jewish culture, emigration vs. the maintenance of Jewish positions, as well as the problems of the Jewish communities (*Gemeinden*), the Jewish woman and, last but not least, the editors of Jewish periodicals – reveals more than just the image of a press in a "state of emergency." Their examination also provides, to a degree, a concrete picture of German Jewry under the Nazi regime at a time when it was still able to express itself ideologically, to organize voluntarily and to adopt practical measures for its own rescue.

The constraints of the situation forced upon them from outside often imbued relations between various Jewish periodicals with a certain militancy. The pressure was so great, the threat so immense, that people were unwilling to accept compromise and partial solutions in the struggle for survival; each believed to be in possession of the sole valid truth, and hence fought for his own standpoint down to the ultimate test of strength. Only later did it become evident that what really mattered was not so much the formulation of Jewish concepts; rather, the politics and policies of the environment were the determinant factor. Yet no mortal has the faculty to presage the vagaries of history.

Nonetheless, it is fair to contend that the discussions in the Jewish press, carried on with conviction, emotion and impatience, made a major contribution toward helping to clarify matters in spheres such as education, culture and the economy, job procurement and welfare services. In particular, the question of emigration – whether to Palestine or other countries overseas – and the professional retraining such emigration often necessitated, was broached at an early point in the press. Indeed, it was the merit of the Jewish press that it provided momentum to push forward with the process of internal centralization of German Jewry, and that it appealed to the Gemeinden to adapt to the needs and exigencies of the hour.

No one is called upon to sit in judgment, neither those who witnessed the events nor the historians who chronicle them. We can only depict and present things as they actually were. Martin Buber once recounted the tale of an old Chinese philosopher who was asked why he was actively engaged in pursuing people, trying to interest them in his teachings. A beautiful maiden should remain at home and be courted; if she were to spend too much time cavorting about in the streets, soon no one would pay her any further attention. The sage answered that in the prevailing corrupt times, the situation when it came to matters of intellect and the spirit was far worse than for beautiful girls: if one did not actively press people, issues of *Geist* would go unnoticed. Political thought, Buber observed, shared a similar fate in eras marked by varying degrees of "corruptedness": "the political idea does not rest contained in itself – it craves realization, and that realization is necessarily one that is determined by history. Thus, the political idea must be fearful lest it perchance miss its hour" (*Jüdische Rundschau*, May 29, 1934).

I would like to take this opportunity to express my thanks to the Leo Baeck Institute, Jerusalem, for having entrusted me with the task of investigating the Jewish press in Nazi Germany, and providing me with helpful and kindly assistance during the course of my work. I am also grateful to my translator, William Templer, for his painstaking rendering of the text into English, and the preparation of a handy glossary.

JERUSALEM, SUMMER 1991

# Introduction

"What the Jewish press is today requires a special explanation, since its image among the general public is misshapen, contorted as if viewed in a distorting mirror. The best approach is to proceed on the basis of a principle of Indian philosophy, stating first what it is not in order to comprehend its nature. By no means is it what is termed the *Judenpresse*."[1]

The term "Judenpresse" is part of the lasting inventory of the vocabulary of German anti-Semitism. It was used in reference to those papers that anti-Semites believed were substantially influenced, published or edited by Jews.[2] In the main, this meant the liberal papers in the larger urban areas catering to the needs and interests of the progressively minded middle classes: papers such as those put out by the publishing houses of Mosse and Ullstein in Berlin, or the *Frankfurter Zeitung* founded by Leopold Sonnemann in 1856. Although it was taken over by the firm of I.G. Farben in the 1920s, the *Frankfurter Zeitung* nonetheless was able to maintain a certain independent attitude up to its prohibition in 1934.

The editors-in-chief of the representative papers published by Rudolf Mosse and Ullstein houses were Jews. Theodor Wolff was chief editor of the *Berliner Tageblatt*, while Georg Bernhard headed the editorial staff of the *Vossische Zeitung*, the oldest existing German paper, acquired in 1913 by Ullstein. In the 1920s, the later Reich Superintendent of Culture, Hans Hinkel, had spoken derisively of the "Jewish *Vossische Zeitung*."[3]

The *Berliner Tageblatt*, founded in 1872, had only three editors-in-chief up to its demise in 1939: Arthur Levyson until 1906, Theodor Wolff up to 1933, and then Paul Scheffer for its last six years, while the Nazis were still interested in maintaining the paper in its old form.

After the change of ownership in the Mosse publishing house, the *Jüdische Rundschau* commented:

> We have often pointed out that the *Berliner Tageblatt* does *not* deserve the epithet of a "Jewish" periodical. A newspaper is a double-edged affair: on the one hand, it is an intellectual tribune; on the other, a business enterprise. The fact that the owners or beneficiaries of the business firm are Jewish does not entitle anyone to regard such an institution as being representative of something "Jewish" in an intellectual sense. We Jews must suffer because this misconception is unfortunately quite widespread among broad segments of the population. For that reason, we should now be especially pleased about this change which has clarified matters. Since the *Berliner Tageblatt* can no longer be viewed by the public as a "Jewish paper" [*Judenblatt*], we have also been relieved of any necessity to object should its position be interpreted as supposedly being a "Jewish" one.[4]

Rudolf Mosse and Ullstein certainly did not enjoy any sort of monopoly in Berlin. The publishing concern founded in 1883 by August Scherl, whose leading paper was the *Lokalanzeiger*, was taken over by the firm of Hugenberg in 1916; that company gradually gained control of some 80 conservative and Deutschnational papers, while also exercising a key influence on a large segment of the provincial press. This position of power was facilitated by a structural circumstance: of the almost 5,000 daily papers in the Weimar Republic, only about 200 had a full editorial staff; the majority of such dailies were local editions of larger papers. The latter furnished the main section, consisting of news on politics, the economy, culture and entertainment, sports and a serialized novel, and all that was added in the respective town were the columns with local items.[5]

Almost 600 papers were Catholic in orientation, closely identified in political terms with the Zentrum party and the Bavarian People's party. The Social Democrats had some 200 papers, the Communists 50. The disproportion in 1932 between newspaper circulation figures and ballots cast at the polls dramatically points up the limits of the influence exercised by the press on the voting public. At the time of the Reichstag elections that year, the national-bourgeois forces (German-Nationals, the German People's party, and related groups) had a daily press with a circulation totalling 3.7 million; they received 2.8 million votes. The

Liberals controlled papers with a circulation of 3.2 million copies, and got only 400,000 votes. In contrast, the Social Democratic press had a circulation of 1.2 million copies, but some eight million votes were cast for the party. The Catholic parties had a circulation figure of 1.7 million for their daily papers, yet received 5.8 million votes. Although the National Socialist press had a mere 700,000 in circulation volume, the party gained 13.8 million votes at the ballot box.[6]

Why were there so many Jews associated with the press in Germany, more so than in other countries? Why did the press hold such a strong attraction for them? Numerous young Jews in the nineteenth and twentieth century had an unmistakable aversion to inherited commercial pursuits, especially the notion of making money as the meaning and purpose of life. Many strove to find a "more idealistic" occupation, in particular to acquire a higher education. However, educated Jews often encountered closed doors barring careers in civil service and university teaching. Such discriminatory practices pushed the young Jew into the political opposition; and the easiest way to articulate that oppositional stance was by means of the pen, possibly even because many young Jews may have had a greater natural facility to express their convictions. "At school, there was a marked aptitude for excellence in German composition among Jewish children, as well as a quite evident pleasure in writing. . . . All this also helped explain why there was such an especially large number of Jews among journalists writing on cultural affairs. However, the noticeably high percentage of Jews among business-page editors can be accounted for by reference to their aptitude for economic affairs."[7] It is no accident that Heinrich Heine and Ludwig Börne can be ranked among the classic writers of German journalism.

German Jewry, as it developed into modernity in the nineteenth century, exercised a formative influence on Jewry in Russia and Galicia.[8] German culture held out such an attraction for Eastern European Jews that a number of Jewish families took the name of Schiller in order to underscore their desire to embrace the freedom of Western culture by choosing the name of a German poet of liberty as their own.

During the years 1933–1938, the Jewish press in Germany developed largely from two principal taproots: the active participation of Jewish journalists in the German press and the time-honored tradition of more than one hundred years of a purely religious/homiletic Jewish press, involving papers founded and run mainly by rabbis. The influence of such periodicals was marginal. The Jewish circles they were able to penetrate were by nature circumscribed, and their readership in any case consisted only of those who were interested in Jewish affairs. One exception to this were Jews living in the smallest Jewish communities in the provinces; for them, the Jewish paper was their only connection with Jewish life. "The general Jewish public before 1933 was unfamilar with the Jewish papers – as unfamiliar with the Jewish press as they were with Jewish life in general. The Jewish papers had no desire to introduce elements from beyond the framework of Jewish matters into the purview of their coverage."[9]

Since emancipation, Jewish papers had been a mirror of Jewish life only to a limited degree. As German Jews began to take part in the political, intellectual and cultural life of their surroundings, they stopped identifying with the narrow parochial interests of Jewish papers. The latter dealt principally with the local Jewish *Gemeinde* and its religious and social functions, and with the religious world of ideas, gradually being eclipsed by mounting secularization.

> Whoever wishes to study Jewry of the nineteenth and twentieth century from the pages of the press would best not occupy himself with those papers that call themselves Jewish. . . . Rather, the real intellectual and political history of German Jews should be extracted from the general press of the age. . . . Viewing the period up to 1933 in retrospect, it is evident that papers such as the *Berliner Tageblatt* and *Frankfurter Zeitung*, the periodicals of publishing houses such as Mosse and Ullstein, and products like the *Neue Rundschau* of the S. Fischer publishing house . . . provide, by their nature, a greater source of testimony as to the intellectual creativity and thinking of German Jews during this period.[10]

Jewish papers under Nazism had to serve two functions: to enhance Jewish consciousness among German Jews, and at the same time to take over the role of the general press for the Jewish reader, because that readership was no longer able to rely for information on papers that insulted and humiliated it – a press of which 82.5 percent had, by 1944, been incorporated into the Nazi publishing conglomerate.[11]

Max Amann, the head of that conglomerate (*Zentralverlag der NSDAP Franz Eher Nachf.* [Central Publishing House of the National Socialist Party, formerly Franz Eher Press]), had, despite his vested business interests, nonetheless been appointed Reich Director of the Press and President of the Reich Chamber of the Press. Hitler sent Amann a handwritten note congratulating him on the occasion of his 50th birthday: "There is no area in which there has been greater implementation of the fundamental principles of National Socialism than the press."[12]

Speaking at the NSDAP Party Convention in 1936, Amann defined the role of the press as follows:

> The press should . . . familiarize the reader, engaged in the daily struggle of his life, with what is happening...in the world around him, in this way providing a prerequisite both for the enhancement and development of the individual reader's life within the framework of the whole and for advancement of the community. . . . The paper should bring the community to the reader, and the reader to the community, thus placing him within the midst of the events of the day. . . .[13]

In the preface to the *Handbuch der Reichskulturkammer*, its editor, Reich Superintendent of Culture Hans Hinkel, who also held the title of "Special Representative of the Minister for Popular Enlightenment and Propaganda, Charged with Supervision of Non-Aryans Active in Cultural and Intellectual Matters within the Area of the Reich," commented: "Within the melting pot of National Socialist ideas, there came into being the Reich Chamber of Culture, and with it the long-desired community of all those who create culture and art. . . .The entire German people owes the fact that all this could become a reality . . . to Adolf Hitler . . . the first artist of the nation."[14]

Writing in his autobiography, Hinkel observed: "Already at an early age, a propitious fate showed me the way to Adolf Hitler. . . . I found that auspicious path as one among a hundred thousand. . . ."[15] His style turns less declamatory when speaking about Jewish matters:

> Actually, we shouldn't have anything against it, should we, my dear friend, if the Rothschilds and Warburgs finally now wish to "build up Palestine," according to the latest reports published in the *Israelitisches Familienblatt* – after they have been "padding" their money pouches for a decade, taking from the nations of their hosts. – O, may you build Palestine quite soon, so you can construct your "tabernacles" there, you "friends of man" and pretentious democratic creeps [*Edeldemokröten*]! – Hooray, hurrah, Israel rejoice!... Yes, and the pictorial supplement of the *Israelitisches Familienblatt* is also stupendous,

really very enchanting (if only it didn't "smell so nice," redolent with the fragrance of garlic). – This is the tone in which I dealt with the products of the Jewish press.[16]

The exclusion of Jews from the newly defined *Volksgemeinschaft*, their systematically implemented social isolation and cultural segregation, brought about an "internal autonomy of organized Jewish life,"[17] necessitating the formation of a "Jewish economic sector" within which Jews worked among and for Jews.[18] The overall picture offered by Jewish reactions in Germany during the period 1933–1939 was recently termed by historians "self-assertion in an emergency."[19]

Within the confines of this sharply circumscribed framework, the Jewish press was entrusted with a difficult task: to inform and encourage its readership, to console and entertain, to provide leadership and serve as a source of warning. Despite its careful reserve under the prevailing pressures, a number of dailies in western Germany published an open attack on the Jewish press in October 1934: "The brazenness of the Jewish papers is becoming downright insufferable. While the government decided to permit the continued publication of these papers on the assumption that it would allow Jews a possibility to exchange views among themselves on cultural and religious questions, the Jews have turned their papers into a political-ideological battlefield. Each week, the rabbis sit there in judgment of National Socialist Germany." The *Israelitisches Familienblatt* commented: "We fail to understand on what basis they can make this accusation." Nothing, the paper averred, was further from the Jewish press than to deviate from its old, time-tested principles and, precisely at that point in time, to inadmissably blur the boundaries erected by the new state between itself and its Jewish population. Yet, the reply went on, reserve and non-participation in German political life did not mean that one should go off into the corner of the disinterested to sulk in silence.[20]

Arno Herzberg observed that the Jewish press had formerly led a quiet life. Back then, the Jewish reader had basically been in the same situation as the German reader: it had been necessary for him to consult several papers in order to grasp "truth" as refracted in the mirror of differing opinion. Now, being Jewish was something no longer open to choice. The Jewish reader, Herzberg stressed, wanted to find the Jewish answer to the events of the time in his paper. Since he felt unable to cope with the situation, he wished to find out if the Jewish press was in a position to do so. He wanted the paper to show him the way to find a meaning in life or see that meaning confirmed. In a word – he wished to recognize himself reflected in the mirror of the paper.[21]

Some three decades later, Robert Weltsch asked if editors had erred: was what we tried to do in those years 1933–1939 mistaken? Had the terrible end that events took exposed our false judgment?

> Those are questions of conscience with which our backward-looking view on history is unavoidably interlinked. Whoever believed that a proper solution to the Jewish question in Germany would be feasible and that the "world" would not permit excesses and infringments of the law beyond a certain measure was mistaken. There were many who falsely assessed the situation at that time, not just Jews. . . . Nonetheless, perhaps it is possible to maintain that it was right to protect the Jews in 1933 from panicking and falling prey to despair, it was right to encourage them to act on their own behalf within the framework of what was possible – i.e., to also create the organizational framework within which they were able to exist. We misused Biblical quotations and lines from the prophets for the purposes of journalism. There were many things that we exaggerated and evaluated in a false light. Yet the objective observer also has to concede that the efforts during those years 1933–1938 were not undertaken in vain. They achieved more...than can be proven by mere facts. . . .[22]

Perhaps it should be recalled in this connection that nearly 300,000 of the approximately 500,000 Jews in Germany counted in the 1933 census[23] were in fact able to emigrate.[24] The contribution of the Jewish press in this specific connection was considerable.

Lived history in retrospect always takes on melancholic undertones. While that history was still the living present, a Jewish journalist attempted to take stock: "A battle is only lost when you *think* it is lost – as a saying goes attributed to the French General Chief-of-Staff Marshal Foch. It is known that this view had a certain effect in various different historical situations, even where it was . . . not a matter of a contest between equal opponents, but involved the acceptance of legislative acts. . . ."[25]

# Notes

1. Bodenheimer, 1928, p. 125, cited in *Documenta Judaica*, Cologne, 1963, p. 415.
2. Ernst Kahn, "Die Judenpresse," *LBI Bulletin*, 5 (1958), p. 13ff.
3. Hinkel, 1938, p. 253.
4. *Jüdische Rundschau*, April 13, 1933.
5. Sonderdienst Inter Nationes, "Die Geschichte der deutschen Presse," SO 4/67/D, Bonn, p. 15; see also H. W. Goldstein, "Die deutsche Presse und die Juden," *Israel Nachrichten*, July 28, 1978.
6. Sonderdienst Inter Nationes, p. 5f.
7. Kahn, "Die Judenpresse," ibid.
8. See Katz, 1986.
9. *Berliner Jüdisches Gemeindeblatt*, September 5, 1935.
10. Weltsch, 1957, p. 105: "In his brochure 'Press and Jewry,' Vienna 1882, Isidor Singer listed a total of 103 Jewish newspapers and journals appearing in 1880. Of these, 30 were in German. . . ." Cited in Fraenkel 1967, p. 7.
11. Sonderdienst Inter Nationes, p. 8.
12. Ibid. Max Amann, Hitler's master sergeant in World War I and party member no. 3, was first managing director of the NSDAP.
13. Hinkel, 1937, p. 209. Law on Reich Chamber of Culture, September 22, 1939: "On the basis of this legislation, chambers are created for the individual branches of culture (literature, press, radio, theater, music, plastic arts). Membership in one of the chambers is a precondition for being active in one of of cultural branches," in Walk, 1981, p. 52. Non-Aryans were not accepted for membership in the chambers.
14. Hinkel, 1937, p. 13. Ibid., p. 242: "Vertrieb jüdischer Zeitungen und Zeitschriften" [Distribution of Jewish Newspapers and Periodicals]. See also "Das Sonderreferat Reichskulturwalter Hinkel," Dahm, 1979, p. 72ff.
15. Hinkel, 1938, "Zum Geleit."
16. Ibid., "Rosinkes und Mandeles," p. 233. Hinkel's manner of expression grew more moderate as a result of his working together with the Reich Federation of Jewish Cultural Leagues [Reichsverband der Jüdischen Kulturbünde], in particular with its director, Dr. Kurt Singer; Hinkel had an interest in preserving Jewish cultural activity, since his job depended on it. See Freeden, 1964, p. 40ff.
17. Herbert A. Strauss, "Jüdische Autonomie im Rahmen der NS-Politik," in Paucker, 1986, p. 125ff.
18. Barkai, "Der wirtschaftliche Existenzkamp der Juden 1933–1938," in Paucker, 1986., p. 153. See also Barkai, 1989, esp. p. 47ff.
19. "Selbstbehauptung in der Not," the title of a symposium organized by the Leo Baeck Institute, Berlin in 1985. See also Reinhard Rürup, "Das Ende der Emanzipation," in Paucker, 1986, p. 97ff.
20. *Israelitisches Familienblatt*, November 1, 1934; the quotation from newspapers in western Germany can also be found there.
21. *Der Morgen*, May 1934.
22. Robert Weltsch, *MB*, Tel Aviv, October 18, 1963. "The newspapers...that are endeavoring to master the situation with a finely tuned sensitivity for what is appropriate each and every day, and in whose columns all the abominations, as well as all the great and heroic aspects of our generation find visible expression, will provide a faithful mirror of this period of our much-agitated history for those who – sometime, somewhere, in another day and age – shall pursue the traces of our fate." Siegfried Braun, in *Frankfurter Israelitisches Gemeindeblatt*, July 1935.
23. *Berliner Jüdisches Gemeindeblatt*, December 8, 1934.
24. Werner Rosenstock, "Jewish Emigration from Germany," in *Yearbook Leo Baeck Institute* (hereafter *YLBI*), 1 (1956), p. 373ff.
25. H.B.[Hans Bach], in: *Der Morgen*, June 1935.

# 1

# Humanism Censored

The fact that there was a Jewish press in Nazi Germany can be compared with the existence of the Jewish cultural leagues (Kulturbünde) – both served as instruments that attempted to inform or entertain a Jewish public by means of media for and by Jews. There were Jewish papers, put out by Jews for a Jewish readership, and Jewish theater, music, fine arts – created by Jews, and aimed exclusively at a Jewish audience. Yet it would be a mistake to regard this as unlimited cultural autonomy. Both the newspapers and Kulturbünde were watched from all sides, threatened and spied upon by the Reich Chamber of Culture, the Nazi party and, of course, the Gestapo.

Contrary to the general view, there was no system of pre-censorship of the Jewish press in Nazi Germany. Rather, there was a procedure of post-censorship, except for the publications of the cultural leagues. Like all public functions put on by the Kulturbünde, they were subject to the censor's red pencil before appearing in print or on the stage.[1]

The practice of post-censorship, "a method of Government control copied from Fascist Italy,"[2] was also applied to the German newspapers; in their case, however, German editors were given guidelines and pointers in the daily official press conferences. "During the twelve years of Hitler's dictatorship, it is believed some 75,000 secret directives, guidelines, 'phraseology prescripts' [*Sprachregelungen*] and prohibitions on reporting were issued to the editorial offices of German newspapers and periodicals. Initially, it was a sporadic procedure, not completely developed until during the war years."[3] Pre-censorship for the German press was introduced on August 26, 1939, a few days before the beginning of World War II.[4]

9

However, Jewish editors were not provided with guidelines or suggestions. They had to rely on their own judgment and the experience of their colleagues in order to discover what it was the censor might possibly object to. A false assessment in that regard could lead to the suspension of the paper or the arrest of those responsible, with the possibility of a prison term or even incarceration in a concentration camp.

"Each writer or editor had to be his own censor. Everyone knew that the sword of Damocles was suspended over his head. If he printed something that displeased the police or the Propaganda Ministry, nobody could protect him against the inferno of the Concentration Camp. This was one of the devilish devices of the regime; sometimes it would have been easier to pass the responsibility to the censor."[5]

Thus, for example, the publishing house Philo-Verlag in Berlin received the following signed confirmation on July 15, 1935 from the office of state police, district Berlin: "This is to confirm the confiscation on July 13, 1935 at your publishing house of issue no. 4 of the monthly *Der Morgen* for July 1935. The confiscation was ordered by the office of the Secret State Police [Gestapo] in the interest of public safety and order, in accordance with para. 1 of the decree of February 2, 1933 for the territory of Prussia, because the magazine contained an assertion that Jews in Germany could boast of 'cultural achievements'."[6]

Fritz Neuländer, of the *Jüdisches Gemeindeblatt* in Cologne, was sentenced to six months in prison and his paper suspended because he had added his own commentary to a quotation from a Nazi newspaper. From that point on, in 1937, quotations from German papers were allowed to be reprinted only without commentary; starting in 1938, Jewish periodicals were prohibited from quoting German papers altogether. Not until 1937 did Hinkel's office issue a list of topics that the Jewish press was forbidden to touch on. Thus, for example, no mention was permitted of the anti-Jewish policies of the Polish government or Italian colonial policies.[7]

A rare case occurred in the summer of 1935: Goebbels wrote personally to a Jewish editor, prompted by a commentary on one of his speeches that had been published by the *Jüdische Rundschau*. On August 14, 1935, the Reich Minister for Popular Enlightenment and Propaganda sent the following communication to its editor-in- chief, Dr. Robert Weltsch:

The *Jüdische Rundschau*, in issue no. 53 of July 9, 1935, contains an article entitled "Der Jude ist auch ein Mensch" [Jews are Human Beings Too] dealing with remarks on the Jewish question I made in a speech on June 29, 1935. The article criticizes the standpoint of the bourgeois intellectuals, which I reject, namely "that Jews are human beings *too*," stating that not only are Jews human beings too, but that Jews must be human beings in a *conscious manner*, and should be *conscious* Jews as well. Your periodical was suspended as a result of this publication. That suspension will be cancelled; nonetheless, I wish to warn you in no uncertain terms about such polemics, and fully expect that I shall have no cause in future to lodge any complaint against your publications. Signed (for the Minister) Dr. Jahncke.[8]

Naturally, the frequent suspension orders issued against the papers had grave economic and psychological consequences. "Each one of the Jewish newspapers, and especially the *CV-Zeitung* and the *Jüdische Rundschau*, had become the only source of income – not only for their small and regular staffs, but also for so many Jewish journalists that the paper's suspension would have meant disaster for hundreds of people. Whenever an edition was confiscated or a paper suspended, the wildest rumors spread among the Jews who believed that the end had come."[9]

It is not always accurate to say that you can rely on what is written in black and white; here and there, reading of such papers could lead to certain misinterpretations. The Jewish press in Germany had two layers. On top lay the conformistic coat of paint, as expected. Yet anyone who scratched off the thin surface layer and peered beneath could read the signs – and understand their meaning. The editors had developed an expertise in appropriating the standard accepted nomenclature in order to satisfy the censor, only then to suddenly drop a backdoor hint; they might make an allusion or suggest a word that served to cast a revealing or ironic light on what had been stated previously.

An apt example of this is the review of the motion picture film "Chicago" on the opening of the "Jewish Film Stage" in December 1938, published in the *Jüdisches Nachrichtenblatt* only six short weeks after the November 9–10 pogroms and the burning of the synagogues: "A city is ablaze, and the fire department looks on with folded hands. All hoses have been connected, the ladders positioned, the pumps made ready – but no one makes a move to turn them on. The firemen wait for commands, but none is sounded. Only after the city has burned down to the ground and lies in smoldering ruins is the order given: the fire department returns back to the fire house. A malicious invention? An ugly fairy tale? No. The truth. And it happened in Hollywood."[10]

People living under totalitarianism speak a special language. One has to formulate things so that those being addressed will understand, yet without the actual meaning of what one wishes to communicate becoming clear to the authorities: "A new, even more deeply concealed insider language had to be found to be able to express the truth."[11] It was crucial to imitate and appropriate the "jargon" of the surrounding linguistic environment and thus to encode one's opposition, a procedure that is one of the characteristic features of any literature of resistance.[12] As Martin Buber phrased it, the important thing was "that those who are currently in power do not immediately see our opposition...[we must] write so cleverly that we will have been read by many before they can call us on the carpet."[13]

The extraordinary phenomenon of the Jewish press during that period was not only the fact that it was allowed to appear, but that it was the only genre in German journalism at the time able to be non-Nationalist Socialist. It is true that the *Frankfurter Zeitung* put up a courageous fight to preserve its intellectual independence right up to its suspension in 1943,[14] yet the Jewish press enjoyed a unique position: Jews were not considered to be Germans, and no Jew was allowed to be a National Socialist; indeed, Jews were even prohibited from hoisting the national flag or displaying the national colors.[15] For that reason, Jews were allowed – and probably were even supposed – to exhibit those traits that had been branded by the Nazis as despicable and specifically "Jewish": liberalism and humanism, belief in the sanctity of life, respect for human dignity. These questions were treated in the Jewish papers in the context of existential principles more generally, extending far beyond the realm of something specifically Jewish. Jewish papers were also permitted to print authors who were otherwise blacklisted in Germany. Just as the theaters of the Kulturbund were given permission to stage plays by Stefan Zweig, Arthur Schnitzler, Richard Beer-Hofmann and other outlawed writers, the Jewish press was allowed to publish reviews of books by Thomas Mann, Romain Rolland or Jakob Wassermann; its pages carried a novel by Franz Werfel, and it was free to discuss, and sometimes even to publish, works by other banned or prohibited authors.

This gave rise to a paradox: the Jewish press was the only segment of journalism in Germany that was able to view world problems from a perspective expressly forbidden to the German papers. The National Socialist ideology was a "privilege" reserved for racially pure Germans.

> Since National Socialism decreed that race was decisive and that a Jew cannot be a German, it follows logically that a Jew cannot be a Nazi, and that a Jewish paper cannot be a Nazi paper. National Socialism had to concede that Jews had a right to express positions on their own affairs in the spirit of a liberal and humanistic "Jewish" outlook on the world. This was accepted in practical terms, at least during the first five years of the regime. The regime could place external restrictions on the Jewish papers, but was unable to issue them any intellectual guidelines.[16]

While the various functions put on by the Jewish cultural leagues were only open to Jews with a proper identification card, Jewish papers were allowed to be sold openly in public until 1935. The reason for this is not clear. Perhaps the authorities wished to demonstrate that Jews were no longer able to hide behind a German paper; they had to make explicit reference in the name of the paper to being "Jewish," in this way documenting the desired clean separation between German and Jewish journalism. Or perhaps those in power assumed that no German reader could ever possibly be interested in such Jewish papers; for that reason, a prohibition on distribution and selling of the paper was regarded as superfluous.

Yet reality had a different face. It was a strange sight that greeted the eye once or twice a week in Berlin at the newsstands on the Kurfürstendamm and in other main thoroughfares around the city, but especially on the west side of town: Jewish newspapers with large banner headlines whose tenor differed substantially from that of their surroundings. The papers were distributed by a wholesaler, and figures for circulation ran into the thousands. The papers were purchased from street vendors not just by Jews (many Jews were subscribers to these publications and thus did not purchase them from newsstands), but by non-Jews as well, who read the papers either out of curiosity or in order to have a respite from the uniformity of the Nazi-dominated German press and to cast a glance into another world, otherwise closed to them. The many letters by non-Jewish readers sent to the editors of Jewish periodicals indicate that there was a kind of defiance and opposition in their choice of such papers. The

*Jüdische Rundschau* was the "bestseller" in such street sales as a result of its title and the fact that it appeared twice a week. Its editors received a letter, for example, from the granddaughter of the poet Hoffmann von Fallersleben, who had composed the German national anthem. Under the impression of the events of the time, she made the offer of a house on the Baltic for potential use by Jewish children.[17]

It is thus not surprising that this "boom" was eventually terminated, although only after a delay of some two years. Non-Jews were enjoined not only from purchasing Jewish papers on the street, but also from taking out a subscription to them. Nonetheless, for a time a few brave souls still ventured to obtain copies "under the counter" directly from the publisher. The directive issued by the President of the Reich Chamber of the Press stated:

> In accordance with para. 25 of the First Decree on Implementation of the Law on the Reich Chamber of Culture, dated 1 November 1933 (RGBl 1/33, p. 797 ff.), I hereby determine as follows: "The public display and sale of papers and periodicals which are addressed wholly or in part, by reason of their title or content, to the Jewish population is forbidden. The Federation of German Newspaper and Periodical Distributors and the Reich Association of German Newspaper and Periodical Retailers are charged with supervising the implementation of this directive, which is effective from October 1st. Berlin, September 6, 1935. Signed Amann."[18]

Under a caption "Cleanliness in All Things," the *Westfälische Landeszeitung* editorialized on September 11, 1935:

> In issuing a decree on the sale of Jewish papers, party comrade Amann has not only moved a further step down the path to eradicating anything Jewish from public life, but has also taken action that will find favor with all National Socialists and fellow *Volksgenossen*. For many of us, it was often a difficult test of patience to have to endure the sight of the Jewish press, with its anything but modest, and indeed frequently polemical headlines, arrayed at public newsstands right alongside the papers of our movement. In addition, it was often times quite evident that certain newspaper dealers, interested in garnering greater profits, gave special emphasis in displaying this Jewish press in cities with a large Jewish population, thus kowtowing in a quite undignified manner to these racial aliens.[19]

According to the Law on Editors,[20] editors had to be of Aryan origin, and were not allowed to be married to a person of non-

Aryan descent. The implementation directive of December 19, 1933, waived this requirement in the case of editors of Jewish papers.[21] What this looked like in actual practice is reflected in the experiences of Dr. Robert Weltsch, editor-in-chief of the *Jüdische Rundschau.* In a letter dated December 12, 1933 and addressed to the Berlin district branch of the Reich Federation of the German Press, he requested to be included in the professional listing of editors, and specified that the category be limited to editors of purely Jewish papers. After presenting his c.v. and outlining his previous work experience, Weltsch continued:

> Taking into consideration the above data, I wish to request the following: 1. A waiver of the requirement of Aryan descent . . . ; 2. waiving of the requirement of being a citizen of the Reich [*Reichszugehörigkeit*] . . . since I am performing my duties employed at a Jewish paper, not a German one. Thus, one can probably assume that the concept "of German racial extraction" [*deutsch-stämmig*], which is not applicable here, should be interpreted as "of Jewish racial extraction" [*jüdischstämmig*] in the case of Jewish papers. Likewise . . . one can assume that it was not the intention of the legislation to prevent a person belonging to a national or racial special group [*Sondergruppe*] from being actively employed on a paper that serves that special group, even if the person is not a citizen of the Reich. I am a Czech citizen, received a German education in Prague and served at the front in a German regiment in the Austro-Hungarian army during the World War.[22]

After receipt of a negative reply and a renewed submission of his application, Weltsch was sent a letter from the Reich Federation of the German Press, dated October 5, 1934 and signed by Professor H. Herrmann: "My Dear Colleague! With approval by the Minister for Popular Enlightenment and Propaganda, the director of the Reich Federation has waived the requirement of para. 5, sec. 1 and 3 of the Law on Editors in your case, while limiting your activity to Jewish papers. Your district association has been informed of this decision, and they will provide you with all further information regarding your rights and duties. With German greetings! Herrmann."[23]

Though Dr. Weltsch had open access to the Ministry of Propaganda, he did not take part in press conferences, and avoided all contact with correspondents of foreign papers, since he knew he was under surveillance.[24] Weltsch reported that in many discussions with younger Nazi officials, he had had an opportunity to elaborate on the theory that Jews, in their own press, should be allowed to develop their own interpretation of events – since they were not Germans in the sense of National Socialism, and were barred from becoming Nazis. Those officials, Weltsch notes, were basically in agreement with him.[25] This tendency was abetted by a series of articles entitled "A Nazi Travels to Palestine" published in the notorious Berlin Nazi party paper *Der Angriff*, edited by Goebbels; the series was featured prominently and ran from September 26 to October 9, 1934. Its author, Baron Leopold Itz von Mildenstein (pseudonym Vom Lim) was deeply impressed by the people he had encountered in the collective settlements there, and wrote enthusiastically: "That is the new Jew – this new Jew will become a people."[26] With requisite reserve, the *Jüdische Rundschau* welcomed the series,[27] which apparently had a certain impact on domestic politics and, for a short time, made it easier for Zionist journalists to pursue their activities.

With the mounting restrictions placed on Jewish life in Germany, the pressure on Jewish papers also increased. On January 25, 1938, a letter was sent by the Berlin district branch of the Reich Federation of the German Press to Dr. Weltsch, though this time it began without the formalities of a salutation and use of his doctoral title:

> By decree of the Reich Minister for Popular Enlightenment and Propaganda, the names of Jews in the professional list of editors maintained by the Reich Federation of the German Press, whose activities were limited to the Jewish press, are to be eliminated and their files transferred to the special office of the Reich Superintendent of Culture Hinkel within the Ministry for Popular Enlightenment and Propaganda. Accordingly, I have deleted your name from the list of editors and forwarded your file to the above-mentioned special office.[28]

This "Hinkel office" was responsible not only for the surveillance of the Jewish press, but for the supervision and control of all cultural activities on the part of the Jewish population in Germany – theater, music, the showing of films, lectures, book distribution and publishing.[29]

One of the paradoxes of National Socialist policy during that period was the fact that an outsider grouping on the extreme right of the Jewish political spectrum, namely the *Verband nationaldeutscher Juden* (Association of National-German Jews), founded in 1920, was one of the first organizations to be banned, along with its periodical *Der Nationaldeutsche Jude*, edited by the association's chairman, Max Naumann.

There's a difference whether a Jew stems from a family that has been settled in Germany for many decades and has its roots in German culture, or is a newly immigrated Eastern Jew from Tarnopol, who has just cut off his temple forelocks, but has preserved his Asiatic character. . . . I have great respect for the Jewish-national Zionists provided they emigrate to Palestine, because they do not belong in Germany. We national-German Jews affirm the national revolution, which is in keeping with our views. We must act to make sure that the National Socialist state recognizes our ideology and does not put its policies into practice against nationalistic, German-minded Jews. . . .[30]

Naumann was of the opinion that "Jewish law" violated "natural law," and he wished for nothing more than to live in a German – indeed, even a Nordic – manner together with other *Volksgenossen*. He maintained that Jewish priests had created the Jewish people artificially, and that racial hatred and religious arrogance had come into being with Ezra and Nehemiah.[31] Judaism in Germany would no longer exist, he claimed, if there had not been rabbis from Eastern Europe to whom the Jewish masses had flocked later on: it was only their influx that had prevented the desired dissolution of German Jewry.[32]

On December 5, 1935, the DNB (German News Agency) announced: "In accordance with para. 1 of the Decree on the Protection of State and People, the 'Verband Nationaldeutscher Juden' has been dissolved due to its subversive views, and its property confiscated." The position taken by the periodical had been repudiated by all responsible Jewish bodies. It was all the more tragic for Dr. Naumann, who was arrested and taken temporarily into protective custody, that he had been accused of "subversive attitudes" specifically by the German authorities. He died in New York in 1939.

The anti-humanist position within the Jewish political spectrum was represented not only by a German-völkisch journal, but could also boast a Jewish chauvinist periodical, namely the Revisionist *Der Staatszionist*, which had to cease publication a short time after its appearance. Max Schulmann, Lieut. (Res.), was the journal's editor and the author of numerous articles published in its pages. It appeared twice monthly in his own printing house in Berlin as *Mitteilungsblatt der Staatszionistischen Organisation und des Staatszionistischen Frontkämpferbundes* (Newsletter of the State-Zionist Organization and the State-Zionist League of Combat Veterans).[33]

The journal, which differed from other Jewish publications in its sensationalist style, advocated the status of minority for Jews in Germany. "There is no spectre that can frighten a member of the CV, an RJF man or any other Jew in 'secure financial circumstances' more than that of minority rights. . . . When the narrow-minded shopkeeper hears that word he begins to take fright instead of thinking. . . . We do not intend to conceal the fact that as state-Zionists . . . our affirmation of the racial-national-Jewish principle is not in contradiction with the similar National Socialist principle."[34]

The disdain for "those in control of the Zionist party machinery," whose "horizon was no higher than the church belfry of their hometowns," was directed in particular against Dr. Weltsch. In an article entitled "Reckoning," he had "brazenly . . . confirmed once again his betrayal of Herzlian Zionism, by recognizing the right of the Arabs to Palestine as . . . their homeland. . . . In the eyes of the *Rundschau*, we are fascists, murderers of workers or whatever the particular flattering epithets may be. . . . The *Rundschau* is something that has to be overcome."[35]

In order to be perfectly clear, a warning was published entitled "Avengers of Israel": "Joseph Flavius tells about the 'avengers of Israel' who, as guardians of Jewish honor at the time, made sure that every person who had betrayed the people was brought to justice and received a proper and befitting punishment. Now that we no longer have this salutary institution, we can but warn the corrupters of the people that they should be careful not to go too far."[36]

# Notes

1. Performances, lectures and publications of the Jewish Kulturbünde were subject to prior approval by the Hinkel office. Freeden, 1964, p. 44ff.

2. Herbert A. Strauss, "The Jewish Press in Germany 1918–1938," in World Federation of Jewish Journalists, 1980.

3. B. Zeller (ed.), *Klassiker in finsteren Zeiten 1933–1934*, Marbacher Kataloge 38, 1983, vol. 1, p. 99.(Lit. Research Center and Archives, Marbach).

4. Sänger, 1975, p. 386.

5. Robert Weltsch, "A Goebbels Speech," *YLBI*, 10 (1965), p. 285.

6. Wulf,1964, p. 217.

7. Arno Herzberg, "Last Days of German Jewish Press," *Contemporary Jewish Record*, April 1942, p. 145ff.

8. Private archive Weltsch, Central Zionist Archives, Jerusalem; see also Weltsch, "A Goebbels Speech," ibid., p. 287.

9. Margarete Edelheim-Mühsam, "Reactions of the Jewish Press," *YLBI*, 5 (1960), p. 328.

10. It is well-known that in the night of November 9–10, 1938, when some 200 synagogues were set ablaze, the fire departments were instructed not to take action unless the flames threatened to spread to nearby property. See also Kochan, 1957, p. 63 and Pehle, 1991, esp. pp. 16, 74, 78.

11. Simon, 1959, p. 75. See also Leo Strauss: "Persecution . . . gives rise to a particular technique of writing . . . in which the truth about all crucial things is presented exclusively between the lines," 1952, p. 25.

12. Franz Meyer, "Bemerkungen zu zwei Denkschriften," in Tramer, 1962, p. 116.

13. *In den Katakomben, Jüdische Verlage in Deutschland 1933–1938* (comp. I. Belke), *Marbacher Magazin* 25 (1983), p. 94 (Lit. Research Center and Archives, Marbach). On the question of censorship of non-Jewish publications as well, there is an interesting letter by Wilhelm Stapel to Will Vesper, dated November 22, 1935, written on the official stationery of the monthly *Deutsches Volkstum*: ". . . Hermann Claudius has brought out a selection of the works of Matthias Claudius with Stalling Publishers. The selection committee of the Ministry of Culture refused to place the book on the list of recommended titles until two poems by Matthias Claudius had been removed: the 'Great Hallelujah,' and the poem about little David and the great Goliath. . . . The first poem should be eliminated because of the two lines: 'The being of all beings, truth, God! His name is Jehovah Lord of Hosts'; the second (literally) 'because of racial considerations.' So literary history is also being purified in terms of its *Weltanschauung*. That is the situation." Cited from Zeller, 1983, Vol. 1, p. 106.

14. "The *Frankfurter Zeitung* had a special status during the years of the National Socialist regime. As a result of the attitude taken by the editors and publishers . . . it was assigned to an historic and lonely place." Sänger, 1975, p. 11.

15. Law on the Protection of German Blood and German Honor, September 15, 1935; see Walk, 1981, p. 127.

16. Robert Weltsch, "Jüdische Presse vor 30 Jahren," in Gärtner, Lamm, and Lowenthal, 1957, p. 111.

17. Archives, Yad Vashem, Jerusalem, doc. 01/40, 1944.

18. Quoted from Wulf, 1964, p. 246.

19. Ibid., p. 256.

20. *Reichsgesetzblatt*, October 1, 1933, valid as law from January 1, 1934. See Walk, 1981, p. 55, and appendix to the present study.

21. Ibid., p. 65.

22. Private archive Weltsch, Central Zionist Archives, Jerusalem.

23. Ibid.

24. Archives, Yad Vashem, Jerusalem, doc. 01/40, 1944.

25. Weltsch, "Jüdische Presse vor 30 Jahren," ibid.

26. *MB*, Tel Aviv, March 14, 1980.

27. *Jüdische Rundschau*, September 28, 1934.

28. Private archive Weltsch.

29. Freeden, 1964, p. 154.

30. "Naumann in Berlin," report on a lecture by Naumann, *Jüdische Zeitung*, Breslau, January 19, 1934. "The hall was decked with a large number of black-white-and-red flags. Before the speech, the 'Hohenfriedberger' and various other military marches were played, and afterwards the 'Deutschlandlied' anthem was sung, with arms raised in salute."

31. Leaders of the religious and intellectual renewal after the return from Babylonian exile in the fifth century B.C.

32. Report on a lecture by Naumann, *Staatszionist*, March 3, 1935.

33. The State-Zionist Organization (United Revisionists) included the groups of the Zionists-Revisionists and the Jewish State Party [*Judenstaatspartei*], and was limited solely to Germany: see Lowenthal, (ed.), *Philo-Lexikon*, Berlin, 1935, p. 688.

34. *Staatszionist*, March 3, 1935.

35. Ibid., May 5, 1935.

36. Ibid., October 13, 1935.

# 2

—

# Structure and Statistics

By 1933, the structure of Jewish periodical publication in Germany was highly differentiated. Five categories can be distinguished: political papers; religious periodicals; periodical publications of the *Gemeinden*; scientific and cultural journals; professional periodicals; and publications of associations.

Let us survey each of these categories in turn. Among the political papers, the oldest was the *Jüdische Rundschau*, founded in 1896, the official organ of the Zionistische Vereinigung für Deutschland (ZVfD, German Zionist Association). It was the only one of the large Jewish papers that appeared twice weekly.

Three years later, in 1899, the *Hamburger Israelitisches Familienblatt* was founded. It had a special distinction: while all other periodicals, with the exception of the small *Jüdische Zeitung* in Breslau, were maintained by Jewish organizations, institutions, Gemeinden and associations, the *Hamburger Israelitisches Familienblatt* (renamed *Israelitisches Familienblatt* after its relocation to Berlin in 1935) was the only major Jewish paper that was privately owned.

The political weekly with the greatest circulation was the *CV-Zeitung*, that had evolved in 1922 from the monthly *Im Deutschen Reich*, founded in 1895; it was published by the Centralverein deutscher Staatsbürger jüdischen Glaubens (The Central Association of German Citizens of the Jewish Faith). Another political weekly with a broad distribution was *Der Schild* (The Shield), founded in 1921 by the Reichsbund jüdischer Frontsoldaten (National League of Jewish Combat Veterans).

In 1934, these four large papers had a combined total circulation of 143,800; that figure declined by 13 percent to 130,000 in

1935 and to 123,000 in 1936. Based on a total Jewish population of approximately 400,000, one can thus assume that virtually every Jewish family read one of these papers.

There were other smaller Jewish political papers, such as the Zionist *Jüdische Zeitung* in Breslau, founded in 1924, and the *Palästina-Nachrichten*, a periodical dealing with economy and politics established in 1934. The *Staatszionist* and the irregular *Der Nationaldeutsche Jude* (founded in 1921), both published in Berlin, as well as *Der Vortrupp* (Advance Guard, established 1933), were closed down by official order in 1935.

In view of political developments during the years 1933–1938, there was a decided decline in the numerical importance of the religious periodicals, although these papers did not limit themselves to religious questions, and also addressed the events of the day. The oldest of such papers, *Der Israelit*, published in Frankfurt/Main and founded in 1860 as the official organ of Agudas Yisroel, was regarded as the most important voice of German Orthodoxy.

The *Laubhütte* was the chief paper within the Orthodox community [*Einheitsgemeinde*]; founded in Hamburg in 1884, it later bore the name *Deutsch-Israelitische Zeitung (Die Laubhütte)* until 1935.

The organ of liberal Judaism was the *Jüdisch Allgemeine Zeitung* (successor to the *Jüdisch-Liberale Zeitung*); it was based in Berlin, where the newsletter *Mitteilungen der jüdischen Reformgemeinde* also appeared.

The monthly *Zion*, published in Berlin, was the official organ of the religious-Zionist Mizrahi movement.

Aside from the *Gemeindeblatt der jüdischen Gemeinde Berlin*, founded in 1910, and the *Verordnungsblatt des Oberrats badischer Israeliten*, established in Karlsruhe in 1884, all of the papers put out by the various *Gemeinden* came into being after World War I. In 1936, there were 23 such Gemeinde periodical publications; five were weekly, 12 biweekly and six were issued on a monthly basis. The largest circulation was that of the Berlin *Gemeindeblatt* at 51,000 copies; the smallest figures were for the periodicals in Kassel and Saarbrücken, each with 450. In order to include the smaller Jewish communities, papers were put out by the regional Gemeinde federations on a regional basis in addition to the periodicals of the individual communities: thus, there were regional Gemeinde papers for Prussia, Bavaria, Württemberg and Hesse.

The 23 Gemeinde periodicals had a total combined circulation of 110,000 copies in 1936.

In the category of scientific and cultural periodicals, the journal *Der Morgen* was the principal cultural-political publication, even though its circulation was only 1,600 copies. Founded in Darmstadt by Julius Goldstein in 1925, it was regarded after its relocation to offices in Berlin (1930) as an elite platform for intellectual and cultural discussion and debate. Beginning in 1933, the cultural scene was enhanced by the appearance of the monthlies put out by four Kulturbünde: Berlin, Cologne, Frankfurt and Hamburg. Though their columns were devoted in the main to commentary on the cultural events staged by the various cultural leagues, they occasionally went beyond this to express views on Jewish cultural problems more generally, as did the mimeographed monthly newsletter of the National Federation of Jewish Cultural Leagues, *Mitteilungen des Reichsverbandes der Jüdischen Kulturbünde* (Berlin) as well.

The principal scientific periodicals were the *Zeitschrift für jüdische Familienforschung* (Journal for Jewish Genealogy, Berlin), the *Monatsschrift für Geschichte und Wissenschaft des Judentums* (Monthly Journal for the History and Science of Judaism, Breslau), the *Zeitschrift für die Geschichte der Juden in Deutschland* (Journal for the History of Jews in Germany, Berlin) and the periodical *Jüdische Wohlfahrtspflege und Sozialpolitik* (Jewish Welfare and Social Policy, Berlin), all of which appeared on an irregular basis.

Among periodicals of professional groups and voluntary associations, whose circulation figures ranged from 10,000 for a masonic journal (*Großloge für Deutschland, UOBB*) down to 250 for a professional journal for cantors (*Der jüdische Kantor*), and which generally appeared on an irregular basis, one should also note the athletics monthly of the sports club *Der Makkabi* (Berlin) with a circulation of 5,000, the monthly for artisans *Der jüdische Handwerker* (Berlin – 3,600), and the women's monthly *Blätter des jüdischen Frauenbundes* (Berlin – 3,600). All figures are for the year 1936.

The most important source of news for the Jewish press was the J.T.A. (Jüdische Telegraphen-Agentur), with branches in Jerusalem, New York, London, Paris, Prague and Warsaw. All major Jewish papers subscribed to their daily package of news. Due to its broad network of correspondents, the J.T.A. was able to provide paper readership with a good orientation. For reports from Palestine, there was a further press service, Palco (Palästina-

Korrespondenz), but the Jewish press did not suffice simply with reproducing the news items and stories received; rather, these were supplemented by reports from their own correspondents in the most important centers. Of course, that was true particularly in the case of the political papers. A number of the Gemeinde papers banded together to produce a general paper with various local editions, such as the communities in Düsseldorf, Essen and Wuppertal, in order to better inform their readership over and beyond a diet of purely local news items.

Advertisements played a major role in the expansion of the Jewish press: the numerous periodicals would not have been able to fulfill their new tasks and functions if they had not been aided by a substantial increase in the volume of advertising. Like the editorial columns, the ad sections gave clear expression to the changing situation faced by German Jewry. Before 1933, advertisements had played a minor role, and the few ads that appeared were more an expression of good will on the part of a particular firm than any form of intentional commercial advertising. The 'want ads' section, that often serves to create a bond between the paper and its readers, was virtually unknown in these periodicals, aside from the *Hamburger Israelitisches Familienblatt*. A Jewish "marriage market" had sprung up inside its family ads – instead of going to a marriage broker, you put a matrimonial ad in the paper.

These advertisements provide a psychological and sociological picture of the Jewish middle class in the decades between the world wars. For example, there was the phenomenon of "marrying into" a business: the parents of the prospective bride would place an ad announcing that they were looking for a suitable husband for their daughter of marriageable age, and that the lucky man would then be taken on as a partner in the business of the bride's father. This practice frequently resulted in ads that sounded almost like a caricature: "Partner sought for successful men's clothing store in a middle-size provincial city. Requirements: commercial experience and marriage with the amiable daughter of the family."

All this changed after 1933. Without expanding its want ad section, the Jewish press would not have been able to fulfill its new functions. The expansion of the editorial section went hand in hand with the growth in ads, which facilitated greater scope and variety in editorial content. Comparative statistics from the years 1932 and 1936 provide a revealing picture:

## Table 1: Comparative Figures for Size of Paper and Advertising Volume, 1932–1936

| PAPER | TOTAL NO. OF PAGES 1ST QUARTER | | PAGES OF ADVERTISING 1ST QUARTER | |
|---|---|---|---|---|
| | 1932 | 1936 | 1932 | 1936 |
| CV-Zeitung | 128 | 310 | 45.9 | 90.4 |
| Jüdische Rundschau | 120 | 516 | 14.5 | 172.3 |
| Isr. Familienblatt (Berlin edition) | 262 | 346 | 39.5 | 84 |
| Berliner Gemeindeblatt | 84 | 286 | 36.3 | 142.9 |

The actual expansion in total size is not accurately reflected in these figures, since in addition to the increased number of pages, most papers also enlarged their format. Taking these changes in format into consideration, one can calculate the increase in total size and in the volume of advertising for the four papers from the first quarter of 1932 to 1936 as follows:

## Table 2: Growth in Size of Paper and Advertising Volume, 1932–1936

| PAPER | INCREASE IN TOTAL SIZE | INCREASE IN VOLUME OF ADVERTISEMENTS |
|---|---|---|
| *CV-Zeitung* | 550% | 450% |
| *Jüdische Rundschau* | 425% | 1200% |
| *Familienblatt* | 150% | 275% |
| *Gemeindeblatt* | 525% | 600% |

A number of papers, such as the *Jüdische Rundschau, CV- Zeitung* and *Berliner Gemeindeblatt,* became financially independent as a result of the increase in advertising, and this also holds true in the case of smaller Gemeinde periodicals that were cheaper to produce due to their size. Moreover, the papers were assisted by an official ruling of June 1934 (Advertising Council for the German Economy) stipulating that papers could no longer be distributed gratis. In particular, that affected the Gemeinde papers, which collected subscription fees as part of the Gemeinde religious taxes. However, there were also some organizations and associations that had distributed their periodicals to members cost-free; they now were obliged to charge for their publications. In addition to the financial benefits for the paper, this also had the advantage that people who received the papers were perhaps more likely to read them.

### Table 3: Circulation Figures for the Largest Jewish Papers in Germany, 1934–1938

| PAPER | 1934 | 1935 | 1937 | 1938 |
|---|---|---|---|---|
| *CV-Zeitung* | 50,000 | 40,000 | 40,000 | 39,500 |
| *Jüdische Rundschau* | 37,000 | 37,000 | 37,000 | 25,300 |
| *Hamburger Israelitisches Familienblatt* | 36,500 | 36,500 | 30,000 | 26,500 |
| *Der Schild* | 19,350 | 17,200 | 14,000 | 15,100 |
| *Berliner Gemeindeblatt* | 46,000 | 52,000 | 46,000 | 40,000 |
| *Frankfurter Gemeindeblatt* | 7,200 | 7,200 | 7,200 | 6,300 |
| *Breslauer Gemeindeblatt* | 5,300 | 5,500 | 5,300 | — |
| *Münchner Gemeindeblatt* | 4,500 | 4,500 | 4,500 | — |

Based on: *Lexikon des Judentums*, Gütersloh 1967

### Table 4: Total Monthly Circulation for Jewish Periodicals by Category

| CATEGORY | 1934 | 1935 | 1936 | 1937 |
|---|---|---|---|---|
| Political | 755,000 | 685,000 | 617,200 | 583,350 |
| Gemeinde | 315,000 | 322,500 | 292,000 | 285,600 |
| Religious | 47,000 | 45,400 | 22,600 | 22,600 |
| Professional organizations | 28,000 | 29,300 | 27,700 | 26,800 |
| Culture, science | 22,000 | 31,000 | 33,800 | 32,850 |
| Other | 15,000 | 21,300 | 5,000 | 5,000 |
| Total: | 1,182,000 | 1,134,500 | 998,300 | 956,200 |

Based on: *Lexikon des Judentums*, Gütersloh 1967

No less so than in other parts of the paper, the social, economic and psychological situation of Jews in Germany at the time was clearly reflected in the advertising sections, especially the columns of small want ads. Thus, in the first quarter of 1936, the *Berliner Gemeindeblatt* published more than 2,300 ads for rooms and apartments. A portion of the Jewish population had to vacate their apartments because German landlords insisted on their leaving; others found they could no longer afford a large apartment, or tried to rent out furnished rooms for extra money. Those furnished rooms, in turn, were in demand among persons who had become homeless. Another factor playing a role was the emigration of younger family members, so that older married couples suddenly found themselves alone in large apartments.

Ads announcing family events also increased dramatically:

## Table 5: Family Announcements

| Paper | 1st quarter 1932 | 1st quarter 1936 |
|---|---|---|
| *CV-Zeitung* | 49 | 283 |
| *Jüdische Rundschau* | 32 | 747 |
| *Isr. Familienblatt* | 84 | 383 |
| *Berliner Gemeindeblatt* | 0 | 517 |

The first death notice in the *Berliner Gemeindeblatt* appeared in the issue dated February 17, 1934; eleven months later, such notices already occupied a full page. Announcements of engagements and marriages multiplied to a similar extent. The practice of informing business friends and other acquantainances, previously done by placing an announcement in the general press, had now shrunk to the Jewish sphere of contacts. Thus, the Jewish paper became the platform for reporting to a now contracted social world about the sad and happy events in one's family life.

There was also a gradual change in commercial advertising. In May 1933, but a month after the public "boycott" of Jewish businesses ordered by the Nazi party on April 1st, there were ads by the large banks, the popular resorts, motion picture theaters and entertainment spots around town. The *Berliner Gemeindeblatt* carried an advertisement for a popular Berlin beer that read: "The cool blond says: my name's Berlin White"; not long thereafter, Jews were officially forbidden from uttering the word "blond" in public. In a performance of a comedy by Franz Molnar put on at the Berlin Kulturbund, the sentence "Farewell, you unfaithful blond briefcase" had to be changed to "beautiful briefcase" to please the censor.[1]

The columns of the Jewish press increasingly contained a new feature called the "Commercial Directory," a section in which retailers, wholesalers and factories introduced their wares and services, generally under the heading "Jewish Community Members Can Supply You With." The Association of Jewish Artisans also made its presence more felt in the Jewish press. In each issue, most of the Gemeinde periodicals published a list of members with their trade or profession and the services they offered readers. This attempt at creating a kind of economic "autonomy" did not find favor with the Nazi party, as reflected in a letter dated November 19, 1934 from the NSDAP, district head-quarters Berlin, addressed to the Reich Superintendent of Culture, Hans Hinkel:

> After reading issue no. 10 of the second volume of the monthly Monatsblätter des Kulturbundes deutscher Juden . . . it appears to me that the ads throughout the paper were of even greater importance. Special attention must be given to slogans tantamount to propaganda, such as: "Jews, buy only from Jews.". . . In a situation where difficulties are now arising, and we are no longer to be permitted to carry out our actions because we might disturb the economic peace, it's an impossible state of affairs when, in contrast, it is perfectly all right for Jews to advertise for their own kind. We are no longer supposed to say: Germans, buy only from Germans, or Christians, buy only from Christians – but the Hebrews are allowed to urge: Jews, buy only from Jews![2]

Only in one area did there seem to be something of a discrepancy between editorial policy and the advertisements section: while ads placed by moving and shipping companies and travel bureaus were on the increase, indicating a more rapid rate of emigration and a concomitant necessary reduction in readership, editors continued to expand the other sections of the paper. Now, almost every larger paper had supplements or special sections on women, children, education, sports, books, the Kultur-bund – and, of course, on Palestine and emigration. Some periodicals even published serialized novels.

1. Freeden 1964, p. 48.
2. *Bulletin des Leo Baeck Instituts*, 5 (1958), p. 18.

## Table 6: The German-Jewish Press 1934

| PERIODICAL | FOUNDED | CIRCULATION OCT. 1934 | MONTHLY FREQUENCY | EDITOR |
|---|---|---|---|---|
| *Esra* (Frankfurt/M) | 1925 | – | | |
| *Der Israelit* (Frankfurt/M) | 1860 | 4,250 | 2x | S. Schachnowitz |
| *Jüdische-Allgem.* (Liberale) *Zeitung* (Berlin) | 1934 | 5,000 | 4x | Dr. E. Tannenbaum |
| *Mitteilung der jüdischen Reform-Gemeinde* (Berlin) | 1918 | 3,000 | 1x | George Goetz |
| *Die Laubhütte* (Hamburg) | 1884 | 3,000 | 2x | Jakob Meyer |
| *CV-Zeitung* (Berlin) | 1922 | 50,000 | 4x | Dr. M. Edelheim |
| *Jüdische Zeitung für Ostdeutschland* (Breslau) | 1924 | 2,000 | 4x | Erich Bildhauer |
| *Jüdische Rundschau* (Berlin) | 1896 | 37,000 | 8x | Dr. R. Weltsch K. Löwenstein |
| *Der Nationaldeutsche Jude* (Berlin) | 1921 | 15,000 | irreg. | Dr. Max Naumann |
| *Der Schild* (Berlin) | 1921 | 20,300 | 4x | Dr. Hans Wollenberg |
| *Der Vortrupp* (Berlin) | 1934 | 1,300 | irreg. | Dr. H.J. Schoeps |
| *Hamburger Israelitisches Familienblatt* | 1898 | 36,500 | 4x | Dr. Alfr. Kupferberg |
| *Zeitschrift für jüdische Familienforschung* (Berlin) | 1924 | 1,000 | 1x | Dr. A. Czellitzer |
| *Monatsschrift für Geschichte und Wissenschaft des Judentums* (Breslau) | 1851 | 1,800 | | Dr. I. Heinemann |
| *Zeitschrift für die Geschichte der Juden in Deutschland* (Berlin) | 1929 | 500 | irreg. | Dr. E.G. Lowenthal |
| *Monatsblatt des Kulturbunds deutscher Juden* (Berlin) | 1933 | 17,600 | 1x | Julius Bab |

## The Jewish Press in the Third Reich

| PERIODICAL | FOUNDED | CIRCULATION OCT. 1934 | MONTHLY FREQUENCY | EDITOR |
|---|---|---|---|---|
| *Der Morgen* (Berlin) | 1925 | 1,600 | 1x | Dr. E. Reichmann<br>Dr. H. Bach |
| *Der jüdische Kantor* (Hamburg) | 1927 | 250 | irreg. | Leon Kornitzer |
| *Jüdische Schulzeitung* (Cologne) | 1924 | 1,100 | 1x | Dr. Siegfr. Braun |
| *Der jüdische Handwerker* (Berlin) | 1908 | 4,000 | 1x | Erich Salinger |
| *Blätter des jüdischen Frauenbundes* (Berlin) | 1924 | 4,000 | 1x | |
| *Schwesternverband der UOBB* (Frankfurt/Main) | 1928 | 5,500 | 1x | Dr. Dora Edinger |
| *Großloge für Deutschland UOBB* (Berlin) | 1901 | 11,000 | irreg. | Daniel Bernstein |
| *Der Makkabi* (Berlin) | 1898 | 44,000 | 1x | |
| *Zeitschrift der Beamten der jüdischen Gemeinde* (Berlin) | 1898 | 750 | | H.H. Altmann |
| *Verwaltungsblatt des preußischen Landesverbandes* (Berlin) | 1922 | – | 1x | George Goetz |
| *Korrespondenz für jüdische Auswanderungsangelegenheiten* (Berlin) | 1905 | 4,000 | irreg. | Mark Wischnitzer |
| *Palästina-Nachrichten* (Berlin) | 1933 | 7,500 | 1x | Dr. Fr. E. Ascher |
| *Band, Zeitschrift für jüdische Gehörlose* (Berlin-Weißensee) | 1926 | 500 | 1x | Dr. Felix Reich |
| *Jüdische Wohlfahrtspflege* (Berlin) | 1929 | – | | Dr. Fr. Ollendorf |
| *Informationsblätter des Zentralausschusses für Hilfe und Aufbau* (Berlin) | 1934 | – | irreg. | Dr. Fr. Brodnitz |
| *Gemeinde-Blatt für den Bezirk Aachen* | 1926 | 500 | 2x | Rich. Heidelberg |

| PERIODICAL | FOUNDED | CIRCULATION OCT. 1934 | MONTHLY FREQUENCY | EDITOR |
|---|---|---|---|---|
| *Jüdisches Gemeinde-Blatt für Anhalt* | 1925 | 500 | 1x | Dr. Walter |
| *Gemeinde-Blatt der jüdischen Gemeinde Berlin* | 1910 | 49,000 | 4x | Leo Kreindler |
| *Gemeinde-Blatt der israelitischen Gemeinde Bremen* | 1929 | 450 | 1x | Dr. Gruenewald |
| *Breslauer jüdisches Gemeinde-Blatt* | 1920 | 7,650 | 2x | Manfr. Rosenfeld |
| *Jüdisches Gemeinde-Blatt Danzig* | 1928 | 2,500 | 2x | Dr. Iwan Grün |
| *Gemeinde-Blatt für die Gemeinde Dortmund* | 1933 | 900 | 2x | Heinz Meyerfeld |
| *Mitteilungen des sächsischen Gemeinde-Verbandes* | 1927 | 2,400 | irreg. | official |
| *Gemeinde-Blatt der jüd. Gemeinde* | 1925 | 2,200 | 2x | official |
| *Gemeinde-Zeitung Düsseldorf* | 1929 | 1,900 | 2x | Rabbi Dr. Klein |
| *Gemeinde-Zeitung Duisburg* | 1929 | 500 | 2x | Rabbi Dr. Klein |
| *Gemeinde-Zeitung Essen* | 1929 | 950 | 2x | Rabbi Dr. Klein |
| *Frankfurter Israelitisches Gemeinde-Blatt* | 1922 | 8,000 | 1x | Dr. H. Gundersheimer |
| *Deutsches israelitisches Gemeinde-Blatt Hamburg* | 1925 | 5,000 | 1x | Dr. N. M. Nathan |
| *Nachrichtenblatt der Synagogen-Gemeinde Hannover* | 1924 | 1,600 | 1x | Siegfr. Bacharach |
| *Verordnungsblatt des Oberrats badischer Israeliten* (Karlsruhe) | 1884 | 1,000 | irreg. | official |
| *Gemeinde-Blatt Köln-Ehrenfeld* | 1931 | 3,000 | 4x | Fritz Neuländer |
| *Königsberger jüdisches Gemeinde-Blatt* | 1924 | 1,400 | 1x | Dr. Reinhold Lewin |

| PERIODICAL | FOUNDED | CIRCULATION OCT. 1934 | MONTHLY FREQUENCY | EDITOR |
|---|---|---|---|---|
| *Gemeinde-Blatt der israelitischen Rel. Gem. Leipzig* | 1925 | 4,250 | 1x | Rabbi Gustav Cohn |
| *Israelitisches Gemeinde-Blatt für die Pfalz* (Ludwigshafen) | 1923 | 2,300 | 1x | Dr. Gruenewald |
| Mitteilungsblatt der Israelitischen Gemeinde Hessens (Mainz) | 1926 | 5,500 | 1x | Dr. Dienemann |
| *Israelitisches Gemeinde-Blatt* (Mannheim) | 1923 | 2,150 | 2x | Dr. Gruenewald |
| *Bayerische Israelitische Gemeinde-Zeitung München* (Munich) | 1924 | 4,600 | 2x | Dr. L. Feuchtwanger |
| *Nürnberg-Fürther Gemeinde-Blatt* | 1921 | 3,400 | 1x | M. Bernheimer |
| *Gemeinde-Zeitung Saarbrücken* | 1928 | 1,100 | 4x | Rabbi Dr. Rülf |
| *Gemeinde-Blatt* (Stettin) | 1929 | 1,200 | 1x | Justizrat J. Moritz |
| *Gemeinde-Zeitung für die Israelitischen Gemeinden Württembergs* (Stuttgart) | 1924 | 22,000 | 2x | Hans Sternheim |
| *Gemeinde-Zeitung* (Wuppertal, Düsseldorf) | 1928 | 950 | 2x | Gustav Sussmann |

SOURCE: *Philo-Lexikon*, Berlin 1935, cols.559 ff.

## Table 7: The German-Jewish Press 1935

| PERIODICAL | FOUNDED | CIRCULATION OCT. 1934 | MONTHLY FREQUENCY | EDITOR |
|---|---|---|---|---|
| *Der Israelit* (Frankfurt/Main) | 1860 | 4,050 | 4x | S. Schachnowitz |
| *Jüdische-Allgemeine Zeitung* (Berlin) | 1934 | 4,600 | 4x | Dr. E. Tannenbaum |
| *Mitteilung der jüdischen Reform.-Gemeinde* (Berlin) | 1918 | 3,000 | 1x | George Goetz |

| PERIODICAL | FOUNDED | CIRCULATION OCT. 1934 | MONTHLY FREQUENCY | EDITOR |
|---|---|---|---|---|
| *Die Laubhütte* (Hamburg) | 1884 | 3,000 | 2x | Jakob Meyer |
| *Zion* (Berlin) | 1928 | 2,000 | 1x | Alexander Adler |
| *C.V.-Zeitung* (Berlin) | 1922 | 40,000 | 4x | Dr. A. Hirschberg Dr. M. Edelheim |
| *Jüdische Zeitung* (Breslau) | 1924 | 2,000 | 4x | Erich Bildhauer |
| *Jüdische Rundschau* (Berlin) | 1896 | 37,200 | 8x | Dr. R. Weltsch K. Löwenstein |
| *Der Schild* (Berlin) | 1921 | 17,200 | 4x | Dr. Hans Wollenberg |
| *Der Vortrupp* (Berlin) | 1934 | 1,300 | irreg. | Dr. H.J. Schoeps |
| *Hamburger Israelitisches Familienblatt* (Berlin) | 1898 | 36,500 | 4x | Dr. Alfred Kupferberg |
| *Zeitschrift für jüdische Familienforschung* (Berlin) | 1924 | 1,000 | 1x | Dr. A. Czellitzer |
| *Monatsschrift für Geschichte und Wissenschaft des Judentums* (Breslau) | 1851 | 1,800 | irreg. | Dr. I. Heinemann |
| *Zeitschrift für die Geschichte der Juden in Deutschland* (Berlin) | 1929 | 500 | irreg. | Dr. Ernst G. Lowenthal |
| *Monatsblatt des jüdischen Kulturbunds* (Berlin) | 1933 | 18,200 | 1x | Julius Bab |
| *Monatsblatt des jüdischen Kulturbunds Rhein-Main* (Frankfurt/M) | 1934 | 3,000 | 1x | Arthur Holde |
| *Monatsblatt des jüdischen Kulturbunds Rhein-Ruhr* (Cologne) | 1934 | 5,000 | 1x | Dr. T. Rosenthal |
| *Der Morgen* (Berlin) | 1925 | 1,400 | 1x | Dr. E. Reichmann Dr. H. Bach |

33

## The Jewish Press in the Third Reich

| PERIODICAL | FOUNDED | CIRCULATION OCT. 1934 | MONTHLY FREQUENCY | EDITOR |
| --- | --- | --- | --- | --- |
| *Posener Heimatblätter* (Berlin) | 1926 | 1,250 | 1x | Dr. H. Berlak |
| *Der jüdische Kantor* (Hamburg) | 1927 | 250 | irreg. | Leon Kornitzer |
| *Jüdische Schulzeitung* (Cologne) | 1924 | 900 | 1x | Dr. Siegfried Braun |
| *Der jüdische Handwerker* (Berlin) | 1908 | 3,600 | 1x | Erich Salinger |
| *Blätter des jüdischen Frauen-bundes* (Berlin) | 1924 | 4,100 | 1x | Hannah Kaminski |
| *Schwesternverband der UOBB* (Frankfurt/Main) | 1928 | 5,500 | 1x | Dr. Dora Edinger |
| *Großloge für Deutschland UOBB* (Berlin) | 1901 | 10,000 | irreg. | Daniel Bernstein |
| *Der Makkabi* (Berlin) | 1898 | 5,000 | 1x | Heinz Engländer |
| *Gemeinde-Blatt für die jüdische Gemeinde Preußens* (Berlin) | 1922 | 6,000 | 1x | George Goetz |
| *Korrespondenz für jüdische Aus-wanderungsangelegenheiten* (Berlin) | 1905 | 5,000 | irreg. | Mark Wischnitzer |
| *Palästina-Nachrichten* (Berlin) | 1933 | 5,000 | 2x | Dr. F.E. Ascher |
| *Band, Zeitschrift für jüdische Gehörlose* (Berlin-Weißensee) | 1926 | 500 | 1x | Dr. Felix Reich |
| *Jüdische Wohlfahrtspflege und Sozialpolitik* (Berlin) | 1929 | – | irreg. | Dr. Fr. Brodnitz |
| *Informations-Blatt des Zentralaus-schusses für Hilfe und Aufbau* (Berlin) | 1934 | – | irreg. | Dr. Fr. Brodnitz |
| *Gemeinde-Blatt für den Bezirk Aachen* | 1926 | 500 | 2x | Rich. Heidelberg |
| *Jüdisches Gemeinde-Blatt für Anhalt* | 1925 | 350 | 1x | Dr. Isidor Walter |

| PERIODICAL | FOUNDED | CIRCULATION OCT. 1934 | MONTHLY FREQUENCY | EDITOR |
|---|---|---|---|---|
| *Gemeinde-Blatt der jüdischen Gemeinde Berlin* | 1910 | 52,000 | 4x | Leo Kreindler |
| *Gemeinde-Blatt der israelitischen Gemeinde Bremen* | 1929 | 450 | 1x | Dr. Gruenewald |
| *Breslauer jüdisches Gemeinde-Blatt* | 1920 | 5,500 | 2x | Manfr. Rosenfeld |
| *Jüdische Zeitung für Mittelsachsen* (Chemnitz) | 1931 | 1,000 | 2x | Rabbi Dr. Fuchs |
| *Jüdisches Gemeinde-Blatt Danzig* | 1928 | 2,500 | 2x | Dr. Iwan Grün |
| *Gemeinde-Blatt für die Gemeinde Dortmund* | 1933 | 900 | 2x | Heinz Meyerfeld |
| *Mitteilungen des sächsischen Gemeindeverbandes Dresden* | 1927 | 2,400 | irreg. | official |
| *Gemeinde-Blatt der jüdischen Gemeinde Dresden* | 1925 | 2,200 | 2x | Leo Anschel |
| *Gemeinde-Zeitung Düsseldorf* | 1929 | 1,600 | 2x | Rabbi Dr. Klein |
| *Gemeinde-Zeitung Duisburg* | 1929 | 500 | 2x | Rabbi Dr. Klein |
| *Gemeinde-Zeitung Essen* | 1929 | 950 | 2x | Rabbi Dr. Klein |
| *Frankfurter Israelitisches Gemeindeblatt* | 1922 | 7,200 | 1x | Dr. Hermann Gundersheimer |
| *Deutsches Israelitisches Gemeinde-Blatt* (Hamburg) | 1925 | 6,400 | 1x | Dr. M.N. Nathan |
| *Nachrichtenblatt der Synagogen-Gemeinde Hannover* | 1924 | 1,600 | 1x | Dr. Siegfr. Bacharach |
| *Blatt des Oberrats badischer Israeliten* (Karlsruhe) | 1884 | 1,000 | irreg. | official |
| *Israelitisches Gemeinde-Blatt* (Karlsruhe) | 1934 | 2,600 | 2x | Paul Steeg |

# The Jewish Press in the Third Reich

| PERIODICAL | FOUNDED | CIRCULATION OCT. 1934 | MONTHLY FREQUENCY | EDITOR |
|---|---|---|---|---|
| *Jüdische Wochenzeitung* (Kassel) | 1933 | 450 | 1x | Jakob Weißlitz |
| *Gemeinde-Blatt Köln-Ehrenfeld* | 1931 | 2,800 | 4x | Fritz Neuländer |
| *Königsberger jüdisches Gemeinde-Blatt* | 1924 | 1,400 | 1x | Dr. Reinhold Lewin |
| *Gemeinde-Blatt der israelitischen Rel. Gem. Leipzig* | 1925 | 3,800 | 4x | Rabbi Gustav Cohn |
| *Israelitisches Gemeinde-Blatt für die Pfalz* (Ludwigshafen) | 1923 | 2,300 | 1x | Dr. Max Gruenewald |
| *Mitteilungsblatt der israelitischen Gemeinde Hessens* (Mainz) | 1926 | 3,200 | 1x | Dr. Hermann Gundersheimer |
| *Israelitisches Gemeinde-Blatt* (Mannheim) | 1923 | 2,350 | 2x | Dr. Max Gruenewald |
| *Bayerische Israelitische Gemeinde-Zeitung München* | 1924 | 4,500 | 2x | Dr. L. Feuchtwanger |
| *Nürnberg-Fürther Gemeinde-Blatt* | 1921 | 2,950 | 1x | M. Bernheimer |
| *Gemeinde-Zeitung* (Saarbrücken) | 1928 | 1,100 | 2x | Rabbi Dr. L. Rothschild |
| *Gemeinde-Blatt* (Stettin) | 1929 | 1,200 | 1x | Justizrat J. Moritz |
| *Gemeinde-Zeitung für die Israelitischen Gemeinden Württembergs* (Stuttgart) | 1924 | 1,850 | 2x | Hans Sternheim |
| *Gemeinde-Zeitung* (Wuppertal, Düsseldorf) | 1928 | 950 | 2x | Gustav Sussmann |

SOURCE: *Lexikon des Judentums*, Gütersloh 1967, cols. 89—896

## Table 8: The German-Jewish Press 1936

| PERIODICAL | CIRCULATION | FREQUENCY | FOUNDED |
|---|---|---|---|
| **I. Political Papers** | | | |
| *C.V.-Zeitung* (Berlin) | 40,000 | weekly | 1922 |
| *Jüdische Rundschau* (Berlin) | 37,800 | 2x weekly | 1896 |
| *Israelitisches Familienblatt* (Berlin-Hamburg) | 32,000 | weekly | 1899 |
| Edition A Berlin | 9,400 | | |
| Edition B Frankfurt | 3,000 | | |
| Edition C Hamburg | 2,900 | | |
| Edition D National | 16,700 | | |
| *Der Schild* (Berlin) | 15,500 | weekly | 1922 |
| *Jüdische Zeitung* (Breslau) | 1,500 | weekly | 1894 |
| *Palästina-Nachrichten* (Berlin) | 5,000 | monthly | 1934 |
| **II. Religious Papers** | | | |
| *Jüdische Allgemeine Zeitung* (New Series of Jüdisch-Liberale Zeitung) (Berlin) | 3,000 | weekly | 1934 |
| *Der Israelit* (Frankfurt a.M.) *Deutsche Israelitische Zeitung* | 4,000 | weekly | 1860 |
| *Die Laubhütte* (Hamburg) | 2,000 | weekly | 1884 |
| *Mitteilungen der jüdischen Reformgemeinde* (Berlin) | 3,000 | monthly | 1918 |
| **III. Gemeinde Papers** | | | |
| *Gemeindeblatt für den Bezirk der Synagogengemeinde Aachen* | 500 | biweekly | 1927 |
| *Gemeindeblatt der jüdischen Gemeinde zu Berlin* | 51,000 | weekly | 1911 |
| *Breslauer Jüdisches Gemeindeblatt* | 5,500 | biweekly | 1920 |

## The Jewish Press in the Third Reich

| PERIODICAL | CIRCULATION | FREQUENCY | FOUNDED |
|---|---|---|---|
| *Jüdische Zeitung für Mittelsachsen* (Chemnitz) | 900 | biweekly | 1931 |
| *Gemeindeblatt für die jüdische Religionsgemeinde Dortmund* | 850 | biweekly | 1933 |
| *Gemeindeblatt der Israelitischen Religionsgemeinde Dresden* | 2,200 | biweekly | 1925 |
| *Gemeindezeitung für den Synagogenbezirk Düsseldorf* | | | |
| Edition A: Düsseldorf | 1,600 | biweekly | 1931 |
| Edition B: Wuppertal | 1,000 | biweekly | 1931 |
| *Gemeindezeitung für den Synagogenbezirk Essen* (Düsseldorf) | 800 | biweekly | ? |
| *Frankfurter Israelitisches Gemeindeblatt* | 7,100 | monthly | 1923 |
| *Gemeindeblatt der Deutsch-Israelitischen Gemeinde zu Hamburg* | 7,300 | monthly | 1925 |
| *Nachrichtenblatt, Amtl. Org. der Synagogengemeinde Hannover* | 1,000 | weekly | 1924 |
| *Israelitisches Gemeindeblatt* | | | |
| Edition A: Offiz. Organ der Isr. Gemeinden Mannheim, Heidelberg u. Ludwigshafen a. Rh. u. des Verb. der Isr. Kultusgemeinden der Pfalz (Mannheim) | 2,100 | biweekly | 1923 |
| Edition B: Offiz. Organ der Israelitischen Gemeind. Badens (Mannheim) | 2,000 | biweekly | 1923 |
| *Jüdische Wochenzeitung für Kassel, Hessen und Waldeck* (Kassel) | 450 | weekly | 1923 |
| *Gemeindeblatt für die jüdischen Gemeinden in Rheinland u. Westfalen* (Cologne) | 2,800 | weekly | 1931 |
| *Gemeindeblatt für die Israelitische Religionsgemeinde zu Leipzig* | 3,700 | weekly | 1925 |

| PERIODICAL | CIRCULATION | FREQUENCY | FOUNDED |
|---|---|---|---|
| *Mitteilungsblatt des Landesverbandes israelit. Religionsgemeinden Hessens* (Mainz) | 1,900 | monthly | 1926 |
| *Bayerische Israelitische Gemeindezeitung* (Munich) | 4,300 | monthly | 1925 |
| *Nürnberg-Fürther Israelitisches Gemeindeblatt* (Nuremberg) | 3,000 | monthly | 1921 |
| *Nachrichtenblatt der Synagogengemeinden des Saarlandes* (Saarbrücken) | 450 | biweekly | 1928 |
| *Gemeindezeitung für die Israelitischen Gemeinden Württembergs* (Stuttgart) | 1,900 | biweekly | 1924 |
| *Gemeindeblatt für die jüdische Gemeind. Preußens* (Berlin) | 7,600 | monthly | 1923 |

## IV. Scientific and Cultural Journals

| | | | |
|---|---|---|---|
| *Der Morgen* (Berlin) | 1,400 | monthly | 1925 |
| *Zion* (Berlin) | 1,200 | monthly | 1928 |
| *Jüdischer Kulturbund Berlin* | 18,000 | monthly | 1933 |
| *Jüdischer Kulturbund Rhein-Ruhr* (Cologne) | 5,000 | monthly | 1934 |
| *Monatsblätter des Jüdischen Kulturbunds Bezirk Rhein-Main* (Frankfurt/M) | 3,500 | monthly | 1935 |
| *Jüdischer Kulturbund Hamburg* | 1,600 | monthly | 1935 |

## V. Periodicals of Associations

| | | | |
|---|---|---|---|
| *Das Band, Zeitschrift für jüdische Gehörlose* (Berlin) | 500 | monthly | 1926 |
| *Blätter des Verbandes jüdischer Heimatvereine* (Berlin) | 1,600 | monthly | 1927 |
| *Blätter des Jüdischen Frauenbundes* (Berlin) | 500 | monthly | 1925 |

## The Jewish Press in the Third Reich

| PERIODICAL | CIRCULATION | FREQUENCY | FOUNDED |
|---|---|---|---|
| *Der Jüdische Kantor* (Hamburg) | 250 | bimonthly | 1927 |
| *Der Makkabi* (Berlin) | 5,000 | monthly | 1900 |
| *Der jüdische Handwerker* (Berlin) | 3,600 | monthly | 1909 |
| *Jüdische Schulzeitung* (Mannheim) | 800 | monthly | 1925 |
| *Die Zeitschrift des Schwesternverbandes der Bne Briss* (Frankfurt/M) | 5,000 | monthly | 1926 |
| *Jüdische Familienforschung* (Berlin) | 1,000 | monthly | 1925 |

SOURCE: Hermann Samter, "Die Jüdische Presse in Deutschland," *Berliner Jüdisches Gemeindeblatt*, August 23, 1936

Figures for the year 1938 cannot be found in Jewish sources, but are available from the files of Hans Hinkel, the Reich Commissar for Jewish Affairs in the Chamber of Culture. According to those files, there were 65 Jewish papers and periodicals in 1938, printed by 53 publishing houses. The figures are valid down to November 10, 1938, when the entire Jewish press was closed down, and also include Jewish periodicals published in Austria, which had been annexed.

## Table 9: Jewish Papers and Periodicals in the German Reich, 1938

| CATEGORY | NUMBER |
|---|---|
| Newspapers | 4 |
| Gemeinde periodicals | 28 |
| Kulturbund periodicals | 5 |
| Religious (Orthodox) publications | 2 |
| Scientific periodicals | 8 |
| Sport bulletins | 5 |
| Professional journals | 3 |
| Sociological journals | 2 |
| Women's magazines | 1 |
| Other | 7 |

Source: Wiener Library, London (now Tel Aviv University)

# 3
—

# Development of a Jewish Press: The Historical Background

It is impossible to comprehend the phenomenon of Jewish journalistic activity under the Nazis without an understanding of the development of the Jewish press in Germany over the preceding one hundred years. Though it had never been condemned to having to function under a regime as uniquely oppressive as that of National Socialism, its periods of flowering and famine had nonetheless provided a reflection of the political and social situation of the Jewish population even in earlier decades.

Whenever Jews were permitted to participate in the public, economic and cultural life of their German environment, then they read the German papers. The greater the restrictions, the more hampered their freedom of movement, the more the Jewish reader turned toward Jewish papers – for advice and edification, and as a source of hope. In other words: the worse the situation Jews found themselves in, the greater was the importance of the Jewish press, and this historical precedent gives an indication of the prominent role it was to play under the Nazi regime.

In 1928, the international press exhibition "Pressa" was held in Cologne. For the first time, the Jewish press also wished to introduce itself to the rest of the world. The question was whether it should appear as a compact unit or scattered according to geographical criteria among the various general papers and periodicals.

An honorary committee was set up in 1927 for the purpose of deliberating on the matter; its members included representatives from all the Jewish political and religious currents, as well as outstanding Jewish personalities in intellectual and economic life, such as Chaim N. Bialik, S. Dubnow, Shalom Asch, Albert Einstein, Max Liebermann, Nahum Sokolow and the bankers Oscar Wassermann and Jakob Goldschmidt.[1] Max Bodenheimer[2] was appointed committee chairman. He complained that preparations in Berlin had been impeded "by the most remarkable struggles between differing camps." The Centralverein deutscher Staatsbürger jüdischen Glaubens (Central Federation of German Citizens of Jewish Persuasion) espoused the view that a separate Jewish section was quite inappropriate.[3] Moreover, Bruno Woyda, a Religious-Liberal member of the executive committee of the Berlin Gemeinde, had already decided to organize an exhibition of German-Jewish periodicals in the section on German journalism.[4]

However, the principal question that had to be resolved was whether a separate Jewish exhibit had any justification whatsoever; after all, it did not represent a unified world view, neither in the religious sense, as among Catholics and Protestants, nor in a political or humanistic respect. The *Kölner Jüdisch-Liberale Zeitung* observed: "In religious, national, political, sociological, cultural, literary and aesthetic terms, it is as the demands of the day require. It [the Jewish press] evinces all possible shades of opinion, from uncompromising orthodoxy to sceptical atheism, from bourgeois capitalism to socialism to communism, from the most narrow and closed nationalism to the most embracing and inclusive internationalism."[5] In the end, however, it was generally agreed that despite all differences, Jewish journalism shared a common basis in the "fundamental moral and social conceptions embodied in Jewish literature."[6] Dr. Bodenheimer called it a "tragic misfortune" that the products of this press had not succeeded in penetrating out beyond the confines of the Jewish population in order to inform the rest of the world about Jewish concerns and ideals, "the ideals of humanity as first proclaimed by the Bible."[7]

In his speech on the opening of the Jewish special exhibit, which was housed in a spacious pavilion and had some 100,000 visitors, Bodenheimer commented: "It sounds almost ironic when people call papers like the *Berliner Tageblatt,* the *Vossische Zeitung* and *Frankfurter Zeitung* . . . the 'Jewish' press. Their founders and directors are very distant from Judaism both in the sense of a religion and an ethnic community. . . . One enjoys labelling the leftist papers '*Judenpresse*,' while completely forgetting that the narrowly conservative *Kreuzzeitung* was likewise established by a baptized Jew."[8] Thus, Bodenheimer noted, while Jewish journalism celebrated its greatest triumphs in the general daily press, the actual Jewish press remained small and without influence; nonetheless, it demonstrated the willingness to sacrifice shared by Jews throughout all eras in their struggle for religious liberty and human and civil rights. "It demonstrates that the Jews take part in the joys and sufferings of the people amongst which they live."[9]

This tendency was already manifest in the earliest Jewish periodicals published in German. The narrow world of small principalities was not advantageous for the development of a Jewish press in Germany. That press had its first beginnings in Holland in the seventeenth century, and its center of gravity did not shift to Germany until the middle of the eighteenth century. After initial publications which appeared in Hebrew and Yiddish, the first Jewish periodical in German, *Sulamith*, appeared in 1806 in Moses Mendelssohn's native town of Dessau, edited by David Fraenkel and Joseph Wolf.[10] Programmatically, it intended to promote the "development of intensive educational abilities among Jews" and, animated by the optimistic faith in progress of the Enlightenment, espoused the new ideals – emancipation, religious reform, Jewish sermons and science in the German language.[11]

Yet upon the heels of early success came a crisis. Looking back at the first two decades of the nineteenth century, the doctor and author Phöbus Philippson remarked: "Those who deemed themselves to be the most progressive, and who were thoroughly weary of rabbinical religion and its excesses, looked to the outside world, and developed an exclusive enthusiasm for the . . . German classical writers. Lessing, Goethe, Schiller, Jean Paul were for them the supreme authors of a general education, while the French writers Voltaire and Rousseau were the outstanding spokesmen of a general natural religion valid for all men. Or, burdened by worldly affairs and concern for their home and hearth, they remained strangers to any and all intellectual perfection."[12] Why, people asked, were there such fearful efforts to spread the benefits of culture and education? "Was it not an arrogant gesture for the only Jewish journal at the time, *Sulamith*, to brandish the tendentious phrase 'for the furtherance of culture and humanity among the Jewish nation' on its title page? Why could this not be left to the workings of time and the powerful influence of social and political life?"[13] Jews in Germany in that era found themselves in an ambiguous situation. As citizens, they wanted an Allied victory and the liberation of Germany from French occupation. But as Jews, they feared an undermining of their equality after the fall of Napoleon. "They will be shackled once again with the old chains, that have been broken or lightened only in a small part of Germany."[14]

And this is indeed what occurred. After the French were routed, a new wave of anti-Semitism engulfed the Jewish community; and as always in such periods of travail, the Jewish press experienced a brief moment of flowering. Journals were founded that seldom survived beyond their first issue, and even when they did, were generally short-lived publications. Their editors were rabbis who endeavored to edify their readership in a popular manner and to inform readers about events in the Jewish world and current issues that had relevance for the Jewish population.

The first issue of the journal *Der Jude* appeared in 1832; it was edited by Gabriel Riesser, an early champion of civil liberties, who also "brought Judaism once again to the level of self-awareness and demonstrated by word and deed the baseness of its disavowal for the sake of advantage."[15] The fact that the periodical only existed until 1835 was due in large measure to the fact that its editor left journalism to later become the first Jewish judge in Germany, a justice of the superior court in Hamburg; in 1848–1849, he served as vice-president of the Frankfurt National Assembly.

Another journal with political overtones, *Der Orient* (1840–1848), edited by Dr. Julius Fürst, addressed itself to the question as to what the victory of reaction had to do with the Jewish interests to which the periodical was committed: "For us, emancipation is a legacy of the revolution, and with the latter, emancipation will probably also be vanquished. . . . We can only trust in the victory of the revolution to bring about a victory for our cause. . . . Let us repeat: as Jews, we stand or fall with democracy."[16]

Although the focal point of journalism in those years was with the scientific periodicals,[17] the establishment of the *Allgemeine Zeitung des Judentums* proved decisive for the development of the Jewish press, both in respect to its editorial breadth of coverage and its durability. The journal's founder and editor, Rabbi Ludwig Philippson, wished to gather in "Israel's dispersion once again by means of an intellectual and literary bond" and to explain the "importance of Judaism in respect to universal history as well."[18] The paper was founded in 1837 and absorbed in 1921 into the new *CV-Zeitung*, which continued to carry its name in its banner.

The *Allgemeine*, styling itself as a "non-sectarian organ for all Jewish interests in respect to politics, religion, literature, history, linguistics and belles-lettres," also was the first Jewish journal to have non-Jewish readers as well. Although it was not actually published three times a week as the advance notice promised, it had a special position as a weekly by dint of its durability over the years. After the death of Ludwig Philippson, the first modern journalist in the Jewish sector, he was succeeded by Gustav Karpeles, a biographer of Heine; Karpeles was followed by Ludwig Geiger, editor of the Goethe Yearbook, and finally by Alfred Katz. Philippson also introduced the practice of the "editorial," political commentary by the editor, a column that was later to play such an important role in the Jewish press in Germany.

After the Jewish press was granted greater freedoms as a result of the 1847 Prussian Law on Jews, its pages soon reflected the wave of disappointment over the events following in the aftermath of 1848, although censorship was not reinstated and several other achievements were also preserved to a certain extent. Efforts for emancipation gradually prevailed in the new constitutions in the individual states, especially in those of the North German Confederation and the Bismarckian Reich.

German citizens of the Jewish faith who were able to take part in the political and intellectual currents of the surrounding world now sought out the general German press as a source for information and opinion, and the Jewish press was pushed off into a narrow and highly circumscribed corner. The centrifugal currents in Judaism were met by forces that viewed the family as the abiding center of stability in Jewish life; hence, a new genre arose in Jewish journalism – the family paper. Once again, as in the case of Ludwig Philippson, it was a rabbi, Moritz Rahmer, in his own right an eminent journalist, who in 1878 added the new supplement "Jewish Family Life" to the *Israelitische Wochenschrift*, which he had taken over ten years earlier. From 1894 on, it appeared as a separate independent publication entitled *Familienblatt*. Others followed his example.

Such family papers had their own special profile – they wished less to inform than to entertain the family sitting together around the table. Its stories and legends, cultural section and serialized novels became the paper's core, and they were careful not to espouse any party or organized persuasion. Even their ads section remained limited to personal notices – family announcements contributed to the intimacy of the publications. On the other hand, they formed a transitional link with the institution of the Gemeinde papers, the first of which appeared in Königsberg in 1876. The family papers constituted a kind of bridge to the Gemeinden in that they were distributed in various localities gratis to community members, even though they were not official publications and continued to be shaped by the decisions of their publishers. The largest of the family journals, the *Hamburger Israelitisches Familienblatt*, was founded by Max Lessmann in 1898 and remained in existence until 1938.

The ambition to enter into German society and the struggle for equal rights were briefly reinforced by a feeling of security within national political life in Germany. That sense of security was soon shattered. Anti-Semitism underwent a resurgence with the appearance of the court preacher Stoecker in Berlin and in the wake of the Dreyfus affair in France, and the Jewish press reacted correspondingly. A gradual differentiation had also occurred within Jewish journalism as a result of the developments in general newspaper publishing and changes in the transmission of news. One segment of the Jewish press countered anti-Semitism with enlightenment and defensive riposte, while another segment pressed on with a thoroughgoing examination of the Jewish question. Both the defensive and the Jewish-national attitude led to a growing politicization of Jewish journalism.

Even before Theodore Herzl published *Die Welt* in Vienna in 1897 and the German Zionists had founded the *Jüdische Rundschau* in Berlin in 1896, the weekly *Die Menorah*, edited by M. Deutschländer in Hamburg, had carried the appeal as early as 1891: "Zionists of all lands, unite! The movement for the Holy Land and Syria has once again taken on a powerful new momentum. . . . There is understanding from all quarters . . . for the aims of the Zion associations.[19] But the mighty hand is still absent which could unite all these efforts into a great and unified whole; the impulse is still lacking for a united, purposeful, practical approach."[20]

In this way, a new type of paper was created, one that remained predominant until the tragic end in 1938, namely the official organs of the Jewish political organizations: the Zentralverein deutscher Staatsbürger jüdischen Glaubens and its *CV-Zeitung*, the Zionistische Vereinigung für Deutschland and its journal *Jüdische Rundschau*, the Reichsbund jüdischer Frontsoldaten (*Der Schild*), the nationalist grouping Nationaldeutsche Juden (*Der Nationaldeutsche Jude*),[21] the short-lived *Der Staatszionist* of the Revisionists and the paper *Der Vortrupp*.[22]

The initiative of the individual publisher and editor was supplanted by the collective initiative of the organization or institution, such as that of the Gemeinden. The only exception to this was the *Hamburger Israelitisches Familienblatt*, that survived as an independent weekly until the bitter end.[23] It was one of the four large Jewish papers and also engaged on occasion in political commentary, though remaining on "neutral" ground.[24]

The columns of the papers of these organizations carried ideological discussions on Zionism and assimilation, anti-Semitism and emancipation, full-fledged citizenship vs. autonomy, Reform Judaism vs. Orthodoxy, German culture and Jewish culture.

In 1933, a radical transformation was wrought in Jewish journalism. Papers that had only addressed themselves to limited segments of Jewish existence now became comprehensive media. The process ran in an opposite direction to what had taken place after achieving emancipation: then the Jewish reader had ceased using the Jewish press as a source of information, since the German media were opening its pages to him, and it was there that he found his economic and cultural interests represented. Now he sought orientation in the Jewish papers, and not just because he had lost his trust in the German press and regarded it as a hostile instrument. It was only in Jewish papers and journals that the Jewish reader could find everything that was of concern to him, that moved him and was relevant. He had come full circle.

## Notes

1. Private archive, Dr. Max Bodenheimer, Central Zionist Archives, Jerusalem.

2. Attorney in Cologne, president of the Jewish Gemeinde, a leading Zionist.

3. Minutes of the meeting held on September 29, 1927, private archive, M. Bodenheimer.

4. Minutes of October 20, 1927, ibid. Woyda later became a member of the Berlin working committee on the special Jewish exhibit.

5. November 11, 1927.

6. Max Bodenheimer, "Entstehung und Bedeutung der jüdischen Sonder-schau," *Menorah* (Vienna-Frankfurt/M), 6 (June–July 1928), no. 6–7, special issue on the Jewish exhibit at the PRESSA, Cologne 1928.

7. Bodenheimer 1958, p. 259.

8. Friedrich Julius Stahl, formerly Julius Joelson, founder of Prussian conservatism and the Conservative Party (1802–1861).

9. Private archive, M. Bodenheimer. See also *Monumenta Judaica*, 1963, p. 414ff; Asaria, 1959, p. 318. The *Hamburger Israelitisches Familienblatt*, in its edition of May 31, 1928, termed the special exhibit "one enormous failure. . . . One really can derive no idea at all of their type of influence . . . of the cultural, literary and political importance of these periodicals from the sample pages that had been included in the exhibit."

10. Later edited by Fraenkel alone.

11. Cf. the exhibition catalogue *Jüdische Presse im 19. Jahrhundert*, issued by the International Press Museum of the City of Aachen, Aachen 1967, p. 13.

12. Philippson, 1864, p. 162f.

13. Ibid., p. 99.

14. Ibid., p. 117.

15. Ibid., p. 100. The journal *Der Jude* was again revived and published in Berlin 1916–1924, under the editorship of Martin Buber and Siegmund Katznelson.

16. November 25, 1848. Quoted from *Jüdische Presse im 19. Jahrhundert*, p. 29.

17. Among others, *Zeitschrift für die Wissenschaft des Judentums*, established by Leopold Zunz, Berlin 1822; *Wissenschaftliche Zeitschrift für jüdische Theologie*, founded by Abraham Geiger, Frankfurt/Main 1834; *Monatsschrift für Geschichte und Wissenschaft des Judentums*, established by Zacharias Frankel, Breslau 1851.

18. Philippson, *1864*, p. 100.

19. Association of "Chowewe Zion," the "Friends of Zion"; their first weekly in German, *Der Colonist*, appeared in Kattowitz in 1876.

20. Hamburg, September 4, 1891, no. 28.

21. 1921–1935, under the editorship of Dr. Max Naumann.

22. The journals *Der Nationaldeutsche Jude*, *Der Staatszionist* (founded in 1933, edited by Georg Kareski) and *Der Vortrupp* (founded in 1924, under the editorship of Hans-Joachim Schoeps) were all officially banned in 1935.

23. Since 1935 called *Israelitisches Familienblatt*; the *Jüdische Zeitung*, Breslau, also survived until 1937.

24. When Schalom Ben Chorin applied as a young man in 1934 for the position of culture-page editor with the *Familienblatt* in Hamburg, he was told: "You could have saved yourself the trip. Our political editor is a Zionist and free-thinker. Now what we need is somebody non-Zionist and Orthodox." Private archive, Ben Chorin. The political editor on the paper was Dr. Alfred Kupferberg.

# 4

## To Stay or Leave?

Journalism has been called the "interpretation of events."[1] The problem of interpretation opens up numerous options for the journalist. There are cases in which he is at the veritable mercy of a kind of psychological "gradient" molding his perceptions, manifested in the general direction taken by his efforts to make sense of the events of the day. This journalistic attitude stands in marked contrast with attempts to interpret events that involve a conscious effort on the part of the commentator to penetrate to the inner mechanism and dynamics operative among the various events. In this sense, those who left a shaping imprint on the Jewish press in Nazi Germany were interpreters of the scene – "able to check the irresponsibility of those in power"[2] – interpreters and admonishers, teachers and consolers. They stood torn between the poles of compulsion and conscience, constraint and knowledge, before the judgment chair of history and the butchers of the Gestapo.

There was a great deal more than mere semantic masquerade or opportunism behind the avowal of loyalty to *Deutschtum* ("Germanism," German culture and mores) expressed by all shades of opinion in the Jewish press in 1933. The German Jews had strong psychological and intellectual bonds with *Deutschtum*, and felt they were an integral part of the German people.[3] As "unpatriotic" and untrue as it may have been to deny those bonds in the first two years after 1933, such an avowal of allegiance was frowned upon and even viewed as dangerous during the course of 1935. Finally, in September of that year, the Nuremberg Laws made it a criminal offense.[4]

This problematic relationship with the German people and culture found greater expression in the pages of the Jewish press than in any other forum. It crystallized in the question: to stay or leave? The various options were discussed, ranging across a broad spectrum of stark hues and the finest nuances: the homeland vs. exile, Germany, Palestine or another country overseas, inner or external emigration. Deliberations were always based on the presupposition that economic survival was still possible.

The Nuremberg Laws brought this controversy to an abrupt end. German Jewry was stripped of its citizenship; the new direction, which until then had been open to differing interpretations, appeared clearly defined: the Nazis apparently now had a definite and set policy toward the Jews. The formerly bright palette of the Jewish press turned monochrome, and the constraints effected an internal Jewish accommodation with the new system.

The liquidation of the business enterprises of German Jews did not follow immediately on the heels of their removal from official positions and from political and cultural life. Rather, that process of gradual liquidation dragged on for some five years, punctuated occasionally by periods of "economic upswing."[5] If they sought a *modus vivendi* in Germany after the initial shock, Jews tended to follow the example of their coreligionists in two other areas, Italy and Eastern Europe. Italian Jews had been living already for more than a decade in a form of accommodation under fascism, and Jews occupied prominent positions in the fascist party.[6] Jews in Eastern Europe had accumulated experience over the decades in developing forms of coexistence with anti-Jewish regimes – without coming to a conclusion that they should emigrate en masse. The fact that the Vatican had concluded a concordate with the new German government on July 20, 1933 was viewed as a sign that the highest levels of the Catholic church had moral confidence in Germany, even under Hitler. Moreover, it seemed unlikely that the Nazi regime would be anything more than a passing episode. Its ultimate fate depended on conflicts in its own internal camp,[7] as well as on the Western powers. Leo Baeck, who in 1933 had predicted an end to the thousand-year history of Jews in Germany, thought a year later that a military coup directed against Hitler was indeed a possibility.[8] From May 1933 until the summer of 1936, there were repeated expectations that the Western powers would introduce sanctions in response to Hitler's treaty violations; it is doubtful whether the Nazi government would have been able to survive such an eventuality.[9]

Under such circumstances, the question of Jewish emigration from Germany was less an expression of ideological outlook than the product of pragmatic considerations. It would be a gross simplification to maintain that the *Jüdische Rundschau*, the official organ of the German Zionist Association, supported emigration to Palestine, and that the non-Zionist press at the time favored the idea of staying on in Germany, or later espoused the idea of emigration overseas and to other European countries. None of the papers excluded any of these options. Discussion about the primacy of emigrating to Palestine was only initiated after 1935. The *Jüdische Rundschau* warned readers not to regard Palestine solely as a continuation of existence in the diaspora. "Zionism is not a welfare office . . . it is an idea. . . . For example, it would be mistaken to say that whoever has lost his job in Germany should go to Palestine. . . . As paradoxical as it sounds, we have to advise many Jews nowadays not to go to Palestine, because there will necessarily be disappointments arising from such decisions. Palestine only gives to those who give to it."[10]

The papers differed in their analyses of the Jewish question. They agreed in the view that a return to Judaism was not identical with a return to the land of the Jews. Their common platform was: Judaism as an intellectual direction, a source of moral strength, a protection against defamation. "Jews in the midst of . . . a world that rejects them are now beginning, intellectually and culturally, to strike out on an inward path."[11] Or, in a formulation with strong religious overtones: "What Germany's Jews need is for a burning wave of *tshuva* (repentance) to now sweep over them. Repentance and renunciation in all Jewish spheres."[12]

Zionists were no different from other Jewish groups in their deep attachment to Germany.[13] "It is no easy task bearing the burden of the fate of an emigrant. . . . We know that generations will remain true to what they have received from the German spirit."[14] The *Jüdische Rundschau* believed there ought to be possibilities for Jews to live in the new Germany as well: "We believe that German Jews also must find their place and be integrated into this state, and we hope it yet proves possible to find the form for this, one that is in harmony with the principles of this new state."[15] What the author meant here was not a "regaining" of rights by Jews, but rather a "new restructuring"[16] of Jewish life: i.e., the Jews would have a possibility, after consolidation of the new state, to live there as Jews – because the path of emigration was open "only to the few, and those who had especially high qualifications."[17] This standpoint was made even clearer: "Many a Zionist . . . may be linked by much stronger ties to the country of his birth than others who openly profess their loyalty."[18] No Jewish group, the paper emphasized, had raised the demand that Jews should forswear their allegiance to *Deutschtum*. The *Jüdische Rundschau* was also the first paper after the horrifying experiences of the national boycott of Jewish firms on April 1, 1933 to state in no uncertain language that the bonds linking German Jews with German culture and the German people could not be sundered – even as a result of such events.[19] However, the paper also called for preserving certain loyalties that could not be put on show and paraded before "those in power" – namely one's loyalty to Judaism. That was a form of faithfulness which demanded greater moral fiber than the repeatedly reiterated loyalty to *Deutschtum*.[20]

The *Jüdische Rundschau* rejected the notion of narrowly pigeonholing the Zionists, placing them, say, in the category of "specialists for migration to Palestine." After all, despite the difficult changes taking place in occupational life, the majority of German Jews, the paper believed, would have to stay on in Germany and succeed there in the struggle for survival. Thus, the Zionist task was to strengthen the backbone of Jews, to bring about a "transformation in the Jewish psyche."[21] "Anyone who has a basic familiarity with the fate of many families . . . knows that the decision to emigrate or stay on is not prompted by considerations of ideology or principle; rather, it is questions of one's economic survival that play the crucial role." The paper was against drawing any conclusions about an individual's ideology and outlook from such a decision.[22]

The journal *Der Schild*, the official organ of the Reichsbund jüdischer Frontsoldaten, occupied the polar opposite end of the internal Jewish spectrum.[23] It asserted that the will to cling steadfastly to every clod of German soil was more powerful than bloodless theory and brilliant literary subtleties.[24] "Germany is not our second home by dint of choice; it is our [only] home and homeland. . . . As Germans who risked their lives on the battlefield for Germany and then reaped this reward, we feel a sense of unspeakable shame."[25] The decision to save *Deutschtum* for German Jews insofar as they desired to be German was, the paper argued, a choice up to the Jews and lay squarely in their hands.[26]

If the present-day generation were to inwardly bury their attachment to German culture and make concessions to the notion of encapsulating oneself off from the surrounding world, then German Jews would, by their own actions, be forfeiting the inner legitimacy for ever again demanding and acquiring full legal equality.[27] The German Zionists, it contended, were committing an error by trying to persuade this segment of German Jews to abandon their German outlook.[28] "This is where the great guilt of Zionism lies. . . . By its struggle against emancipation, which it erroneously regards as a struggle against assimilation, it has endangered the very meaning of emancipation."[29]

The *CV-Zeitung* reached similar conclusions.[30] "The German Jews who are members of the CV differ from the Zionists living in Germany by the fact that, going beyond strict adherence to their duties as citizens, they follow what is taking place in Germany with great emotional interest."[31] In its overwhelming majority, German Jewry was, the paper asserted, determined to remain in its homeland for reasons of powerful inner psychological attachment, and not because of economic expediency; it was ready to serve the "ordered principle of the state." German Jewry did not want any solution that would dissolve its ties with Germany.[32] "The more and more the National Socialist state is strengthened and made a concrete reality as a result of its decisions, the more unthreatening for its expression and survival must the integration of a portion of the population be whose hearts have always beat strong with patriotic feeling for Germany. . . . For us, Germany is our historical place."[33] Zionism, the paper went on, viewed the eventual separation of German Jewry from its German context – be it by emigration to Palestine or while staying on in Germany itself – as inevitable, regarding only the specific point in time as uncertain. The CV, in contrast, regarded a later reintegration as definite and only a matter of time, though its precise hour remained uncertain.[34]

The *Jüdische Rundschau* countered: "What dialectic? . . . Zionism has called for 'strengthening Jewish consciousness' . . . the CV-Zeitung calls this a 'separation . . . from its German context,' and in a certain respect that is correct, because a conscious Jew will no longer see himself as part of a German context the way an assimilationist used to."[35] The *CV-Zeitung* had stated: "We regard the strengthening of Jewish consciousness . . . as the intellectual and psychological foundation stone for our remaining on in Germany."[36] To this, the *Rundschau* replied: "We fail to comprehend what can be meant by the proclamation of a strengthening of Jewish consciousness as a foundation stone for staying on in Germany, unless this means to say: a Jew can live in dignity in Germany only as a Jew who is fully and constantly conscious of his being a Jew. But that is a Jewish nationalist position, adopted from us quite literally."[37] Was it true that the German Jews had been guilty of "transgressing beyond a certain limit," i.e., had they been active in German political life over and beyond their numerical importance, failing to find the requisite reserve and tact to avoid assuming public office, something which "astonished the people, injuring its feelings"?[38] The national chairman of the Reichsbund jüdischer Frontsoldaten, Cpt. (Dr.) Löwenstein, answered in reply: "A widely read Jewish paper in Berlin . . . has recently accused Jews of such a failing. We feel it necessary . . . to point out that the accusation which this paper believes it is obliged to hurl against the so-called 'assimilationists' cannot fail to boomerang, falling back on its own group. The fateful fact . . . was that it was specifically persons who said they were national Jews – and did not regard themselves in national terms as Germans – who were the ones holding public office."[39]

The *Hamburger Israelitisches Familienblatt*, not affiliated with any organization or party, did not enter the fray of internal Jewish disputes. Nonetheless, on occasion it provided representatives of various political directions with a platform for discussion. Thus, Heinrich Stern, chairman of the Association for Liberal Judaism in Germany, wrote that German Jews should be careful to avoid incurring the criticism of their children that they had been guilty of casting aside an inalienable treasure: their beloved fatherland. Dr. Alfred Hirschberg, editor of the *CV-Zeitung*, also declared that a Jewish community which voluntarily forfeited its German position could never have an inner justified claim to rectifying its situation. That view was seconded by Dr. Ludwig Freund, national executive director of the Reichsbund: "Today we are engaged in a struggle for the final, outermost positions of German Jews in the German world. If we willingly surrender the outposts we can maintain, then we will forfeit any prospects for the future." Among Zionist spokespersons, Georg Kareski, member of the executive board of the Jüdische Volkspartei, blamed the fact that Palestine had not yet become the home of the Jewish people on the "indolence shown by broad segments of German Jewry." He argued that at the very least, there should now be an attempt to provide as large a number of German Jews as possible with the opportunity to begin a new life in Palestine. To accomplish this, it would be necessary to transfer Jewish assets from Germany, Kareski added, and that could only be implemented, of course, after reaching an agreement with the German government. Rabbi Pinchas Cohen, executive chairman of the World Organization of Agudas Yisroel, had a different view: he argued that since the religious idea towered far above any racial and national elements in Judaism, to accept the "Jewish nationalist curia" would be tantamount to acceptance of the racial conception.[40]

In the summer of 1933, the then rector of Frankfurt University, Dr. Ernst Kriegk, commented on the Jewish problem in his journal *Volk im Werden*: "It is our desire to reach an understanding with the Jews, and some day we shall. But that will not come about by treading the path of Jewish emancipation attempted in the nineteenth century; rather, it will be realized by constituting the Jews as a people in the sense of Zionism, and thus as a national minority here in our country. We are speaking here as one people to another, and it is on that new basis that we must resolve the Jewish problem."[41] A similar idea was also broached by the Deutschnational Reichstag deputy Freiherr von Freytag-Loringhoven, who suggested the possibility that the Jews might be declared a foreign people in complete accord with völkisch-racial principles; they could then be granted cultural autonomy under supervision of the state.[42]

The Jewish press rejected such conceptions. Commented the *CV-Zeitung*: "To the extent that this is . . . a psychological decision and not something decreed by the state, we must reject . . . the solution. Moreover, the sense we have that we . . . are facing an uncertain future and difficult fate can change nothing in this regard. . . . We do not wish to live in this country, on whose soil our fathers have lived and suffered . . . as a national minority, but rather as German citizens – of Jewish extraction and Jewish faith."[43] Dr. Alfred Hirschberg wrote in the *Hamburger Israelitisches Familienblatt*: "There is no need to waste words on the utopian scheme of a total resettlement. . . . In accordance with the law of polarity, the counterproposal has been made that we should lead an autonomous existence within the borders of Germany in line with the example . . . of national minorities elsewhere. Palestine, as it exists today, cannot now, and will not for a long time to come, be able to constitute the homeland for Jewish minorities that culturally are on a Western European level."[44] The position of the *Schild* was unambiguous: "The RJF had to decide whether it was in favor of the homeland or opted for being considered a foreign element [in Germany]. . . . It goes without saying that for us, our claim to the soil we have fertilized with our blood and defended with our bodies shall never be extinguished."[45]

The same problem was treated by Max Hildebert Boehm in his book *Das eigenständige Volk*.[46] Boehm's approach proceeded on the basis of the assumption that national minorities should demand state protection in order to ensure the vital preservation of their own national-ethnic culture [*Volkstum*] within an alien environment. Commenting on this, the *Jüdische Rundschau* noted that German Jews wanted just the opposite, namely not to be disturbed in their assimilation. Yet the current policy of the German government amounted to dissimilation of Jews.[47] The *Jüdische Rundschau* also rejected the conception of a national minority. It argued that not only the CV, but all other Jewish groups in Germany as well, including the Zionists, had always espoused the view that Jews there could not be regarded as a national minority in the sense of the Treaty of Versailles, since they lacked the usual features of a national minority in a democratic state. Yet now the situation had changed: "The state, whether the Jews wished so or not, had transformed them into a group that was also special and recognizable in terms of national law. Today they are no longer equal individuals before the law in a liberal state, but rather are characterized by their group affiliation, both legally and politically. Yet the import of this should be clear: Jews do in actual fact constitute a minority in Germany, whether they like it or not."[48] The *Schild* reminded the *Jüdische Rundschau* that it had recently rejected the idea of setting up a Jewish minority group, despite all its earlier[49] pronouncements: "according to this, what else can Zionism offer the great mass of German Jews but the inorganic status of being a foreign element in Germany, which . . . will necessarily be harmful for all sections of the population, Aryan and non-Aryan alike?"[50]

Along with the question of national minority and group affiliation, the concept of "group emancipation" also surfaced in public discussion. In a report on a Berlin public meeting held by the CV, Dr. Bruno Weil, one of the leading personalities of the organiza-

56

tion, declared that at the present moment, the lines of difference within German Jewry no longer followed the divide between Zionists and non-Zionists. Rather, the line of fissure ran between those who supported a new emancipation, and those who rejected the idea. "We intend to wage the new struggle for emancipation as Germans and German citizens in Germany."[51] The *Jüdische Rundschau* also voiced a position on this problem: "The goal of the new struggles for emancipation cannot be the equality of the individual, but emancipation as a group. . . . In the new Germany, we will . . . only be able to achieve a true and genuine emancipation by restoring an intellectual visage to our Jewishness. . . . In the old mode of emancipation, the slogan was to make Judaism as inconspicuous as possible. Today it is to make Judaism conscious."[52] That prognosis was not shared by the *Israelitisches Familienblatt*. "The new emancipation – as bitter that awareness is, as difficult it remains to enunciate and put down in writing – is but a dream."[53]

The *Israelitisches Familienblatt* was a unique case within the Jewish press in that it was the only one of the large Jewish papers unaffiliated with an institution or organization. An advertisement on its own behalf read: "Today a Jewish paper has to have absolute editorial independence, and not be subservient to any party or large organization; it must take a clear and unequivocal stand on the issues and concerns of the day."[54] Although its publisher M. Lessmann had tried hard to give the paper a nonpartisan flavor, the personal outlook of the four subsequent chief editors made itself felt in the paper's orientation.[55]

In 1933, young people finishing their school exams were advised by the paper to come to a realization "that the Jewish craft trades and agriculture in Germany need new blood"[56] and that "we Jews cannot be torn from the body of the German people without leaving lasting, bloody wounds."[57] Even after being temporarily shut down by the Hamburg police, the paper stated that "after [occupational] restructuring has been completed, we shall present ourselves to those of our fellow German *Volksgenossen* as the kind of individuals we always were: an integral part of the German people – full of strength, ready to engage in reconstruction, a segment that cannot be discouraged or kept down long by any blow of fate."[58]

The first article of the paper on emigration opportunities, with reports from Denmark, England, Holland, Yugoslavia, Lithuania,

Luxembourg, Austria, Portugal, Sweden, Switzerland, Spain and Czechoslovakia, carried the pessimistic caption: "Abandon all Hope . . . No Possibilities to Survive Economically for German Jews Abroad." The paper noted: "We did not request information from our staff correspondents in the Holy Land because anyone desiring to go there can obtain comprehensive information from the Palestine Office, Berlin W15, Meinekestraße 10."[59] A short time thereafter, the paper published a full-page spread "From the Holy Land," with reports and information.[60] That column became a regular feature and was further expanded, though the section on Palestine was incorporated as part of a new page entitled "Occupational Restructuring and Emigration."[61]

The initially negative attitude toward emigration was amended that same summer by other reports: "Are There Prospects for Emigrants After All? What Foreign Countries Need and Don't Need,"[62] an article in which Belgium and Morocco were added to the above list of countries. In September, the paper conducted a large-scale survey, "The Situation of Emigrants in Various Countries," including ten countries in Europe, along with Palestine, the United States, Egypt and Latin America.[63] An editorial at year's end concluded: "Though it is certain that the inexorable constraints of living will drive a good many of the younger generation of Jews to embark upon the building of their economic existence far from their homeland, the destiny of the greater majority of German-Jewish youth will, of necessity, be played out here on German soil. . . . Over the past six months, Palestine, the land of our fathers, has demonstrated both its Jewish and practical economic importance for a substantial number of German Jews. For that reason, the heavy burden of concern for an undiminished continuation of Jewish immigration to Palestine . . . rests upon the entire Jewish community."[64]

In early 1934, the paper dispatched two correspondents to study the situation of Jewish emigrants from Germany in European countries as well as the situation and prospects in Palestine. The reports appeared in a double series, one entitled "German Jews Abroad" and the other "German Jews in the Jewish Country." The first began with the question: "Did they burn all bridges behind them, or had they only been seized by that old wanderlust which reverberates through the lines of both German and Jewish folksongs? . . . Are others helping to look after you, are you able to provide for yourself, are you happy or would you like to return home?"[65]  An editorial in the second series, which later was issued in book form by the publishers of the *Israelitisches Familienblatt*, distinguished between "those who don't care which particular country can offer new opportunities for living and those for whom, if forced to depart from their German homeland, there can be only one destination: the Holy Land."[66] Without touching on emigration, the article "Taking Stock After Two Years" dealt with "new forms of our Jewish communal life . . . a strengthening of Jewish consciousness."[67] There was a nonpartisan call for religious renaissance and a distinctive Jewish cultural life. A month later, the paper sent another reporter, Doris Wittner, to Palestine on special assignment. "The Berlin Jewish author of novels and travel literature, for years a quite well-known writer, has been dispatched by us on assignment. She is now on board the ship 'Tel Aviv,' that steamer of the new and the first purely Jewish Palestine Shipping Co., and has begun the initial leg of a 'Contemplative Trip to the Land of the Jews'."[68]

Following its relocation to Berlin,[69] the paper commented in its issue for the Passover holiday: "It is precisely our tragedy as Jews that we are forced again and again, without wanting to do so, to pick up the wanderer's staff."[70] The editors prefaced extracts from Fritz Theilhaber's book *Untergang der deutschen Juden?* (The End of German Jewry?) with some advice: "Let's be optimists! Let's assess the future of German Jewry without any illusions far removed from the real world, yet likewise devoid of that paralyzing absence of hope, completely lacking any basis in reality."[71]

With the exception of the *Jüdische Rundschau*, Palestine was not a topic occupying the center of attention of the Jewish press in the two years immediately following Hitler's takeover of power, even though it was repeatedly touched on from various perspectives. Kurt Blumenfeld sketched the Zionist standpoint: "The true great renewal can only come about in and through Palestine. In Palestine, one can see the clear proof refuting the injustice of the anti-Semitic criticism that Jews are 'parasites.' Zionism brings about a new evaluation of everything that is Jewish. We respond to the hatred round about us with a new love for Judaism, by building a new Jewish reality."[72] "Zionism," stated the *Jüdische Rundschau*, was not one gigantic "transport effort," but rather a "movement encompassing all spheres of life."[73] "It would be mistaken to assume that it is our task today to propagandize for emigration to Palestine. Where propaganda must be used is in publicizing the presence of a new spirit in Judaism. . . . Hence, it is absurd when some German-Jewish groups want to limit the Zionists, whom they find annoying, to the organization of emigration to Palestine, while claiming for themselves the prerogative of leadership for the German-Jewish community."[74] On a number of occasions, the *Jüdische Rundschau* voiced its opposition to the tendency to make a distinction between Jews prepared to emigrate and those remaining on in Germany,[75] though not without admonishing its readers: Palestine was not a country of immigration comparable to other destinations. "The possibility for leading a 'comfortable' life in the cultural and intellectual sense does not exist in Palestine. . . . We fear that the old outlook and attitudes of the diaspora are being taken along to Palestine, and that the country and its conditions are not powerful enough to stimulate an inner spiritual change in a person's character."[76] Dr. Arthur Ruppin advised against any hasty immigration to Palestine and suggested keeping in mind countries such as the United States, Brazil, Argentina, Canada and South Africa.[77] At a conference of British Zionists in London, Harry Sacher emphasized that from the Palestinian point of view, the quality of immigration was more important than its quantity, and that one should not contemplate a mass immigration of German Jews.[78]

In a discussion between Heinrich Stern and Dr. Robert Weltsch, Stern, chairman of the Association for Liberal Judaism, voiced his view that virtually nothing had taken place as yet in Palestine that could be of any significance for world Jewry. In his opinion, Palestine had not generated a single great or creative idea about Judaism. Dr. Weltsch countered by arguing that "Judaism was not a question of utility." It did not matter what Palestine had given the Jews up to then; rather, what was important was what Jews had done for their part to advance the construction of Palestine, and what they were willing to contribute.[79] In an editorial, Weltsch commented: "The strict division some would like to make between Palestine and the diaspora does not exist. . . . The entire Jewish people today is confronted with great problems . . . in Palestine those problems are . . . of a special kind. There, everything that is masked by the situation in the diaspora becomes palpably visible and manifest. For that reason, the basic spirit and character of the Jewish people must prove themselves there more than anywhere else."[80]

*Der Schild* had a different perspective on Palestine. "The

German Jew who goes to Palestine only wishes to work there and create a basis of livelihood for himself. Even in the distant foreign land, he retains his loyalty to his old homeland. . . . Even long after he has learned the local language and acquired the citizenship of his new country, he will continue to be a German Jew."[81] The paper came out even more forcefully against a politicization of the idea of Palestine: "On the one hand, Palestine for us is a place of refuge, a haven for a small proportion of German Jews. According to authoritative Zionist sources, Palestine has no capacity to absorb a substantial number of German Jewry in the foreseeable future. On the other hand, it is the sacred site of religious traditions. Yet we would regard it as a serious blow to Jewish interests were . . . Palestine to be made into a political center. It is unacceptable that representatives of national-Jewish Zionism should have an active hand, openly or behind the scenes, in the formation of our relation to the German state and the German nation."[82]

Dr. Alfred Hirschberg arrived at similar conclusions: "There is no doubt that it would be better for the country if there were no politicization of the construction of Palestine. Jews have always preferred to open their pocketbooks more for Jews than for Jewish ideas."[83] If a person, in his search for a place to continue on with his life, considered Palestine – as well as England, Spain or North America – among the options, that said nothing against his German outlook, nor did it mean that he was a proponent of Jewish nationalist conceptions.[84] This prompted a protest on the part of the *Jüdische Rundschau*: "Whenever Palestine is mentioned, then it is only in order to belittle that country, even today. There is not a single word of understanding or appreciation for what Zionists have created there by arduous effort over the course of decades."[85]

An editorial by Dr. Hirschberg sparked a further exchange between the two papers. Hirschberg formulated a provocative comparison: "At a certain point in the road on which German Jews are passing through the German present, there is a fork leading off to the outside world. . . . Today, to venture outside means to choose the path that leads to foreign countries, especially Palestine. In earlier periods, it was the road leading out of the Jewish community by means of baptism or formal resignation from the Gemeinde. Compulsion and one's own free will, then as now, combine in shaping the decision."[86] The *Jüdische Rundschau* responded angrily: "This surprising formulation must be countered with the most forceful objection. . . . If nothing else, it is at least a highly original notion to compare the Jews going to Palestine in order to create the preconditions there for a full Jewish life with those individuals who broke with the Jewish community by the act of baptism."[87]

Dr. Bruno Weil recognized Palestine as a fact and conceded that in such trying times, it was a source of consolation and strength even for those who were not emigrating; nonetheless, one should not close one's eyes to the dangers lurking in the Arab world.[88] In a report about a meeting of the working committee of the CV in Berlin, M.E. (Margarete Edelheim, co-editor) indicated that Palestine was more and more a focus for deliberations, especially as a place for young people to build a new life. This was a change in the old basic principle espoused by the CV that saw Palestine primarily as a haven: a place of refuge for all Jews who were homeless, or would become so, as a result of political or economic reasons. It was stated that Palestine today was not an ideology, but a fact. In the same way, Germany was not a mere ideology, but the actual and concrete homeland for the German Jew: he had been at home in Germany for generations and had his roots there.[89]

On the occasion of the tenth anniversary of the Hebrew University in Jerusalem, A.H. (Alfred Hirschberg, editor) commented on the "strange contradiction" that people would have to try to comprehend as a kind of "dispensation": in the midst of a world that rejected them, the German Jews were beginning to embark upon a cultural and intellectual path leading inward,[90] and Jerusalem had initiated the development of a new cultural life, planned and conceived as a site from which once again "the teachings of Judaism," a thousand years of Jewish fate, would go forth.[91]

Dr. Friedrich Brodnitz, member of the CV board and the initiative committee of the Jewish Agency, felt that the question as to who should be advised to resettle in Palestine was one that could only be answered on an individual basis.[92] Commenting on a trip to Palestine, he noted:

> No matter how cautiously you assess the role that Palestine will play within the framework of solutions for the practical question . . . of German Jews in the near future, I think there can be no serious discussion of the Jewish question that does not take Jewish accomplish-

ments in Palestine into account as one of the most important factors. . . . The first element is the quiet strength and certitude with which the best portions of Germany Jewry are setting about the project of dignified self-assertion and Jewish renaissance in Germany. The second is the quiet strength and certitude with which the best segments of Jewish Palestine . . . are creating a Jewish life, and living it there.[93]

Even Dr. Alfred Hirschberg felt obliged to concede: "Perhaps the magic attraction which Palestine has had for each and every Jew, by dint alone of its emotional appeal . . . has been too powerful over the past three years. Maybe it has not left sufficient attention, financial means and Jewish courage – out of concern for the idea of Palestine – for considering other immigration and settlement options."[94]

*Der Israelit* had been publishing news on Palestine, including political and economic items, since February 1933. In response to a statement by the then High Commissioner for Palestine, Sir Arthur Wauchope, that the absorptive capacity of the country was the principle guiding policy in the eyes of the British government, the paper wrote: "One can only hope that Sir Arthur Wauchope . . . will also soon put an end to the monopoly of the Jewish Agency on immigration certificates, and will open the gates of the Holy Land to Orthodox youth as well."[95] In an appeal by the settlement fund of Agudas Yisroel, the demand was voiced that "care should be taken to create conditions so that Jews, on its sacred soil, are given the possibility of creating a life for themselves based on Torah." The following comment of *Der Israelit* could probably be regarded as a kind of motto on the question of the Palestine problem: "Many roads lead to Rome, but only one to Jerusalem – this path of a return to God and his Law."[96]

However, the route taken by the onset of reconciliation between the standpoints of the various Jewish groups was not a straight one. Both at the end of 1933 and in 1934, verbal clashes erupted between the *Jüdische Rundschau* and *Der Schild*. The ruling that "membership in the ZVfD [German Zionist Association] . . . was incompatible with membership in the Reichsbund Jüdischer Frontsoldaten and its athletic groups"[97] was the product of a heated polemic debate. In an editorial entitled "The Deep Gap," the editors of *Der Schild* termed the ZVfD ruling "possibly the most important internal Jewish event since the great upheaval in our lives in 1933," and continued: "As paradoxical as it may sound, although German Jews now for almost a year and a half have been nothing but an object . . . they nonetheless are faced with a highly personal decision . . . whether or not . . . to opt for Germany. Were we to give up our Judaism, we would forfeit ourselves. Yet if we were to inwardly relinquish our living connection with Germany, then that likewise would be no less a forfeiture of our own selves."[98]

This was the climax of a development whose contours were already clearly discernable even as early as 1933. "We conceded the Zionists a right to their world view," wrote *Der Schild*, "but the Zionists were not satisfied with that. They were not inclined for their part to allow us that same right to our own Weltanschauung." The paper accused Zionism of "intellectual arrogance," and of putting forward a "claim to exclusivity." "Doubts were raised about the character" of whomever failed to go along with this, non-Zionists were depicted as "simpletons . . . incapable of doing justice to issues of the day and of life." The paper went even further, accusing the *Jüdische Rundschau*, though in veiled language, of "acting in a völkisch manner," and of having adopted the conceptual system of the Nazis.

> The Zionist press espouses the view that the aforementioned terminology . . . of our age was invented by them. . . . In so doing, Zionist spokesmen completely forget that their own conceptual apparatus is not an independent invention by any means or manner, but rather was borrowed in virtually all instances from the ideas and conceptions of the surrounding world . . . it is quite obvious that at the present moment in Germany, there is no Jewish institution more assimilated than the *Jüdische Rundschau*. Since it is precisely Zionist functionaries who enjoy using expressions like "fawning behavior" and "undignified action," it is worth pointing out that never has Judaism been explained to such a degree by utilization of contemporary concepts as nowadays – at the hands of Zionist functionaries.[99]

Benno Cohn, executive chairman of the ZVfD, later commented that there was the danger of a "possible, though distant ideological accommodation with the Nazis . . . so that Zionist spokesmen ought to be very much on their guard . . . not to allow any association to arise with the slogans of the Nazis, for example, or their racial legislation." Nonetheless, he concluded that, "after an honest self-examination," one could maintain that Zionists had never taken advantage of their better strategic and tactical position vis-à-vis the German authorities for obtaining any political benefits for themselves.[100]

While the Reichsbund accused the Zionists of allowing them-selves to be used by the Nazis against the non-Zionists, the *Jüdische Rundschau* accused the RJF of precisely the same practice. They claimed that the national head of the RJF had published an article in *Der Schild* that formulated the thesis in quite open and unmistakable terms: German Zionists could not be equated with members of his own organization when it came to their patriotic loyalties. "Similar comments have continued to appear in the press of the RJF, and they can hardly conceal the fact that the agi-tation of the RJF is aimed at creating a more favorable position in Germany for the Jews who were its members – at the expense of other Jews. This is intended to influence those who are perhaps easily intimidated . . . to accommodate their internal Jewish atti-tude accordingly."[101]

This press campaign prompted the national Jewish organiza-tion, the Reichsvertretung der deutschen Juden (Reich Representation of German Jews), in an appeal signed by Dr. Leo Baeck, to issue the "urgent warning" to put a halt to the "polemi-cal struggle over political directions." "A patriotic outlook, loyalty and devotion to the German fatherland are, like a Jewish outlook and loyalty to Judaism, not the special possession of any one group within German Jewry. . . . There has never been a lack of patriotic loyalty on the part of members of any group within the German-Jewish community. No group can claim for itself alone to represent the full sum of patriotic tasks of German Jewry. That right is the sole prerogative of the Reichsvertretung der deutsch-en Juden."[102]

The constantly mounting pressure against German Jews and the lack of willingness on the part of the free nations to accept a sufficient number of these harassed individuals as immigrants led repeatedly to speculative projects. The former Italian foreign minister Count Sforza revealed in the Paris biweekly *Revue Bleue*[103] that Jewish immigration was not only possible in Trans-Jordan but in Syria as well, and that it was even deemed desirable there. While on a visit to Syria, he himself had heard prominent Moslems suggest that tens of thousands of Jews should be permit-ted to settle in the region of the Euphrates. Similar rumors were in circulation regarding Cyprus. "Whoever is familiar with Jewish emigration knows that this specific region is a hotbed of all sorts of people who love to dream up new projects . . . quixotic politi-cal dreamers and groups that make no secret out of their animos-

ity toward Palestine and welcome any and every path for emigration – as long as it does not lead to Palestine," observed the
*Jüdische Rundschau* in a commentary. "It is regrettable that . . .
such an area of work is being made into a focus for new illusions
as a result of unobjective propaganda."[104]

In London in 1934, a conference was held of the Freeland
movement, according to its program a successor to the Territorial
Organisation founded by Israel Zangwill. Its goal was to locate an
autonomous area for Jewish settlement outside of Palestine.
Under the caption "No Illusions," the *Israelitisches Familienblatt*
issued a warning both about the territorialists and the limits that
had been placed on emigration as a solution to the question of
the German Jews.

> There is no need to prove the importance of Zionism for Jews in
> Germany during a period in which Jewish emigration from the Reich
> to Palestine is increasing from month to month. No comment will be
> made here on the extent of possible success the territorialists meeting
> in London at the "Freeland Conference" will have in supplementing
> this emigration by one directed to overseas countries. . . . Yes, even if
> a much larger number . . . should leave their old homeland year after
> year – this still would not solve the "German Jewish question" in its
> totality.[105]

The *Jüdische Rundschau* was not surprised that the idea had
resurfaced of finding an autonomous territory outside of
Palestine – in order to make a clear distinction between the splin-
tered emigration wave that was dependent on the willingness of
other countries to admit immigrants and a territory allocated
under international law to Jews, which they would administer
themselves. The paper reminded readers of the Uganda project
aired at the Sixth Zionist Congress in 1903 and the defunct
Territorial Organisation, disbanded in 1925. Such ideas were now
being propagated as though they had had no predecessors.
Among their proponents was the well-known novelist Alfred
Döblin.

> It is distressing to see how a man like Döblin, who . . . always felt he
> was a German, has gradually come round to recognizing the incon-
> testable fate of the Jews.[106]. . . Döblin was recently in London where
> he gave lectures on behalf of the so-called "Freeland Movement,"
> which is nothing but a new version of the old territorialism. He stat-
> ed: "I believe in Palestine, a country that has proven itself to be a
> haven for Jews. But the territory of Palestine is limited, and can only

accommodate a fraction of the Jews compelled to emigrate. For that reason, another country must be found for the rest. There are countries without any native population and without a foreign government, where land does not have to be bought and where cooperative colonization as an autonomous company under the aegis of the League of Nations can also be developed." Unfortunately, it must be pointed out that Döblin's references . . . are very vague and unclear. The danger exists that Jewish energies will be siphoned off into projects that have no basis in reality, but are merely a fantasy. . . . We fear that the leaders of this new territorialist movement, no matter how well-intentioned their aims, will have the same sad experience as their predecessors thirty years ago.[107]

The confusing course of anti-Jewish measures generated a sense of bewilderment, and often led to contradictory reactions among Jews in Germany;[108] these were reflected in the pages of the Jewish papers. The Jewish press evolved into a pillar of moral support for the Jewish public as it grappled with the demands placed upon it.[109] The proof of that was manifest in the autumn of 1935, when the Nuremberg Laws stripped Jews of their citizenship, insulting and humiliating them in the Law for the Protection of German Blood and German Honor. The Jewish press then faced its greatest test.

In the summer of 1935, the *CV-Zeitung* and the *Israelitisches Familienblatt* were suspended for a period of three months, the *Jüdische Rundschau* for one month; although the suspensions of the first two papers were subsequently shortened, the *Rundschau* was the first able to comment on the new legislation. "Everything depends now on giving careful and thoughtful consideration to the new situation," it admonished, courageously raising three demands: Jews should not be subjected to insult and defamation; there should be guarantees for their economic livelihood and for their own sphere of culture, especially in the school system; finally, Jewish emigration, especially of young people, should be promoted by the responsible authorities.[110]

These demands were based principally on a commentary by the chief editor of the DNB (German Press Service), Alfred-Ingemar Berndt, who had termed the Nuremberg Laws a "therapeutic and useful action" for Jews in Germany. He made specific reference in this connection to the Nineteenth Zionist Congress that had just ended in Lucerne "at which an end had likewise been put to all the talk about Judaism being nothing but a religion. The speakers asserted that the Jews were a people in their own right, and they underscored anew the völkisch national claims of Judaism." Germany, in declaring the Jews living in the country to be a national minority, was only drawing the practical consequences from this position and attempting to meet Zionist demands. "The Jewish minority will be granted . . . its own cultural life, its own völkisch life as a people. . . . By giving the Jewish minority an opportunity to live its own life, Germany . . . was promoting the process among Jews of becoming a people, and contributing to rendering the relation between the two nations more tolerable."[111]

The *Berliner Jüdisches Gemeindeblatt* referred to a remark by Hitler made to key party officials after the session of the Reichstag. He had emphasized that in the wake of the laws now promulgated, possibilities had been opened up for Jews to develop an ethnic völkisch life of their own that had no parallel to date in any other country. In regard to this, he had renewed his directive to avoid any individual actions of violence against Jews. "We can build on the following basis: that there will be no interference with possibilities for economic existence, and this will be recognized by both sides as the prerequisite for a tolerable relationship," wrote Heinrich Stahl.[112]

After a few days, the *CV-Zeitung* also had an opportunity to respond. In an editorial, it came out in favor of the program of the Reichsvertretung, which had been reprinted by the entire Jewish press: "emigration according to a plan, principally to Palestine, giving special consideration to youth; intensification of training in the fields of agriculture, craft trades and language skills; expansion of Jewish employment bureaus, occupational counseling and credit institutions; increased activity by the Kulturbünde and in the sphere of adult education."

The paper called on the Jewish population to demonstrate discipline, terming any internal Jewish dispute a betrayal. "We don't know what it [the new Jewish year] will bring, but we know what we want from that year: to live in dignity and decency as Jews."[113]

*Der Morgen* suggested that Jewish minorities were distinguished from other national minorities by the fact that they had no country of origin behind them which could exercise concrete power on their behalf.[114]

The *Jüdische Zeitung* in Breslau termed the legislation a "historical highpoint": national-minded Jews in Germany would presumably have to deal with the difficult task of facing up, at the proper time and with full political responsibility, to the facts now shaping the fate of all Jews in Germany; they would have to increase the functionality of Jewish organizations to the highest possible level.[115] In Jewish life in Germany, those Zionists should take over the reins of power who would really be able to implement the program of the Reichsvertretung.[116]

The paper warned its readers against schematic application of concepts and theories of law that had proven themselves elsewhere to the situation of German Jewry. The textbook interpretation of people, nation or state had also failed when attempts were made to utilize these definitions in the case of the Jews. That is why the valid existing notions of minority rights could not simply be transferred and applied to the Jews as well. Their uncritical adoption was neither in the interest of the German Jews nor that of the German Reich.[117]

While the implementation directives for the Nuremberg legislation were being awaited, the *Israelitisches Familienblatt* remarked that only after it was known what options still remained for Jews in German economic life would an element of insecurity be dissipated – one that affected German as well as Jewish interests. "In this connection, we have in mind the now ever more frequently noticeable sales of Jewish businesses and factories to Aryans. The daily press has pointed out . . . with some justification that it is in the interest of the sellers, business relations, the workers and even the competitors of formerly Jewish firms to avoid hasty sales and the associated selling off of valuable assets at below-market prices."[118]

*Der Israelit* was the only Jewish paper that could see a positive side to the racial legislation. It welcomed the legal prohibition against mixed marriage and sexual relations between Jews and non-Jews.[119]

The new situation was viewed by the head of German Orthodox Judaism, Dr. Isaac Breuer, in a far more differentiated light. Writing in *Nachlat Z'wi*, he argued that the Nuremberg Laws had revoked the emancipation of German Jewry, and Orthodoxy had been warning Jews for more than a century that emancipation could not lead to a solution to the problem of exile and the diaspora – rather, quite on the contrary, it would result in its terrible worsening. This warning had also been issued by Zionism right from its inception, although not in the name of the Torah, but on the basis of its own ideology. However, Dr. Breuer went on, it was questionable whether Zionism could generate a dynamics of renewal given the already very advanced process of assimilation among German Jews. The Zionists were also aware, he noted, that only by linking up with Jewish culture could values be created for the Jewish personality. He arrived at a negative assessment of Jewish cultural life.

> When artists of Jewish extraction appear as actors, singers, virtuosi performers, when writers of Jewish origin compose novels, yes even when Jewish schools bring together Jewish children – is that product something which can be called Jewish culture? . . . The Torah is the culture of the Jewish people. . . . Therefore, whoever returns to the Jewish people, but not to the Jewish Torah, is left standing before a cultural vacuum. Whoever ventures back to the Jewish country without the Jewish Torah will find that he's ended up – in Asia.[120]

The Nuremberg Laws constituted a watershed for the Jewish press: from that juncture on, it was the complex of questions relating to emigration that came to dominate its pages. There were only small differences of nuance now in the issue of destination: whether they should be directed toward Palestine or other overseas countries. While the *Jüdische Rundschau* viewed emigration overseas as individual migration as contrasted with group migration to Palestine,[121] the *CV-Zeitung* felt that migration overseas as a group, after completion of a common shared training program for young people in artisan trades and agricultural skills, was also feasible to a certain degree.[122]

When the refugee commission, assigned by the League of Nations with the task of dealing with the legacy of the James G. Macdonald commissionership met in November 1935, the *Jüdische Rundschau* issued an appeal: "By the very nature of things, Palestine cannot absorb all the emigrants. . . . But there can be no emigration without a country for immigration. For that reason, the problem being dealt with in Geneva is: create more opportunities for immigration! Tens of thousands don't know where to go. Open the gates!"[123]

Leo Baeck spoke about the "spirit of reflection" that was beginning to awaken in the two large organizations which, through their official publications – the *CV-Zeitung* and "most especially," the *Jüdische Rundschau* – had the possibility to speak to the Jews of Germany. "Both these papers have experienced an outstanding period during days of extreme distress."[124] Max Gruenewald also called attention to the important role played by the Jewish press during those days: "Finally, one of the factors that helped the 'Reichsvertretung' to exert its influence was the existence of a nationwide Jewish press. *Jüdische Rundschau, CV-Zeitung* . . . *Israelitisches Familienblatt,* etc. reached and informed almost every Jewish family, except for the periods of enforced silence when one or several papers were temporarily suspended, and in times of persecution silence too is eloquent."[125]

# Notes

1. Kurt Löwenstein, "Historiker und Publizist," in Tramer and Löwenstein, 1961, p. 84f.

2. *Time,* December 23, 1983.

3. "The Zionists did not differ from the anti-Zionists or non-Zionists in respect to their deep attachment to Germany," Dawidowicz, 1977, p. 221.

4. Walk, 1981, p. 127.

5. Freeden, 1963, p. 7ff.

6. *Lexikon des Judentums,* Gütersloh 1967, pp. 201, 551f.

7. "General von Blomberg . . . informed Hitler that he was authorized by the Field Marshal that unless the present state of tension in Germany was brought quickly to an end, the President would declare martial law and turn over the control of the state to the Army. When Hitler was permitted to see Hindenburg for a few minutes in the presence of Blomberg, the old President confirmed the ultimatum. This was a disastrous turn of affairs for the Nazi Chancellor . . . if the Army took over, that would be the end of him and of Nazi government." Shirer, 1968, Book II, "The Blood Purge of June 30, 1934."

8. Dawidowicz, 1977, p. 238.

9. "As Jodl testified at Nuremberg, 'Considering the situation we were in, the French army could have blown us to pieces.'. . . That almost certainly could have been the end of Hitler . . . for the dictator could never have survived such a fiasco," Shirer, 1968, Book III, "A Coup in the Rhineland," pp. 403, 405. In March 1936 the two Western democracies were given their last chance . . . as we have seen Hitler admitting – to bring the Nazi dictator and his regime tumbling down," p. 405.

10. *Jüdische Rundschau,* October 20, 1933.

11. A.H., in *CV-Zeitung,* April 4, 1935.

12. *Der Israelit,* March 30, 1933.

13. "In truth, there is less indication that the average Zionist was in any way less devoted to his German homeland than the average non-Zionist, or that he was in any fundamental sense opposed to the ideals which secured Jews their freedom," Jacob Boas, "Germany or Diaspora," *YLBI,* 27 (1982), p. 117.

14. *Jüdische Rundschau,* April 13, 1933.

15. Ibid., August 29, 1933.

16. Ibid.

17. Ibid., November 14, 1933.

18. Ibid., July 31, 1934.

19. Ibid., June 16, 1933.

20. Ibid.

21. Ibid., November 17, 1933. Robert Weltsch later regretted that, in his well-known article "Wear the Yellow Badge with Pride" (*Jüdische Rundschau*, April 4, 1933), he had called upon the Jews to demonstrate pride instead of encouraging them to leave the country as soon as possible (Dawidowicz, 1977, p. 223).

22. *Jüdische Rundschau*, March 6, 1934.

23. "The Jewish organization . . . which restructured itself after 1933 in accordance with the "principle of the leader" [*Führerprinzip*] . . . and that wanted to integrate all Jews into this state was the Reichsbund jüdischer Frontsoldaten with its 30,000 to 40,000 members. . . . But that attitude was 'acknowledged' by the Nazis only for a short period of time. Starting with the end of 1935, the Reichsbund also dealt with the question of emigration and Palestine; in 1937, it reached a reconciliation with the ZVfD, an organization it had previously waged a bitter struggle against." Alexander Schölch, "Das Dritte Reich, die zionistische Bewegung und der Palästinakonflikt," *Vierteljahreshefte für Zeitgeschichte*, 1982, Heft 4, p. 654f. Cf. also Dunker, 1977, pp. 113–185.

24. *Der Schild*, July 27, 1933.

25. Ibid., April 13, 1933.

26. Ibid., April 27, 1933.

27. Ibid., May 11, 1933.

28. "German outlook" has been used here and elsewhere to render the distinctive expression "*deutsche Gesinnung*," which denotes a complex of attitude, ideology and patriotic sentiment [trans. note].

29. Ibid., September 14, 1933.

30. "Hardened by previous ordeals, the readers of the CV-Zeitung were resolved to ride out the storm in Germany. Hence, for Alfred Hirschberg the question of a Jewish future in Germany hinged on finding a place 'inside the German order,' in accordance with the state's new principles," Jacob Boas, "Germany or Diaspora," *YLBI*, p. 112.

31. *CV-Zeitung*, December 14, 1935.

32. Ibid., August 17, 1933.

33. Ibid., October 19, 1933.

34. Ibid., September 20, 1934.

35. *Jüdische Rundschau*, November 15, 1934.

36. *CV-Zeitung*, September 20, 1934.

37. *Jüdische Rundschau*, November 15, 1934.

38. Ibid., October 20, 1933.

39. *Der Schild*, November 12, 1933.

40. *Israelitisches Familienblatt*, May 26, 1933.

41. *Heft 2*, 1933, Armannen Verlag, Leipzig.

42. *Berliner Lokalanzeiger*, quoted in *Jüdische Rundschau*, May 12, 1933.

43. *CV-Zeitung*, August 10, 1933. "The CV Zeitung still hoped that an 'undiminished life' could be led by Jews in Germany, not as a national minority but as a cultural and religious group whose economic life – as was also the official Nazi deception of those early years – would remain undisturbed," Herbert A. Strauss, in World Federation of Jewish Journalists, 1980, p. 338.

44. *Israelitisches Familienblatt*, May 26, 1933.

45. *Der Schild*, February 16, 1934.

46. (The Autonomous People), Boehm, 1932.

47. *Jüdische Rundschau*, May 12, 1933.

48. Ibid., June 13, 1933. "Those Jews with nationalist feelings in Germany, who banded together in the Zionist movement . . . had no aims in respect to German domestic politics, least of all those of a legally recognized national minority." Weltsch, 1963, p. 13.

49. Referring to an article in the *Jüdische Rundschau*, December 29, 1933.

50. *Der Schild*, January 12, 1934.

51. *CV-Zeitung*, December 7, 1933.

52. *Jüdische Rundschau*, June 16, 1933.

53. *Israelitisches Familienblatt*, November 15, 1934.

54. Ibid., January 11, 1934.

55. "The 'Hamburger Israelitisches Familienblatt' resembled nothing so much as the *gemütliche* middle-brow journal written for the average petit-bourgeois family in city and country, the Sunday paper that wants to edify, educate and comfort, the Jewish equivalent of the (anti-Semitic) Gartenlaube." Herbert A. Strauss, in World Federation of Jewish Journalists, p. 323.

56. *Israelitisches Familienblatt*, March 9, 1933.

57. Ibid., April 13, 1933.

58. Ibid., April 20, 1933.

59. Ibid., June 2, 1933.

60. Ibid., June 29, 1933.

61. Ibid., October 19, 1933.

62. Ibid., July 6, 1933.

63. Ibid., September 14, 1933.

64. Ibid., September 28, 1933.

65. Ibid., February 1, 1934.

66. Ibid., March 8, 1934.

67. Ibid., February 7, 1935.

68. Ibid., February 14, 1935.

69. Last issue in Hamburg, March 28, 1935; first issue in Berlin, April 4, 1935.

70. *Israelitisches Familienblatt*, April 17, 1935.

71. Ibid., June 11, 1935.

72. *Jüdische Rundschau*, February 28, 1933.

73. Ibid., October 4, 1933.

74. Ibid., October 20, 1933.

75. Ibid., November 17, 1933; January 9, 1934, among others.

76. Ibid., November 28, 1933.

77. Ibid., August 29, 1933.

78. Ibid., February 2, 1934. An editorial comment in the *Jüdische Rundschau* noted: "It is a serious error on the part of the CV Zeitung if it believes it can find here the 'heroism of an idea at the expense of those affected'."

79. *Israelitisches Familienblatt*, January 25, 1934.

80. *Jüdische Rundschau*, March 28, 1934.

81. *Der Schild*, February 9, 1934.

82. Ibid., June 1, 1934.

83. *CV-Zeitung*, October 3, 1935.

84. Ibid., April 13, 1933.

85. *Jüdische Rundschau*, May 9, 1933.

86. *CV-Zeitung*, November 8, 1934.

87. *Jüdische Rundschau*, November 9, 1934.

88. *CV-Zeitung*, December 6, 1933.

89. Ibid., October 26, 1933.

90. "The CV's formal break with 'Germanism' came in 1935. On the 4th of April its paper featured a new subheading. . . . The time of creative synthesis was over, conceded Alfred Hirschberg on the Nazi-ordered substitution, leaving Jews no alternative other than that of taking the Weg nach innen," J. Boas, op. cit., p. 113. The concept of "inner emigration," mentioned on various occasions in the *CV-Zeitung* and *Der Schild*, was picked up later by German intellectuals who stayed on in Germany and described their distance from National Socialism as "inner emigration."

91. *CV-Zeitung*, April 4, 1935.

92. Ibid., December 7, 1933.

93. Quoted in *Jüdische Rundschau*, November 12, 1933.

94. *CV-Zeitung*, October 3, 1935. See also Herbert A. Strauss (World Federation of Jewish Journalists, 1980, p. 339): "In the end, the CV Zeitung . . . accepted the central role of Palestine in Jewish migration."

95. *Der Israelit*, March 30, 1933.

96. Ibid., June 6, 1933.

97. *Jüdische Rundschau*, June 12, 1934.

98. *Der Schild*, June 22, 1934.

99. Ibid., December 17, 1933. See also Herbert A. Strauss, op. cit.: "Zionists too, it (i.e., Jüdische Rundschau) claimed, accept race, history and Volkstum as the constituent bases of a nation. Separation would end 'decomposition' ('Zersetzung') of German culture," apparently referring to Kurt Blumenfeld (*Jüdische Rundschau*, February 28, 1933).

100. Benno Cohn, "Einige Bemerkungen über den deutschen Zionismus nach 1933," in Tramer, 1962, pp. 46, 52f.

101. *Jüdische Rundschau*, July 3, 1934.

102. Ibid.

103. Ibid., May 4, 1935.

104. Ibid., June 4, 1935.

105. *Israelitisches Familienblatt*, August 1, 1934.

106. Döblin later converted to Catholicism in 1940, see *Lexikon des Judentums*, Gütersloh 1967, p. 168.

107. *Jüdische Rundschau*, June 28, 1934.

108. Herbert A. Strauss, "Jewish Emigration from Germany," *YLBI*, 25 (1980), p. 338.

109. Margarete T. Edelheim-Mühsam, "Die Haltung der jüdischen Presse gegenüber der nationalsozialistischen Bedrohung," in *Deutsches Judentum, Aufstieg und Krise*, p. 368.

110. *Jüdische Rundschau*, September 17, 1935.

111. *Der Israelit*, September 29, 1935.

112. *Berliner Jüdisches Gemeindeblatt*, September 22, 1935.

113. *CV-Zeitung*, September 26, 1935.

114. *Der Morgen*, November 1935.

115. *Jüdische Zeitung* (Breslau), September 20, 1935.

116. Ibid., September 27, 1935.

117. Ibid., September 15, 1933.

118. *Israelitisches Familienblatt*, November 14, 1935.

119. *Der Israelit*, November 19, 1935.

120. *Nachlat Z'wi*, 1935/36, p. 1ff.

121. *Jüdische Rundschau*, November 15, 1935.

122. *CV-Zeitung*, November 22, 1935.

123. *Jüdische Rundschau*, November 26, 1935.

124. Leo Baeck, "Gedenken an zwei Tote," in Weltsch, 1963 p. 310.

125. Max Gruenewald, "The Beginning of the 'Reichsvertretung'," in *YLBI*, 1 (1956), p. 60.

# 5

# Controversy on Culture

" **W**hat is Jewish? Answer: the achievements of all Jews from all eras lumped together. . . . The total sum of what all Jews accomplish in the cultural sphere, that would be a Jewish culture. . . . We deem it tragic that Jewish achievements cannot be separated off from the rest – because they are closely interwoven with what other peoples have achieved. . . . Yet the separation that the authorities have introduced and are subjecting us to in Germany is not creating a living and vital special character, but one that is merely legal and organizational in nature."[1]

This question and its debatable answer did not exist in a vacuum. They were part of a controversy on Jewish culture that had raged for five years in the pages of the Jewish press and around an institution established in 1933: the Kulturbund deutscher Juden.[2] With some justification, the *Jüdische Rundschau* spoke of a "certain sense of confusion" that had arisen as a result of the exclusion of Jews from the pale of German culture. On the one hand, that move had prompted emphatic expressions of an unaltered continuing adherence to German culture and its values; on the other, the paper observed, it was leading to bitter resentment that resulted in a false negative assessment and consequent devaluation of the German intellectual world.[3]

The cultural debate waged in the Jewish papers remains a unique testimony to the controversies and cleavages of opinion that marked the period. It bespeaks the presence of a powerful reservoir of intellectual and moral strength within German Jewry, given manifest expression in its press. Despite the threats to property and life, the German Jews did not cease in their search for final definitions of what constituted intellectual creativity, and the discovery of Jewish elements in it. For the span of a century, they had "enjoyed participation in the European life of the spirit as a comfortable right." Now they had been pushed into a situation "where heroism was required to continue that participation."[4]

On April 1, 1933, "Boycott Day," and in the subsequent months, Jewish civil servants were removed from their posts, Jewish employees dismissed, teachers and university professors fired, judges sent on "mandatory leave"; lawyers found themselves locked out of their offices, and editors were unceremoniously given the sack. Jewish actors, musical directors and conductors, theater and motion picture directors, stage designers, singers and instrumentalists also lost their positions. An organization, the Kulturbund deutscher Juden,[5] was set up in order to absorb a portion of the numerous Jewish artists who suddenly found themselves without employment.[6] Many emigrated abroad, especially musicians and those in the fine arts, whose work was not dependent on language. Others learned a new profession. Yet far in excess of 2,000 applications were received in response to the first public announcement of the Kulturbund.[7] The task of this organization, which supported three acting ensembles, a standing opera company, two symphony orchestras, a theater for Jewish schools, a cabaret theater as well as choirs, lay orchestras and numerous chamber music groups, was to bring together two segments of the Jewish population: unemployed artists and a now homeless public. Until November 12, 1938, Jews were still allowed to frequent public performances and exhibitions,[8] but a discomfiting sense of uneasiness often prevented them from walking through the front door of a theater that had unceremoniously tossed its Jewish staff and actors into the street out the stage door in back.

The approval for establishment of the Kulturbund was signed on June 16, 1933 by State Commissar Hans Hinkel, in the name of Minister Rust, the Prussian Minister for Art, Science and Popular Education. The stipulation was included that only Jews could become members of the Kulturbund, and admittance to closed performances was open solely to members.[9] Its charter stated: "In particular, it will put on theatrical performances and concerts, lectures and art exhibitions for the benefit of its members; in principle, the artistic and scientific aspects of these activities will be handled by Jews."

Hinkel remarked at the time: "Moreover, let me point out that Jewish artists . . . judged on the basis of their personal ability and achievement, shall always have an opportunity in the future to realize their ambitions. Especially in this sphere, we emphatically repudiate all manifestations in any way associated with vulgar violent anti-Semitism."[10]

Since the events put on by the Kulturbund were necessarily closed to the German public – members of the German press were also refused admittance – it seemed appropriate to speak about the danger of a cultural-intellectual ghettoization, long before separate Jewish residential quarters were established in Germany.

Julius Bab, one of the leading theater historians and drama critics in Germany, and a founder of the movement for popular theater as well as a founding member of the Kulturbund, was the first to comment on these problems. In an essay entitled "The Cultural Problem Facing Jews in Germany Today," he proceeded on the basis of the thesis that the Jewish theater-going public had previously not sensed any need to be entertained exclusively, or even preferentially, by Jewish artists. Yet since the wish among Jews to attend cultural performances had by no means disappeared, Bab believed the problem of the Jewish cultural consumer was now assuming gigantic proportions. "If there is going to be a solution," he continued, "it will evidently also have to include a solution to the problem of the producer. The intellectual sustenance acceptable to Jews will in future have to be furnished them solely by other Jews." He posed the question whether this did not mean that Jews had already begun to retreat from the German cultural community into the confines of a ghetto – a circumscribed domain of life, thought and work that was exclusively by and for Jews. In regard to the outer form, he felt Jews had no choice: they had to accept the form of activity forced upon them in the sphere of culture and the arts – or go down in cultural ruin.

Yet it was their prerogative to decide on the content that this form would have, and he came to the conclusion that ghettoization in the "old, dangerous sense" was much more a question of content than of form. "They can banish us from active life as citizens in Germany, but they cannot ban us from German intellectual and cultural life, and from the world in which we are rooted and have lived for more than five generations. . . . We cannot and shall not cease regarding . . . the works of Lessing and Goethe, Kant and Humboldt, Rembrandt and Beethoven as the fundamental foundation of our being and action. . . . Moreover, we declare our allegiance to that community of European nations whose essence has been shaped and determined by Leonardo and Michelangelo, Cervantes and Shakespeare, Voltaire and Rousseau, Dostoyevsky and Ibsen." Even if by reason of compulsion there would only be Jews to provide for cultural life, this, to Bab's mind, did not yet mean the existence of an intellectual-cultural ghetto. "We shall remain members of the German and European community of culture, and in this way . . . fellow workers engaged in promoting the common cause of humanity."[11]

In contrast, the *Israelitisches Familienblatt* broached another question: to what extent was the theater of the Kulturbund in keeping with the views prevalent in the Jewish public about the nature of a Jewish theater? Should the theater of the Kulturbund be a specifically Jewish stage or basically a German theater, distinguished from other German theatrical houses only by the fact that its actors and audiences were Jewish?

> What do we mean by Jewish theater, what warrants its being accorded this attribute? . . . The core of the problem lies in the decision as to whether one demands nothing but Jewish plays from the Kulturbund – or recognizes that its task in putting together its program should be guided by purely artistic criteria. Nonetheless, the paper came to the conclusion that the responsibility of the Kulturbund was to emphasize the Jewish line in its program content, and to serve Jewish writers and playwrights as a home for their plays.[12]

To a certain extent, Bab agreed with this view. "We must give special consideration to works by Jewish authors that have no other place nowadays [for possible performance] – even if those works have *no* specifically Jewish character; such consideration should also be given to all high-level products that treat a topic of special interest to Jews."[13] Yet he noted that the number of suitable Jewish plays was not particularly large; moreover, not all dramas that were possible candidates would be approved by the authorities or released by their authors for performance. For example, Richard Beer-Hofmann refused to give permission for the staging of his drama "Der junge David."[14] The *Berliner Jüdisches Gemeindeblatt* observed: "In answer to the question whether we already have a Jewish theater and Jewish plays today, an unbiased observer would have to reply with an emphatic 'no.' Because there was no self-contained and integral Jewish culture in Germany, there could not be a Jewish theater in the true sense of the word; a play was not Jewish solely by dint of the fact that it had been written by a Jewish author or had characters with Jewish names."[15]

The *Jüdische Rundschau* warned that nothing was more dangerous than to breed a hot-house variety of unauthentic culture in this sphere. Such a false reality would suggest that German Jews, when restricted to the confines of their own circle, were unable to maintain any cultural productivity without going down a creative path meant specifically for them. "For that reason . . . the cultural achievements of German Jewry must stem from the Jewish element . . . and not simply be the mechanical attempt, unfortunately quite in evidence nowadays, to continue on with what was previously done outside – but now within a Jewish ambience." According to the author of the article, Kurt Löwenstein, the essence of German Jewry was not something that could be easily grasped. German Jewry had expended its best powers to the outside world, and was in a sense alienated from itself intellectually and culturally – this to a far greater degree than any other important group within the Jewish world. For that reason, he believed there was no shortcut to achieving a genuine expression of Jewish intellectual and cultural values. "We are not people who knock impatiently at the door every day, demanding manifestations of the Jewish spirit from persons who can only achieve that spirit by means of a slow process, by learning."[16]

The danger of "unreality" was touched on in connection with a performance of Ibsen's "Wild Geese."

> We certainly do not want to be party to forcing an interpretation [of plays] that tries to find elements somehow related to our Jewish fate in everything we see or hear. Nonetheless . . . virtually all the characters shown to us here by Ibsen take flight into a world that exists only *in themselves*. This formation of a realm of pure fantasy . . . seems strangely familiar to us. There was a generation of Jews who constructed such an artificial "life in the test tube" and believed it was real. . . . A person fled from reality into a domain that he had created for himself. Yet that domain could only continue to exist until it was demolished by a powerful wind coming from the outside.[17]

The *CV-Zeitung* viewed matters differently. It felt that there would be no great regrets about the selection "because the vital force, its fire still unquenchable in the torrent of time, had been put to the test and proven its worth."[18]

Since one could choose between neither "engaged theater" nor "art for art's sake," Leo Kreindler suggested accommodating the repertoire of the Kulturbund to the views prevalent in the Jewish public about the nature of a Jewish theater.[19] In this way, the task of defining "Jewish theater" was passed on to the public, and that public had even more vague notions about this than its spokespersons in the press. But what if, nonetheless, a work was staged that neither had a Jewish author nor dealt with Jewish matters? Well, then it would have to be "so completely infused with Jewish passion in its staging and acting – thus being transcribed, as it were, into a Jewish idiom – that its performance would constitute a powerful Jewish experience for the audience."[20] There was no answer to the question of how one might imbue a play such as Shakespeare's "Midsummer Night's Dream"[21] with the requisite "Jewish passion." It was thus not surprising when the founder and artistic director of the Kulturbund, Dr. Kurt Singer, answered in a quite piqued tone that people should not badger him with well-meaning but unsubstantiated concepts like the communication of "Jewish" works, "Jewish" art and "Jewish" content. "Whatever is genuine and true, noble and humane, whatever can be communicated intellectually and morally as idea and word, as sound and scene by Jews whose language is German to a German-speaking Jewish audience, whatever is aesthetically wellwrought and can excite and amuse their souls – all that is part of the job of our Kulturbund."[22]

This dispute called for some sort of compromise, and compromises were in keeping with the nature of the *Israelitisches Familienblatt.* If it was not possible to create one's own Jewish culture, then why not at least a "special Jewish cultural atmosphere"? That ought to be easy enough to generate, since Jews were performing for Jews.[23]

Milieu, interpretation, atmosphere – what else could make the Kulturbund into a *Jewish* stage?  Arthur Eloesser believed that what was important were the thematic concerns that the theater treated. "When Greek theater was still young and closer to its orgiastic origins, Athenians loyal to tradition used to voice the criticism 'That's nothing for Dionysos' whenever a drama did not seem to be infused with elements of that mythical undercurrent. In modern terms, the equivalent shout of the people would be: 'so what about our concerns?' The same question mark can be found wherever Jews today put on theater for other Jews."[24]

Are "concerns" and "content" the same? The question as to whether the content made a work Jewish triggered a discussion that went on for years and lay at the heart of attempts to "Judaize" the repertory. One can hardly maintain the notion that a play or other literary work is rendered "Jewish" solely by its content. The number of dramas is legion in which biblical figures have the main role, but no one would classify Hebbel's "Judith," Wilde's "Salome" or Otto Ludwig's "Makkabäer" as "Jewish" dramas. The Biblical characters are employed as vessels for presenting historical topics or themes of general human interest, and the plays are composed by authors with no connection to Judaism.

Thus, making content the criterion for Jewishness can lead to rather dubious results. On the one hand, figures created by non-Jewish authors, even if they have Jewish names, are still not Jewish; on the other, plays by Jewish authors, even if they have Jewish characters, are not always in keeping with Jewish "concerns." Robert Weltsch pointed this out when the Kulturbund put on Semyon Yushkevitch's play "Sonkin und der Haupttreffer" (Sonkin and the Jackpot). "The play . . . has an element that is insulting for us. The way in which money is worshipped here is disconcerting. . . . Is this what we Jews in 1933, whom one falsely characterizes as being members of a materialistic people that is only interested in money, should accept as a Jewish performance?"[25] The *CV-Zeitung* likewise had its reservations regarding a performance of this play in the Kulturbund RheinRuhr: "The tragicomedy 'Sonkin und der Haupttreffer' takes place in the milieu of Eastern European Jewry. The danger is that a person can lose one's way caught up in the depiction of the milieu . . . a depiction that awakens feelings of distance rather than affinity in the Western Jew."[26]

But there were also experts who felt that the content or theme had a major importance. "In the beginning was content," wrote Hermann Sinsheimer. In his view, the content had educative properties and an educating effect. A Jewish public cannot absorb Jewish values if it doesn't have Jewish content. "Jews in Germany today should not rack their brains yet about the problem of Jewish form. First of all, they must fill their heads with Jewish knowledge. And to present that knowledge . . . to the Jewish public – that today is the duty and job of . . . Jewish journalism."[27] Sinsheimer felt that since there was no Jewish drama – aside from the beginnings of drama in Palestine and plays from

Eastern European Jewish theatrical literature – drama, in order to be in keeping with modern-day Jewry, had to be a drama that dealt with the path, the way. "It is no accident that such an instinctive writer as Franz Werfel called his dramatic tableau 'Weg der Verheißung' (Path of Promise). In so doing, and by the inner nature of the work, he struck the very heart so to speak, of Jewish dramaturgy. The drama of Jewish paths and the Jewish way. . . . For a people that has taken so many fate-laden routes, 'path' is a suitable theme."[28]

The lack of appropriate themes led to a reinterpretation of dramas that did not pass the test of thematic relevance. One example is Shakespeare's "Othello"; Dr. Hugo Lachmanski stated that (when properly interpreted) it fit in with the program of the Kulturbund just as well as Lessing's "Nathan der Weise." "The decisive element in the play is not the marriage between a Venetian woman and a man of another race. . . . Othello knows he is different, and in that he is vulnerable. . . . Don't we all, after being badly treated by a non-Jew, initially assume that the reason has something to do with our being Jewish?"[29] The external situation was so compelling that comparisons suggested themselves that were indefensible from a literary point of view. "Jewish audiences are often enough inclined to replace the word 'Jew' for 'Moor,' and to relate the meaning of the tragedy of Othello to themselves."[30]

Indeed, it was primarily the public that harbored a tendency toward interpreting plays in terms of their "current topicality." Even a few lines in Bruno Frank's innocuous comedy "Sturm im Wasserglas" (Tempest in a Teapot) gave rise to new interpretations. "The audience . . . at points where it could construe a topical reference, expressed its agreement – such as when in reference to a dog the statement was made that it's breed or race wasn't important, what mattered was the heart. Indeed, the public here, more than in any other theater, is a part of the whole performance and itself plays a role. You can often note how satisfied the audience becomes after it thinks that it has garnered a special meaning from some lines."[31] A new "topical" interpretation was also given to a scene in Shakespeare's "The Winter's Tale," when Autolycus approaches front stage, and declaims his lines (IV. iv) "I see this is the time when the unjust man doth thrive" – the audience broke out in spontaneous applause.[32]

The cultural conference put on in September 1936 in Berlin by the Reich Federation of Jewish Kulturbünde dealt, among other topics, with the question of content. Dr. Joachim Prinz argued that content did not determine culture. Rembrandt was not a Jewish painter because he did a painting of the Jewish ghetto in Amsterdam; the master craftsmen who created the Bamberg cathedral had not become Jewish sculptors by dint of the fact that they had chiselled Jewish figures into the choir. In contrast, Saul Tchernichovsky, whose works were distant from Jewish themes, was nonetheless a Jewish poet – because it was the Jewish person that determined the value of Jewish culture, and not the theme or content. The choice of Jewish content in the Jewish theater in Germany had, in Prinz's view, a national educative function, and this required the actor to be a Jewish teacher.[33]

For this purpose, attempts were made to "school" the actors in things Jewish. Along with rehearsals for "Shabbatai Zwi" by Nathan Bistritzki, the actors were instructed about the Jewish historical background to the play – the imparting of knowledge along with artistic interpretation. This "enlightenment" provided for the actor was to be supplemented by a program to educate the public by means of lectures. But that effort proved a failure; Kulturbund lectures had little impact. On the one hand, this was due to the small number of lecturers asked to speak[34] and, on the other, to the fact that the typical audience of the Kulturbund, generally older people, actually felt no real "inner need" to deal with Jewish problems.[35] Another reason was that persons desirous of acquiring Jewish knowledge could satisfy their interests by means of the highly developed network of Jewish adult-education centers.

The Jüdisches Lehrhaus in Frankfurt, founded by Franz Rosenzweig in 1920 and closed after his death in 1929, was reopened again by Martin Buber at the end of 1933. In the spring of 1933, Buber had suggested the setting up of a Bildungsamt der Juden (Jewish Educational Office), and had worked out the basis for a program of Jewish adult education. The Mittelstelle für Jüdische Erwachsenenbildung (Bureau for Jewish Adult Education), set up within the framework of the Reichsvertretung, dominated the Jewish lecture scene until 1938 with its array of seminars, conferences and training courses. In the autumn of 1934, two Jewish education centers were established almost simultaneously in Berlin: the Jüdisches Lehrhaus, not associated with any Jewish political party, whose opening was inaugurated with a lecture by Leo Baeck on "History and the Present,"[36] and the Zionist center Lehrstätte Ch. N. Bialik, at whose opening Kurt Blumenfeld spoke. "We are a nation without the cultural content appropriate to our nature," he said. "Now, in this time of crisis, there are many who would like to conjure up an additional cultural content, as if by magic."[37] In 1935, another center was added: the Rambam Lehrhaus of the Mizrahi party. All three institutions were located in Berlin and addressed a similar audience. Making the intellectual menu offer something external and superficial is in keeping with that same tendency in intellectual-cultural life among the audience, complained the *Jüdische Rundschau.*[38]

Can culture be "organized"? This question was repeatedly raised. The mutual impact between culture and organization was both doubted and overestimated. Some believed that cultural values could only be created by organizational means; others argued that cultural creation was not possible unless it was included in a web of social contexts. "There is no question that the imparting of culture and its presentation must be organized," one paper commented.[39] But there was also an unmistakable warning that culture could not be created "on the spur of moment," and by decree – it had to grow organically from below.[40]

Where and when does organization deteriorate into a kind of "business," more bustle than substance? Ernst Simon pointed to the equally promising and dangerous signs marking Jewish cultural work at the time. "The swiftness with which some people know how to readjust can occasionally be embarrassing; the rigidity of the 'old die-hards,' in contrast, may seem quite attractive. It's not always value-enhancing to swim with the current."[41]

Leo Hirsch also conceded that it was only right and proper to criticize the hectic bustle of organizational activity, "but without it we cannot exist in a totally structured, mechanical, rationalized world – they are indispensable for us as forms for living."[42] There was no lack of warning and words of caution about an excess of Jewish cultural performances that necessarily had to result in a weariness, a satiety when it came to absorbing artistic products.[43]

> The fear is arising that our efforts to build up a German-Jewish cultural life of our own are beginning to suffer from too much frenetic flurry and hectic bustle. Wherever we look in the city and provinces . . . there are performances that are cultural or claim to be, lectures and concerts by both capable and less gifted artists, recitations and theater

presentations of all manner and type. . . . We have nothing against the extremely laudable work of the cultural leagues. . . . But precisely for that reason, the directors should make sure that the masses flocking to their cultural functions are not "overfed" to the point of surfeit. We know that the Kulturbund has "excessive influence" only on the smallest segment of the people.[44]

The tone became sharper, the language more frank. There was no longer any mention of "hectic bustle," now it was a veritable "boom." "It's alarming to hear all the nonsense being propagated by these 'culture-boom' Jews. . . . Have they really forgotten that we're also Europeans, and that what is important is an interaction between Jewish and European culture? . . . But what do they care! Now the big thing is Judaism!"[45]

The excessive growth in Jewish cultural performances prompted a critical commentary by a respected Jewish organization: "The Jewish experience that has brought the artist to his momentary situation is a negative one. But people can only build constructively based on a positive experience. . . . We will have to continue to concede an important point: the fact that Jewish artists are acting, singing and speaking in front of a Jewish audience does not qualify that as a Jewish experience by any means."[46] Quite naturally, the abundance of offerings – especially performances arranged by associations and organizations, lodges and Landsmannschaften, Gemeinden and the local branches of political parties – had a negative effect on the artistic level. These developments were worrisome to the writer Jakob Picard. In his view, it was imperative to eliminate a pressing danger, namely that artistic creativity among German Jews might – for material or personal reasons, and as a result of the contemporary situation – cheapen its standards, because there was a lack of creative artists ready to accept genuine criticism. Moreover, the personal environment of those who felt qualified only applauded such artists – because they were a part of that environment, one of their own. By no means should Jewish themes be the only ones chosen. "To quickly recite a bit of Dubnow, a little Graetz, or even offer up some Kastein, in catchily rhymed verses. No, that's not the way," he admonished. It can't be done overnight, as some hastily prepared artists have apparently believed in the past two years – and as an easily satisfied public . . . exercising quite understandable indulgence, has been willing and ready to tolerate." Naturally, the reader or spectator would be doubly moved should Jewish characters and fate be presented, but only on the condition that high-quality art is offered. "Why shouldn't we also have our national trash? . . . Kitsch that has to be combatted! A person who wasn't a writer before won't become one now, even as a result of the most severe anti-Jewish legislation."[47]

The *CV-Zeitung* called for similarly strict criteria. Max Spanier remarked that poetry written just for the day was not worth writing. German-Jewish literature should not lose its way by developing a provincial character; it had to take its place in the ranks of the literature of the nations, be part of the poetic creation of all mankind. Michelangelo's Moses was immortal not because it depicted a Jewish figure, but because his character expressed something superhuman. "Away with all the mediocrities and technicians! Our creations must not be inferior to the best of non-Jewish writers!"[48] Warnings about a "counterfeit-Jewish" tendency and an "inflation of Jewish formulations and professional shingles and calling cards" became more and more pointed. "Recitations, cabaret performances, song programs, variety shows that often mention the word Jewish without necessarily being it. . . . As a criterion, just leave out the Jewish nouns in a song or poem. If nothing is missing, then it simply was not genuine. In this way, the public is being fed a phoney kind of Jewishness."[49]

The lack of distance and the monopoly enjoyed by the Kulturbund made the work of the critics more difficult. People had stopped focusing in purely aesthetic terms on a work of art in a relational vacuum. Now the question was always: how does it fit in with our specific existential situation? The reviewers had the weighty responsibility of keeping the purely artistic element constantly in mind – while simultaneously doing proper justice to the unique situation of the producers and consumers, the artists and their public. On the one hand, there was a danger that an artist, struggling to survive, often expected that what he should get from the critic was pure and unreserved positive promotion instead of a critical judgment; on the other hand, there was the danger of overestimating the value and quality of a given performance.[50] "The public . . . will be all the more disappointed if it thinks it was deceived by a critique. And if experience teaches that the Jewish audience assumes the critic is probably expressing measured and polite disapproval in the case of limited praise, this is an indication of just how much the activity of a critic has been altered by the fact that he is writing for a specific public."[51] The

*CV-Zeitung* warned against debasing and devaluating criticism by dishonesty; critics were no longer believed, even when they praised good work. Criticism was not the product of a "destructive spirit," nor did it derive from any pleasure in the activity of criticizing. Rather, it arose from a recognition that Judaism in Germany could only be capable of development if each person, working at his individual post, gave the very best of "what God had endowed him with. The sense of isolation, of being 'among friends,' easily tempts one into letting oneself go, into being satisfied with mediocrity. . . . Are we really helping a 20-year-old poet whose work is banal and derivative when the Jewish press heaps inordinate praise on his writing – solely because he's Jewish? . . . Over time, even the most patient public will not let itself be forced into accepting poor performance, no matter how positive the criticism."[52]

The reserve of critics went to such extremes that a Jewish paper believed it had to issue an apology after it had written a caustic review of a young poet on the occasion of an evening of readings of contemporary Jewish lyric poetry; she had replied in a pained letter to editors. The paper responded:

> Of course, it was certainly not our intention to make it impossible for a young artist to continue to work as a result of our critique, as biting and negative as it is. However, we believe that precisely at a time like the present – when there is a danger that the Jewish public may tolerate artistic inadequacy for the sake of good will – that benevolence cannot be the sole consideration guiding the pen of the critic. . . . We must make sure that the level of artistic work in the Jewish milieu is not substantially lowered.[53]

"The Jewish public, Jewish artists, Jewish stage designers – . . . are hungrily clamoring for Jewish content."[54] But did the public really want Jewish plays? Statistics indicate that they were among the most poorly attended functions put on by the Kulturbund. The only opera with a Jewish theme, "Joseph in Ägypten," attracted a mere 8,688 visitors during the course of a month, while other operas had total audience figures of over 14,000.[55] In other words, when the Jewish theme, long struggled-for and demanded, finally appeared in the program, the public response was hesitant; this was markedly in evidence in figures on attendance at plays as well. Not even all Zionists applauded, as indicated by the letter from one of their functionaries after a performance of Leiwik's "Der Golem": "The world of the Golem is alien to the

Western Jew . . . the abstract language remains incomprehensible to a Jewish public that has not had a Jewish education. . . . Thus, one does injustice to the audience by criticizing its supposed lack of the proper attitude toward the Jewish theme."[56]

The director of the Kulturbund Rhein-Ruhr came to a similar conclusion: "One can note here . . . that Eastern European Jewish artistic elements are met by a certain lack of comprehension on the part of the audience."[57] A person who attended a performance of the "Goldene Kette" (The Golden Chain) by I.L. Peretz openly declared that you could just as easily offer him Chinese theater. "In dealing with a public whose broad masses remain very distant from Jewish life, we quite naturally are faced with an educational challenge that is certainly anything but easy."[58]

Analogous phenomena were evident in the fine arts as well. The art historian Professor Franz Landsberger felt obliged to comment that there was a tendency among contemporary artists to intentionally avoid the Jewish theme. "Perhaps the explanation for this is that people who were quite distant from Judaism before have still not developed any inner relationship toward the plethora of experiences of the past three years."[59] The monthly *Blätter des Jüdischen Frauenbunds* also pointed out that in the field of conscious Jewish art, "people were entering it only with great hesitation on their part."[60]

In 1933, Jews made up 1.5 percent of all students enrolled in art, and Jewish instructors played virtually no role on the staff of departments and academies. The political shift had its major impact primarily in the artists' associations, which gradually were brought into line and integrated into the Nazi-dominated system. A number of Jewish artists emigrated. Four years later, in July 1937, the number of Jewish painters, sculptors and graphic artists in Germany stood at 217.[61] "It is especially important . . . for Jewish artists to display their work in special exhibitions. The Kulturbund in Berlin has already put on such an exhibition in the halls of the theater, but it would be desirable if an exhibition that included all of Germany could circulate to the larger Jewish communities." Another suggestion concerned the establishment of Jewish art associations; in order to avoid splintering, these art associations should be linked up with museum associations in localities where such groups existed.[62]

"What is the situation in regard to the artistic niveau?," asked Professor Landsberger. He was concerned that there should be a halt in the declining level of exhibitions. "During the winter, it nearly reached the limit of what was tolerable." He accounted for this fact by alleging that due to reasons of social welfare, too much space had been accorded to the weaker talents.[63] On the occasion of a visit at the end of 1933 with Max Liebermann, he told the artist how much the mere fact that he was alive was an inspiration for Jews who were endeavoring to vitalize Jewish artistic values under the prevailing circumstances. Liebermann replied: "You know, that's like when someone is sick with a deadly illness and also has caught a cold – and he lets the doctor treat the cold."[64]

Problems were different when it came to the field of music. There, the principle questions were: "What is Jewish music? Does it exist? Can Jewish music be created, and if so, how? To what extent can the music of Jewish composers from the past be regarded as Jewish music?"[65] These questions were never satisfactorily answered. Dr. Singer declared categorically: "There is no such thing as a Jewish opera. . . . One hears no criticism when in the Palestinian opera 'Rigoletto' is performed, but here people resist the world-embracing spirit of 'Figaro.'. . . Don't bother us with the well-intentioned but unsubstantiated concepts about the communication of 'Jewish' works."[66] Dr. Singer attempted to show that Jewish music was vocal, not orchestral: impassioned prayer, the singing of an individual or a group of many, but nothing instrumental. "The fact that we regard certain melodies in the realm of the Kulturbund as being Jewish, or that we term orchestral works by Jewish composers Jewish, is an embarrassment. Based on the knowledge and experience of genuine experts, Jewish music exists only in synagogal music and in the Jewish folksong."[67]

An essay by Müller-Hartmann gives an indication of just how difficult it was to put together a musical program: "Thus, two orchestral songs by Mahler came to stand sandwiched in between the superb suite movements by Bizet and the ouverture to the 'Zigeunerbaron,' performed again by popular request. Gustav Mahler and Johann Strauss – criticism would be justified to a certain extent in classifying that combination as a less-than-ideal solution."[68] Commenting on a rendition of the oratorio "Avodat Hakodesh" by Ernst Bloch, it was noted: "It is the first oratorio by a great musician, a Jew, that does not only have a Jewish content, but a Jewish soul; moreover, it draws on Jewish life for its material, even borrowing from Jewish religious liturgy."[69]

The call for "Jewish" art took on a cacophonous note, if not sinister undertones, due to the fact that the Nazi authorities were themselves pressing for the production of "Jewish culture." Thus, Alfred Rosenberg wrote in the *Völkischer Beobachter*:

> By no means have the Kulturbund deutscher Juden in Berlin and its branches and parallel organizations throughout the Reich . . . completely comprehended to date the nature of their task. For example, the fact that the Berlin Kulturbund has put on a series of performances that have virtually no connection with anything Jewish is really just as little a contribution as are the extremely inspiring and highly artistic concerts in which Jews perform for Jews, but do not actually impart anything that could be called Jewish to their audience.[70]

At an annual meeting of the Reich Chamber of Culture, Goebbels observed that the Jews had been generously given various possibilities for promoting their own life as a group. All they had been denied was the option of fostering German culture – just as vice versa, no German artist had any ambition to take part in Jewish cultural life.[71] In connection with a cultural convention of the Reich Federation of Jewish Kulturbünde in September 1936, the DNB reported: "A significant fact is that Jews among themselves can pursue the furtherance of Jewish culture in an unimpeded manner . . . this was also reflected, among other things, in remarks on program creation, where a tendency is evident toward a return to a special Jewish-völkisch character."[72]

The *Jüdische Rundschau* objected to the practice of depicting nationalist-minded Jews as persons who wished to satisfy all cultural needs exclusively by means of "Jewish" products. It also took issue with the mistaken belief that people thought it necessary to apologize to such Jews every time works were performed written by non-Jewish authors.[73] In an earlier article, the paper stressed that the German Zionists did not deny they owed their intellectual education to German culture: indeed, the Jewish element of the Kulturbund should not consist in some narrow practice of poking around in the background and family tree of one or another artist. Rather, that element should be manifested in the league's consciousness, which it also aimed to enhance in its members, that they had banded together as Jews, and that it was as Jews that they were being afforded the experience of this art or other cultural experiences. The enumeration of the accomplishments of various Jewish composers or virtuosi was not at all in keeping with national-Jewish sentiments, but was a leftover from the apologetic dialectics of assimilation. The article concluded: "To be open to the world, yet as Jews – that is what differentiates the new Judaism from the old Judaism of assimilation."[74]

During those years, the Jewish press played a decisive role not only as a forum for discussion on Jewish culture, but also as a direct platform for the publication of Jewish literature and art. The majority of papers published serialized novels, novellae and short stories by authors ranging from Joseph Roth, Stefan Zweig and Franz Werfel to the young writers just setting out, and opened their pages to translations from Hebrew and Yiddish. By means of such pre-publications, which reached a broad reading public, it supported the Jewish publishing houses. It also provided considerable column space for reviews of works by Jewish authors around the world that were no longer available in Germany. More and more, its "literary supplement" became the criterion for assessing the *niveau* of a given paper. One-page or two-page selections of Jewish contemporary lyric poetry, otherwise published nowhere else, were often included as a supplement in the paper, such as that edited by Kurt Pinthus which appeared in the *CV-Zeitung*, entitled "Contemporary Jewish Lyric Poetry."[75] Some papers gave special attention to literary and artistic developments in Palestine. The *Israelitisches Familienblatt* often ran two serialized novels simultaneously. The response to the novel *Weg ohne Ende* (Unending Road) by Gerson Stern serialized in 1934 prompted the *Jüdische Rundschau* to commission the author to write a new novel for the paper.

Aside from shorter stories and novellae, the following longer literary works were published in the *Jüdische Rundschau* (in chronological order): Franz Werfel's *Weg der Verheißung* (Path of Promise), Yizchak Toral's *Traum im Abgrund* (Dream in the Abyss), Gerson Stern's *Auf drei Dingen steht die Welt* (The World Stands upon Three Things), Ever Hadani's *Das Werk im Ödland* (The Project in the Wilderness, translated from Hebrew), Leo Hirsch's *Die letzte Station* (The Last Station), Hermann Sinsheimer's *Die Abenteuer der Grazia Mendez* (Adventures of Grazia Mendez), Josef Patai's *Die Mittlere Pforte* (The Middle Gate, translated from Hungarian), Moshe Smilanski's *Chawadja Najar* (from Hebrew), Herbert Friedenthal's *Die unsichtbare Kette* (The Invisible Chain), Salman Schneur's *Noah Pandre* (translated from Hebrew), Stefan Zweig's *Der begrabene Leuchter* (The Buried Candelabra, banned by the censor on February 23, 1937), Chaim

Schwarz's *Volk Israel lebt* (The People of Israel Lives), and Franz Werfel's *Damit Du lebst* (So That You May Live), from his Jeremiah novel *Höret die Stimme* (Hear the Voice).

The question was repeatedly raised about the relevance of contemporary literature: could a Jewish writer possibly sidestep having to deal directly with the situation of Jews in Germany? Shouldn't his work necessarily provide some hint of a direction, some modicum of clarification? Gerson Stern, who broached this problem, commented: "What are Jews reading nowadays in Germany? Someone recently said to me: 'If I do in fact read, then what would I prefer? You'll laugh: I would like to laugh!' The fact is that a certain proportion of the Jews are looking for more books that do not deal with a Jewish topic."[76]

Leo Hirsch gave some indication of the nature of reception of literature at that time by the Jewish reader. "We would be devoid of feeling and unworthy of our fate were we able to read even a novel the same way we used to before. . . . Ortega y Gasset once wrote that someone should investigate whether Goethe's work still stands the test if read with the eyes of a drowning man."[77] Joachim Prinz called the cultural situation of German Jews a "tragedy of persons who are living *at* a time but not *in* it." "We have no temporal value in this German present . . . only too quickly, we separate off the great literary works of the past, to which we are devoted, from today's literature, music and painting – for which we are not permitted to harbor feelings of devotion." He dubbed that situation being "culturally out of joint," a condition that no activity, association or Kulturbund could remedy.[78]

The conclusion drawn was that all those who felt that the state of cultural transition should be bridged by a diet largely consisting of Jewish works and performances had been mistaken, just like all those who equated realistic portrayal of life and contemporaneity with the artistic products of a cultural boom that had nothing in common with genuine art. "The slogan 'Judaization' of the theater was a bit of cultural-political romanticism. That romanticizing attitude, which we have all been victims of, more or less, in recent years, had necessarily to yield to a realistic approach in art policy. Such realism, while utilizing the Jewish stage in German as an instrument for education, does so only in carefully measured doses."[79]

A growing sense of resignation – or, more accurately, a feeling of sober disillusionment – made itself felt as the noose of restrictions placed around the Jewish community in Germany was increasingly tightened; that disenchantment also derived from various negative experiences in the sphere of culture. People began to speak about a "blurring of distinctions," a "lack of perspective" in respect to the Jewish component, and claimed that these had spawned a discussion devoid of prospects, and had increased the sense of uncertainty. "Whoever had been initially inclined to accept, say, nothing but Yiddish folksongs and synagogue liturgy as Jewish music soon felt so restricted that he was once again even ready to tolerate Meyerbeer, Mendelssohn and Mahler as part of the Jewish musical legacy." This blurring of distinctions was regarded as symptomatic of the crisis and the sense of enhanced uncertainty about what might be termed the "Jewish weltanschauung."[80] Hence, it was no surprise that the conclusions drawn by the *Jüdische Rundschau* were rather negative: "The initial enthusiasm for the Jewish idea has sunk only shallow roots in the hearts of most people. There may have been no year since 1933 in which Jews in Germany went their own way to such a degree as in 1937: often times, the path they took did not lead back to Judaism. Each and every one of our cultural institutions should clearly realize today that the overwhelming majority of Jews in Berlin still feel distant from – or reject – all attempts at intellectual and cultural activity in the Jewish sphere. We have not succeeded in reaching these 'Jews at the periphery'."[81] So what remained? – a psychological and social function. The *Berliner Jüdisches Gemeindeblatt* singled out loneliness as one of the most lamentable phenomena marking Jewish life. "A program put on by the Kulturbund leads people directly into the circle and life of the community."[82]

The mood of resignation deepened in the course of 1938. The Anschluß of Austria in March of that year sent shock waves reverberating through the already unstable foundations of Jewish life in the *Altreich*. In April, registration of all Jewish property and assets was ordered;[83] whoever did not perceive the handwriting on the wall, could nonetheless not fail to note the increasingly frenzied tone evident in the official press. In an infamous series of three articles, the official SS organ *Das Schwarze Korps* called for the expropriation of all Jews, the destruction of their property and their liquidation as an economic factor. The first attacks on synagogues, months before the November pogrom, took place in the summer with the destruction of the synagogue in Nuremberg.

There were persistent rumors about feverish construction efforts to expand the concentration camps in Buchenwald, Sachsenhausen and Dachau. All this occurred under the oppressive cloud of an international crisis that exacerbated the danger of possible war and ultimately led in September to the Munich Agreement. This diplomatic victory of the Nazis had a staggering effect on German Jewry, which now saw itself defenseless and at the mercy of the full violence of hostile actions.

> Along with worry about a visa and a sufficient amount of cash, there is – indeed must be – concern about one's own self and mental identity. That sense of self must not be allowed to be ground down and pulverized between the millstones of the struggle for survival and the struggle to emigrate. German Jewry has . . . a weapon against this danger of being ground down psychologically, against this threat of progressive mental obtuseness: the Jewish Kulturbund. . . . What is aesthetic lives through its own self and does not need to be promoted and legitimated in the theater. The task of Jewish education had to fight for its legitimation . . . that line of approach . . . derives from the fact that it is a Jewish cultural league. . . . Concept and ideology alone are not sufficient to awaken this adjective to life. Feeling and idea must here contribute their utmost to the effort . . . To be deeply moved, to sense dramatic relief – these are both psychological needs. The experience of the tragic and the comic – both release, both set free.[84]

On July 2, 1944, *MB*, the Tel Aviv newsletter of the Association of Immigrants from Central Europe, published an appreciation of Kurt Singer, who had died in Theresienstadt five months before. In that article, it noted: the "positive value of the Kulturbund was so fundamental that it was even necessary to accept as part of the bargain, so to speak, the fact that Nazi propaganda utilized this institution for its own campaign of lies – by attempting to create the impression that Jews in Nazi Germany . . . actually had some sort of independent cultural life of their own."

# Notes

1. Moritz Goldstein, *Jüdische Rundschau*, July 28, 1934.
2. I.e., Cultural League of German Jews. After 1935, it bore the official name Reichsverband der Jüdischen Kulturbünde in Deutschland (Reich Federation of Jewish Cultural Leagues in Germany).
3. *Jüdische Rundschau*, ibid.

4. Moritz Goldstein, ibid.

5. Cf. DNB statement: "The guidelines of special officer Hinkel, which have now been given full confirmation by the Office of the Secret State Police and lead to [the establishment of] the unitary organization . . . are proof that the National Socialist state is providing its non-Aryan members with all possibilities for activating their own cultural and artistic life – if they cease efforts to force their way, openly or covertly, into the artistic and cultural life of the German people." Quoted in *Jüdische Rundschau*, August 20, 1935.

6. Official opening on October 1, 1933 in Berlin.

7. Of some 8,000 Jewish artists, or artists of Jewish extraction (*jüdisch-stämmig*). See Freeden, 1964.

8. Ibid., p. 144.

9. Ibid., p. 22.

10. Quoted in *CV-Zeitung*, April 5, 1933. Hinkel at that time was a special state commissar in the Prussian Ministry of Culture. On July 25, 1935, he was appointed by Goebbels to a post in the Reich Propaganda Ministry as Superintendent of Culture, with the special additional task of "monitoring of Jews active intellectually and in the sphere of culture in the territory of the Reich," Freeden, 1964, p. 42.

11. *Der Morgen*, 9 (August 1933), Heft 3, pp. 185ff. A similar comment was published by Julius Bab in *Der Schild*, September 14, 1933: "Ghetto in the sense of a constrictive Jewish separation from the world . . . that is a matter of outlook and inner will. We won't have such a ghetto, because we do not intend in any way to pursue a one-sided emphasis on Jewish culture in our Kulturbund. Rather, we wish to promote the great German culture on whose soil we have been brought up."

12. *Israelitisches* Familienblatt, January 11, 1934.

13. Ibid. "It was a theater existing under special historical, political, social . . . and existential conditions. It could hardly afford any theatrical attractions." Huber, 1979, p. 13. "This means an absolute break with previous reality, it means being excluded from the familiar cultural ambience. . . . It means the abandoning of the previous obvious identity. Or at the very least, it demands a search for a compromise between experience up to that point and new necessities." Hans-Christian Wächter, "Theater im Exil – Initiative und Provokation," ibid., p. 21.

These quotations can be seen as a kind of definition of the Jewish Kulturbund, but they are not. Rather, they are taken from a symposium of the Academy of Arts on "Theater in Exile, 1933–1945" held in Berlin in 1973, whose papers were published in book form in 1979. The Jewish Kulturbund is not mentioned anywhere, although exile in this case would have to refer not only to geographical banishment, but to a cultural expulsion as well. The Kulturbund was certainly not an expression of "inner emigration," yet did share certain features in common with a theater in exile.

14. On March 28, 1939, the General Secretary of the Reich Federation of Jewish Kulturbünde, Dr. Werner Levie, received a letter from Dr. Grün, stating that Dr. Richard Beer-Hofmann did not wish his drama "Der junge David" to be performed in the theater of the Kulturbund, and that in his interest, all efforts should cease that might lead to a mention of his name in public. The author at that time was still in Vienna (Archive, Jewish Gemeinde, Berlin, cited in Freeden, op. cit., p. 157). In January 1935, after a full year of negotiations, Beer-Hofmann agreed to the staging of his drama "Jaakobs Traum" in the Berlin Kulturbund theater (Freeden, op. cit., p. 69). "It is gratifying that, on this occasion, the author has been able to overcome repeated doubts and hesitations, this time in our favor" (Arthur Eloesser, in *Jüdische Rundschau*, February 8, 1935).

15. *Berliner Jüdisches Gemeindeblatt*, August 11, 1934.

16. *Jüdische Rundschau*, May 4, 1934.

17. Ibid., March 6, 1934.

18. *CV-Zeitung*, March 15, 1934.

19. *Israelitisches Familienblatt*, January 11, 1934.

20. Ibid., March 15, 1934.

21. Performed during the program year 1936–1937.

22. *Israelitisches Familienblatt*, March 15, 1934.

23. Ibid., April 19, 1934.

24. *Jüdische Rundschau*, May 15, 1934.

25. Ibid., February 19, 1934. Semyon Yushkevitch (1868–1927) was an Odessa-born Russian-Jewish writer.

26. *CV-Zeitung*, December 14, 1933.

27. *Jüdische Rundschau*, May 7, 1937.

28. Ibid., January 14, 1936.

29. *CV-Zeitung*, December 14, 1933. The Kulturbund was opened with Lessing's "Nathan der Weise."

30. *Israelitisches Familienblatt*, December 21, 1933.

31. Ibid., August 7, 1934.

32. Freeden, op. cit., p. 1. The same problem was touched on by the *CV-Zeitung* in connection with the performance of Hauptmann's "Michael Kramer" in the Kulturbund Rhein-Ruhr: "If we sense any distance from the work . . . it derives from the fact that Gerhart Hauptmann made clear that one ought to be familiar with suffering and admit it. Since that time, we have gone through such difficult experiences that there are some words we would rather not hear spoken on the stage – they sound sentimental – because we have a direct experience of their concrete content" (January 31, 1935).

33. Archive, Alfred Klee, quoted in Freeden, op. cit., p. 84.

34. "The Kulturbünde did not utilize more than 19 of the 44 lecturers available throughout the Reich," *Mitteilungen des Reichsverbandes der Jüdischen Kulturbünde*, May 1938.

35. *Jüdische Rundschau*, July 28, 1936. See also *Der Schild* (August 19, 1934): "In contrast, more than half of all lectures had dealt with specifically Jewish themes. . . . Yet here too, one must note that among the best-attended lectures was a series on world literature and one on musical history dealing with the Romantic song. . . . The need to take part in world culture and, especially, in German culture has by no means disappeared among German Jews, it continues to search for proper sustenance."

36. "Some 2,200 membership cards were issued. . . . The institute does not wish to impart Jewish materials exclusively, but also to introduce students to general, neutral fields of knowledge," *CV- Zeitung*, April 4, 1935.

37. *Jüdische Rundschau*, October 30, 1934.

38. "Three teaching institutes in Berlin are courting the favor of the Jewish public. If we did not find ourselves in such a special situation, that circumstance would merit scorn and derision," ibid., February 20, 1937.

39. A.H., in: *CV-Zeitung*, August 27, 1936.

40. *Israelitisches Familienblatt*, October 11, 1933.

41. *Jüdische Rundschau*, May 17, 1935. "In the beginning there was an organizational boom," "Jewish Theater in Germany" (n.a.), *Der Morgen*, 12 (June 1936), Heft 3, p. 111.

42. *Jüdische Rundschau*, September 17, 1937.

43. *Israelitisches Familienblatt*, January 31, 1935.

44. Ibid., February 7, 1936. The *CV-Zeitung* commented: "The Reichsvertretung has contacted the editorial offices and publishing houses of the various Jewish journals and newspapers and proposed a number of suggestions regarding reporting of cultural functions. In future, there are to be reports only on functions which are artistically or intellectually significant, or important from the standpoint of organization" (January 31, 1935).

45. *Israelitisches Familienblatt*, May 9, 1935. This chaotic situation was put to an end with the creation of the Reichsverband der Jüdischen Kulturbünde in 1935. Some 112 independent organizations in 100 cities and towns were affiliated with the Reich Federation (cultural leagues, cultural departments of Gemeinden and associations active in the arts). By official order of the authorities, all programs had to be submitted to the Reich Federation's central offices. See Freeden, op. cit., p. 110.

46. *Blätter des Jüdischen Frauenbundes* (Berlin), 9 (September 1935), no. 9.

47. *Jüdische Rundschau*, November 22, 1935.

48. *CV-Zeitung*, April 4, 1935. Note also: "The Jews are borderline Germans [*Grenzdeutsche*], but their border is not bound up with a country; it is a state of marginality of the spirit," Ernst Lissauer, quoted in: *CV-Zeitung*, June 22, 1936, on the question "German Jew, German Literature."

49. *Mitteilungen des Reichsverbandes der Jüdischen Kulturbünde*, November 1937.

50. *Jüdische Rundschau*, March 19, 1937.

51. Weltmann, 1937, p. 61.

52. Dr. M.E., "Kritik als Aufgabe," *CV-Zeitung*, January 17, 1935.

53. *Jüdische Rundschau*, September 10, 1935.

54. *Israelitisches Familienblatt*, March 13, 1934.

55. Freeden, op. cit., p. 94.

56. Dr. Hans Capell, *Jüdische Rundschau*, November 5, 1937.

57. Dr. Heinrich Levinger, *Mitteilungen des Reichsverbandes der Jüdischen Kulturbünde*, August 1937.

58. Benno Cohn, *Jüdische Rundschau*, December 18, 1936.

59. Ibid., August 21, 1936.

60. *Blätter des Jüdischen Frauenbundes*, 13 (May 1937), no. 5.

61. Freeden, op. cit., p. 127.

62. *Jüdische Rundschau*, January 5, 1934. According to a report in the *CV-Zeitung* (December 24, 1934), the Reich Federation of Jewish Kulturbünde had, together with the Artists' Aid of the Jewish Gemeinde in Berlin, set up an Office for the Fine Arts.

63. *Jüdische Rundschau*, August 21, 1936.

64. Ibid., January 5, 1934.

65. Peter Gradenwitz, *Jüdische Rundschau*, March 16, 1934.

66. *Israelitisches Familienblatt*, March 22, 1934. Cf. also: "The special emphasis on a Jewish note is a rare occurrence in the concert program," *Der Schild*, August 19, 1934.

67. Freeden, op. cit., p. 125f. See A.H. in *CV-Zeitung* (on the occasion of Singer's fiftieth birthday): "No one – with perhaps the exception of those who are always perfect, and who for that very reason will never attain perfection – would utilize the fact that he required supplementary information on Jewish matters as an argument against the value of this man. We all are more or less in the same intellectual and psychological situation that Singer. . . . is now setting out to master" (October 10, 1935).

68. *Monatsblätter des Jüdischen Kulturbundes Hamburg*, March 1937.

69. *Israelitisches Familienblatt*, July 5, 1934.

70. Quoted from *Israelitisches Familienblatt*, March 15, 1934.

71. Quoted from *Jüdische Rundschau*, November 19, 1935.

72. Quoted from *Jüdische Rundschau*, September 18, 1936.

73. *Jüdische Rundschau*, July 25, 1933.

74. Ibid., March 5, 1933.

75. *CV-Zeitung*, April 6, 1936.

76. *Israelitisches Familienblatt*, April 28, 1938.

77. *Jüdische Rundschau*, December 6, 1935.

78. "Leben ohne Nachbarn," ibid., April 17, 1935.

79. Werner Levie, *Jüdische Rundschau*, August 20, 1937. Fritz Friedländer spoke about the "limits of cultural autonomy," *Der Morgen*, 10 (February 1935), no. 11, p. 492.

80. Leo Hirsch, *Jüdische Rundschau*, September 17, 1937.

81. Gerhardt Neumann, ibid., January 1, 1938.

82. *Berliner Jüdisches Gemeindeblatt*, August 22, 1937.

83. On this and other economic measures against Jews in 1938, see Barkai, 1989, pp. 117ff.

84. W. G., *Jüdische Rundschau*, September 2, 1938.

# 6

—

# Voice of the Gemeinde

"Little of the struggle (ideological, political, religious, religio-political) found its way into the Gemeindeblatt. It was, after all, the official organ of the whole community . . . neutral ground. Every group got a hearing. The reaction of the Gemeindeblatt went seldom beyond gentle rebuke. Personal controversies and rebuttals were rare. Its neutrality was dictated by the character and function of the Gemeindeblatt."[1]

The *Frankfurter Israelitisches Gemeindeblatt* reached similar conclusions, though with certain provisos. The special character of the Gemeinde papers as official organs and as reading matter for various circles lay in their middle-of-the-road position. To find this position in the middle was now more difficult than ever, the author contended, and a number of such Gemeinde papers had been unsuccessful in that regard. They had become information sources about events that had their proper place in Jewish weeklies.[2] Undoubtedly, the *Gemeindeblatt der Jüdischen Gemeinde zu Berlin* was also in that category. Since it was published on a weekly basis, it felt obliged to comment on topical events, especially those pertaining to Jewish politics.

## Berlin

Whether due to the size of its readership – a third of all German Jews lived in Berlin – or because of the specific conditions prevailing in the administration of the Berlin Gemeinde, the paper took part in the political struggles within German Jewry and was a peculiar mixture, something of a hybrid between a communal-official organ and a political pamphlet. Nonetheless, the paper repeatedly underscored that its aim was preservation of the unity of the Gemeinde.

To that extent, it was in agreement with what the *Gemeindeblatt* in Frankfurt maintained, namely that most readers of Gemeinde papers were actually somewhat biased as a result of their experience with Jewish papers, and had certain preconceptions. They expected to find an answer to political questions of the day in the Gemeinde papers, the same questions and issues they were familiar with from the publications of the various Jewish ideological camps.[3]

In January 1933, the *Berliner Gemeindeblatt*, then in its 23rd year, was still appearing as a monthly, with a total of 28 pages, nine of which were devoted to advertisements. Beginning with the issue dated February 2, 1934, the paper went weekly, and adopted a larger format.

The January 1933 issue still contained no reflection of the events that were already beginning to shake Germany and its Jewish community. The contents consisted of essays such as "The Personalities in Jewish History" (J. Ellenbogen), "Moses and the Kingdom in Ancient Israel" (Elias Auerbach), "Jeremiah and Prophetic Judaism" (Rabbi Josef Lehmann), "Ezra and Post-Exilic Judaism" (H. H. Schaefer), "Rabbi Akiva and Talmudic Judaism" (Josef Kastein), "Moses Mendelssohn and Emancipated Jewry" (Selma Stern-Täubler), as well as the calendar for religious services and announcements by various sections of the Gemeinde.

Since the paper was produced by the method of deep copper plate printing (a technique retained until the final issue), it was more suitable than any other Jewish paper in Germany for printing illustrations. In the early numbers, the illustrations it carried were religious in nature, and later it featured reproductions of works by Max Liebermann, Jakob Steinhardt, Lesser Ury, Ludwig Meidner, Eugen Spiro and others. In the years 1935–1938, reproductions predominated of works by artists who had taken part in the exhibitions in the Jüdisches Museum, the Kulturbund Theater and other Jewish institutions, for the main part arranged by the Artists' Aid of the Jewish Gemeinde.

The first issue to comment on events in the surrounding world was the April 1933 number. Together with the Reichsvertretung der deutschen Juden, the Berlin Gemeinde had issued an appeal disseminated by telegraphic news services, daily papers and in part via radio as well (at that juncture, these media were still available to the Gemeinde): "German Jews feel deeply shaken . . . The allegation that we have done harm to our people is a deep offense to our sense of honor. In the name of truth, we solemnly protest against this accusation." The paper appealed to the Jewish community in Warsaw, the American Jewish Committee (New York), the Jewish Board of Deputies (London), the Chief Rabbi in London Dr. Hertz, and Grand Rabbin Israel Levy (Paris) to try to help bring an end to the "atrocity propaganda" against Germany. The German-Jewish community was being held responsible for every word of accusation by these bodies and personalities, and saw themselves as hostages in the hands of the new rulers. That same month, the *Gemeindeblatt* published a special number carrying reports on the work of the welfare office, the Jewish Winterhilfe relief program, and made reference to the "Guide for Seekers of Advice and Assistance."

The two April issues reported a growing number of Jews who had renewed their membership in the Gemeinde. Each day, the Gemeinde office received mail from persons who had formally left the Gemeinde or renounced their Judaism in earlier years, and who now declared they were rejoining the community. Among these letters were also some from well-known personalities who stated their willingness to work as volunteers. One letter to the editors read:

> I left the Gemeinde more than 30 years ago. Explanations about my reasons then seem inappropriate today. I am 64 years old. . . . My son was in the war from the start right down to the end, serving in a field artillery unit. . . . He was awarded the Iron Cross First Class for bravery and sacrifice. In the depths of my being, I remain a Jew, and I believe that today it is my duty to rejoin the community. . . . I have found the way back not as a person who desires something, but as one who wishes to help, and will do whatever I can to assuage the pain and distress.[4]

In May 1933, the paper began publication of a list of Jewish artisans, "so that one can frequent their premises as a customer"; that list was constantly expanded in subsequent issues, supplemented by a "Directory of Commercial Supplies." An appeal to Gemeinde members urged them to preserve a "dignified, reserved behavior in public." This advice was aimed especially at readers "who are in a position to spend their summer weekends at favored recreation spots in the vicinity of Berlin."

In June 1933, the newly elected chairman of the Gemeinde,

Heinrich Stahl, introduced himself in an appeal: "Suppress what is divisive! . . . every view, every direction, every party is welcome!"

Apparently that wish for unity remained nothing but good intentions. The first public dispute developed from an article in October 1933 by Bruno Woyda, member of the board and representative of the Religious-Liberal faction. He contended that only those suffering from false illusions could believe that a solution to the "Jewish question in Germany" could be brought about by external forces. "We can and should gain what is our right from one source alone: the German people and its leaders. Nothing can cause us to waver in our belief that this German people and its chosen leadership acknowledge the fact of the presence of the Jewish Germans – and are attempting to do that fact justice."[5]

A month later, in November 1933, a report on a rally held by German-Jewish youth in the community center noted that there was a need for more forceful representation of German-Jewish identity, so that the preponderant majority of German Jews – who wished to live in Germany, with Germany and for Germany – would have some institution appealing to their sense of nationalism, and thus not be driven into the arms of those who seek their salvation in a new homeland. Aside from the fact that Zionism sprang from a pessimistic view of the situation and was based on a misconception of the actual concrete facts, the danger existed that German-Jewish youth might become homeless, losing the ties that bound it with the past and future as part of German Jewry.[6]

A report on the session of the representative council of the Gemeinde held on January 18, 1934 contained a response to this point of view:

> Associated with the discussion is a proposal by the faction of the (Zionist) Jüdische Volkspartei regarding the restructuring of the editorial commission. In the proposal, the faction states that it is in disagreement with the contents of the issues for October and November 1933. . . . The first speaker to respond was Dr. Rau, who criticized the Gemeindeblatt for only publishing articles with a German-Jewish orientation, while failing to take into proper consideration the outlook and philosophy of the Gemeinde members represented by the Zionist faction. . . . The Zionist faction demanded that the Gemeindeblatt should be managed differently from in the past.[7]
>
> In reply, Herr Kreindler[8] took issue with the view that a paper can be properly judged only on the basis of two numbers. . . . If certain articles that Herr Rau felt were lacking did not appear, then the reason

for that was because such articles were not submitted to the paper. Dr. Alfred Klee and Dr. Siegfried Moses thought it was peculiar that the accusation of onesidedness had not been challenged by anyone. After closing the discussion, the Zionist faction withdrew its proposal to express dissatisfaction with the manager and editor of the Gemeindeblatt. Dr. Klee was elected to the editorial commission.[9]

Thus, for the first time, a Zionist had a vote on the editorial committee.

With its expanded format, now as a weekly, various changes were introduced, such as literary contributions; among the first authors published were Arno Nadel, Hermann Sinsheimer, Arthur Silbergleit, Doris Wittner and Martha Wertheimer. Also included were critical essays on literature, by writers such as Kurt Pinthus, Julius Bab and Arthur Eloesser, a page entitled "The Voice of the Gemeinde," and a column of "Letters to the Editor." A substantial section of the paper was devoted to discussion of upcoming attractions in the Kulturbund and Artists' Aid programs, and evaluations of functions already held.

The advertisements section offered a rather broad array of advertisers, and the paper promoted it by reminding readers: "The *Gemeindeblatt*, as a new weekly, has by far the largest Berlin circulation of any Jewish paper."[10] In July 1933, one could still find ads of the Dresdner Bank, restaurants and cafés along the Kurfürstendamm and hotels in resort spots and spas once in great favor with the Jewish public, such as Heringsdorf, Bad Nauheim, Bad Kissingen, Wiesbaden, Bad Wildungen, Bad Harzburg – and even Berchtesgaden, later notorious for Hitler's "Adlernest" retreat. On March 1, 1934, the paper ran an ad placed by the cabaret "Tingel-Tangel," known for its subtle political satire and starring Kate Kühl and Ellen Schwanneke; on September 29, 1934, the motion picture theaters "Marmorhaus" (Kurfürstendamm) and "Titaniapalast" (Berlin-Steglitz) lauded the new movie "Die große Zarin," featuring Marlene Dietrich in the lead role. An appeal to readers urged: "Stay at the Jewish hotels in Germany . . . in the light of the special difficulties currently faced by the Jewish hotel industry."[11]

The census of June 16, 1933 gave a figure of 499,682 for the total Jewish population in Germany.[12] Of these, 160,564 (32.1 percent) lived in Berlin, as compared with 172,672 Jews there in 1925. While the decline in Jewish population in other parts of Germany was around 15 percent or more, the number of Jews in

Berlin had dropped by seven percent over the previous eight years.[13] At that time, there were some 1,000 Jewish associations in Berlin, and Heinrich Stahl announced that the Gemeinde was taking over responsibility to see to it that superfluous organizations disappeared.[14] "We have read of instances at Jewish meetings where Jewish groups have insulted and attacked one another; it is our view that such incidents deserve the most forceful condemnation."[15]

However, that did not put an end to the controversies in the Berlin *Gemeindeblatt*. On the occasion of the 25th anniversary of the city of Tel Aviv, a report received from Palestine[16] was commented on in an editorial entitled "Palestine and Us" signed by B. W. It argued that the Palestine question had long been a controversial issue in present-day Jewry and that the reason for the dispute was not the project of construction, but the national Jewish slogan accompanying that enterprise. It was understandable that German Jews also judged the Palestine question from the perspective of German politics. Yet now there had been a decision on the Jewish question in the wake of the victory of the concept of race, so that anti-Zionism was no longer a factor. In the radical German-Jewish camp, the view was that it was not the task of the community to care for those who wished to separate from it. A similar extremism could often be encountered in the ranks of the Zionists. Given the economic situation of Jews in Germany, no one was asking that the Gemeinde demonstrate its interest in the construction of Palestine by financial contributions. Precisely for that reason, the dispatching of a Zionist board member to the celebration festivities of the city of Tel Aviv had a justifiable symbolic value.[17]

Not long thereafter, there was an editorial for the first time by a Zionist. He was pleased to note that the paper had recently commented that opposition to Zionist work among the German-Jewish community no longer existed; it could only be hoped that the task of the Gemeinde was not merely to provide practical assistance for the emigration of large numbers of Jews to Palestine – its intellectual attitude toward Palestine also had to be reexamined.[18]

Yet there was no sign of this, and the *Gemeindeblatt* was quite militant, for example, in voicing a demand, led by the Religious-Liberal faction, for expanded representation on behalf of the Gemeinde in the Reichsvertretung, using figurative phraseology like: "If a central organization wishes to have vitality, it must draw its strength from the Jewish Gemeinden, must grow out of them, like a tree from its roots."[19]

What it actually boiled down to was a political power struggle for the leadership of the Reichsvertretung. The task of the central organization was to make sure there was a "dignified" cooperation between all Jewish currents, the paper wrote; but it rejected the Zionist demand that the board of the Berlin Gemeinde had to adjust to the changed circumstances before attaining the desired organizational unity between the Gemeinde and Reichsvertretung.[20] "It is abundantly clear that objective necessities cannot be answered by party concerns that stem from dissatisfaction over the attempt to avoid an election struggle in the Berlin Gemeinde; thus, any polemics would be inappropriate here."[21]

Yet polemics by the *Gemeindeblatt* continued. "No one is better aware than we are that the position of Jews in Germany is a matter for the state and that we should not offer ourselves where we are not wanted." Yet here the question at issue was "whether we should affirm our removal voluntarily and based on inner conviction – or whether we still feel emotionally that we are a part of Germany." It was disconcerting, the paper noted, if any and every attempt to express such ideas was deemed unpleasant by the representatives of a certain Jewish ideological current.[22]

This editorial generated some opposition, and shortly thereafter the editors published a short comment: "In the issue before last, we voiced the position held by the majority of the Gemeinde board. We shall now publish the minority opinion of a Zionist representative in the Gemeinde administration."[23] The article, written by Dr. Hans Klee, affirmed work in the diaspora in line with the program of current activities formulated during the initial years of the Zionist Congress; it came to the conclusion that work for Palestine, seen in a broader perspective, had an impact on the strengthening of Jewish community life in the diaspora and that in turn was ultimately beneficial for Palestine.

Yet this did not put an end to the dispute by any means, and dissension was aggravated at the beginning of 1936. After noting that it was a harmful practice to disparage the opinion of others just in order to put forward one's own view as the only correct one,[24] Heinrich Stahl rejected criticism of the *Israelitisches Familienblatt*,[25] alleging that the spirit of the Gemeinde had not

undergone any change, the development of the Jewish school system had not been the result of any fundamental attitude in the
Jewish community but had been the product of pressure from on
high – and that all this was the fault of certain persons in the
Gemeinde who had failed to comprehend the new times. Stahl
commented:

> The board is neither blind nor deaf in regard to the tenor of the
> times and the burden of fate placed upon us . . . we are promoting
> the Jewish school not only in a formal sense, but by undertaking the
> greatest of efforts . . . as we see it, our ties with Jews everywhere – and
> especially with Palestine – are not merely some sort of friendly gesture
> or even a compromise, but are the expression of our conviction.
> When we celebrate the anniversary of the Hebrew University, this is
> not for economic reasons; rather, it is an act that comes straight from
> the heart.[26]

The Zionists were still in the minority on the Gemeinde board
and in the council of representatives. Of the 12 members of the
board, four belonged to the Jüdische Volkspartei, and one was a
member of the Zionist faction[27]; of the 41 representatives in the
council, 12 were members of the Jüdische Volkspartei and three
came from the ranks of the Zionists.[28]

Tensions finally came to a head. An announcement appeared
on the front page of the paper stating that the editors felt it was
necessary and proper to keep Gemeinde members exhaustively
informed about important developments in the various institutions of the Gemeinde; this immediately prompted declarations
issued by the two Zionist groupings (Jüdische Volkspartei and
ZVfD) and the Religious-Liberal faction.[29]

First declaration: "The factions of the Jüdische Volkspartei and
the ZVfD in the Berlin Jewish Gemeinde do not regard it in the
interest of the Jewish community as a whole for the present composition of the board of the Gemeinde to continue; it no longer
reflects the true will of the Jewish population. The two factions
are aware that they have the support of the preponderant majority of Jews in Berlin, and call for an immediate change in the composition of Gemeinde representative bodies."

Second declaration (Religious-Liberals): "Despite the growing
distressful situation now afflicting every Jewish family, the Zionist
factions deem it once again fitting and proper to inject Jewish
partisan political disputes into Gemeinde affairs. . . . In addition,
they are demanding a 'restructuring of the central and local

authoritative bodies of German Jewry in terms of personnel and organization.'. . . In contrast, we declare the following: we shall not allow . . . work in the Gemeinde to suffer from such disputes. We shall continue to fulfill the tasks that must be addressed given the present situation faced by Jews in the Berlin Gemeinde, and will do so free from any party-political dogma."

In the three subsequent issues, the paper published a detailed report on the activities of the Gemeinde. An understanding was not reached until November 1935.[30] New appointments to the board and a corresponding redistribution of control of various departments were carried out based on a principle of fifty-fifty representation.

In the meantime, there had been a new turn in the fate of German Jewry with the passing of the Nuremberg Laws. On the eve of the National Socialist Party congress, which stripped the Jews of their citizenship and proclaimed the Law on Preservation of the Purity of German Blood, the Berlin *Gemeindeblatt* emphasized the role to be played by the Jewish press at that difficult hour. Jewish papers, it stressed, had the task of preparing the way for the reorganization of Jewish life. For that reason, Jewish papers did not wish to be – and should not be – a repository for past events. The task should be focused on striving to push forward toward new developments in a changed situation.[31] "Don't lose heart!" urged an appeal published by Heinrich Stahl after passage of the new legislation,[32] followed by an announcement from the press office of the Reichsvertretung: "In its capacity as the official leadership of Jews in Germany, the Reichsvertretung, operating on the basis of the new national legislation, has initiated measures that will be of decisive importance for the planned and orderly restructuring of Jewish life."[33]

How was the reaction of Berlin Jews to their new status reflected in the *Gemeindeblatt*? The fact that they were being squeezed out of the economy and society was becoming increasingly evident. One might have expected some manifest expression in the press of their degrading loss of civil rights and the new racial legislation, which had such tragic consequences for so many. Yet instead, the main topic of discussion was the question of household maids. In Jewish households headed by a male, it was no longer permitted to employ Aryan maids under the age of 45. The Jewish employment office felt it necessary to make the following announcement: "The new legal regulations of September

15th obligate the employment bureau to reorganize the procurement of Jewish domestics for Jewish households. We will have to try new approaches here, and determine which families are prepared to engage women or girls with no previous experience as domestic help, and to train them on the job. . . . In consideration of the particularly heavy demand . . . we request that persons refrain at the moment from contacting us by phone."[34]  At the same time, an appeal was addressed to Jewish housewives:

> Housewives will have to try to shift the schedule for domestic help to a nine or ten-hour workday. . . . This adjustment naturally necessitates a simplification in the way the household is run and the additional utilization of children for chores around the house. None of this is easy for the housewife. . . . Daughters of working age have been restricted to a small number of professions as a result of the general limitations placed on options for existence. The job of household servant offers good prospects for earning a living; it is a profession that can serve as a source of livelihood in any country.

The section "small want ads" for household personnel expanded to such an extent that the paper felt it had to comment on the matter in an editorial: "Nowadays it seems there is no more lively topic in many Jewish families than talking about the problem of supply and demand in the labor market for domestic help. . . . Nonetheless, we believe that this question, though not unimportant, is being terribly exaggerated. One should not overlook the fact that we have had to adjust in recent years to many changes of a quite different sort."[35]

The impression that a certain stratum was quite well-off was enhanced by the presence at year's end of a whole page of announcements for New Year's parties. In subsequent years as well, until 1937, a few more such ads appeared, though the expression "New Year's Eve party" (*Silvester-Feier*) was replaced by the more neutral term "social gathering." Jewish cafés with dancing continued to place ads, some of which carried the additional notice: "For members of the Jewish community only, upon presentation of proper identification." Others included the letters M.d.J.G. (*Mitglied der Jüdischen Gemeinde* – member of the Jewish community) after the name of the proprietor, but not all ads contained such added features.

An appeal urged reserve when appearing in public places: "This is the self-evident obligation of every responsible-thinking Jew. Such a Jew should avoid the large restaurants and cafés, and refrain from superfluous strolls, preferring the privacy of his own home."[36] Two years later, however, the Jewish Women's League felt it necessary to issue the warning:

> As summer approaches, Jewish organizations, especially the Jewish Women's League . . . have been receiving letters critical of the behavior of Jewish women. These letters generally mention the outdoor gardens of cafés along the Kurfürstendamm, and women with a Jewish appearance who sit there at the front row of tables dressed in a way that is, to say the least, conspicuous. One can only react to such letters with a sigh. Unfortunately, their content is only too familiar. But none of their authors can suggest what should be done to combat such excesses.[37]

A request was made not to park one's car in front of the synagogue on Rosh Hashana.[38]

These signs of prosperity contrasted with the increasing destitution of broad segments of Jewish society, a situation reflected in almost every issue in the appeals to support the Jewish Winterhilfe relief fund. For the winter 1935–1936, figures of the Jewish Winterhilfe in Berlin indicated it was providing aid to a total of 27,508 persons, who received coal, food certificates, potatoes, bread and packages of essential foods.[39]  One year later, the report noted that more than four thousand volunteers, along with the regular staff of the Gemeinde, had assisted a total of 29,610 individuals through the Jewish Winter Relief. 144,193 food certificates with a total value of 288,386 reichsmarks were distributed, redeemable in 193 stores. The number of food packages distributed amounted to 80,782, with a total value of 232,227 reichsmarks; these included 8,343 packages for those on special diets or with medical problems. Some 441,980 kg (486 tons) of coal were distributed, and clothing worth more than half a million reichsmarks. The clothing room was visited by more than 100 indigent persons daily. A charity benefit concert was even organized for a highly respected and previously well-paid profession, namely "doctors in distress."

Family announcements were becoming more frequent in the advertisements section, especially death notices, and the listings under the caption "Members of the Gemeinde Can Supply" now covered more than six pages. Shipping companies and travel agencies were more conspicuous in their representation, offering their services to prospective emigrants and travellers who wanted more information about a potential land of immigration. New sections were added by the editors: "Palestine and Immigration," "Jewish Books," and a growing number of stories, short stories, novellae and legends. Now as before, the Kulturbund and Artists' Aid were of central importance. There were various special articles in installments, running over a number of issues, such as "New Culture on an Ancient Soil," a report on a trip to Palestine by Dr. Werner Levie, "Personalities in the Jewish Community" by Abraham Heschel, and a series by Julius Bab entitled "Jewish Figures in German Literature."

At the beginning of the Festival of Tabernacles in 1937, it was announced that official regulations for the days of planned air-raid drills had necessitated changes in times for the start of holiday services. "The ritual booths will remain closed in the evening, but can be visited during the day."[40] Seen in the light of future events, the following official announcement takes on an eerie note: "There will be distribution of gas masks among the Jewish population (via the central welfare office of the Berlin Jewish Gemeinde) on orders from the Main Welfare Office of the NSDAP, in cooperation with the Reich Ministry of Aviation."[41]

## Bayerische Israelitische Gemeindezeitung

The *Bayerische Israelitische Gemeindezeitung* was the polar opposite of the Berlin paper. "In artistic design and in size it was surpassed by the Gemeindeblatt of Berlin, but as to content it was superior to that of all the other communities."[42] Compared with other Jewish periodicals at that time, it resembled the monthly *Der Morgen*, a cultural journal whose articles dealt with theological, sociological and literary topics.

Naturally, one function of the *Bayerische Gemeindezeitung* was to serve as an organ for the Gemeinde, faithfully publishing official Gemeinde announcements and local news. Yet these items were not the main body of the paper; moreover, aside from several exceptions, the paper did not comment on political questions. When it did, that was usually an official declaration by the Gemeinde board or the Reichsvertretung.

In one of its rare editorials, it called for "absolute concentration on the independent life of the Jewish community," aiming at cultural autonomy, a separate Jewish elite after as many as possible had emigrated, and a correspondingly intensive expansion of Jewish schools and all options for training that could be of use to potential immigrants.[43] Soon after the Nazi takeover, the paper commented: "The legality of the anti-Jewish authorities makes any opposition to injustice and illegality itself 'illegal'. . . . The ancient problem of opposition and resistance to injustice and the abuse of state power still remains."[44]

The paper tried to bolster inner resistance by maintaining a high intellectual level. To name only a few of the articles it carried: "Reason and Science" (Ernst Cassirer), "Agnon's Jewish World" (Ernst Simon), "Morality and Religion" (Martin Buber), "Thoughts on Our Educational Goal" (Martin Buber), "The Task of Jews in Europe Today" (Romain Rolland), "Religion and Reality" (Alexander Altmann), "The Concept of *Volk*" (Romano Guardini), "The Concept of Justice" (Jakob Wassermann), "The Jewish Question" (Gerhard Kittel), "On the Decline in the Art of Reading and the Philosophy of the Half-Educated" (unsigned), as well as a three-page critique of Maimonides and a discussion about "Jewish poetry in German." Dr. Willy Cohen (Breslau) was also a regular contributor.[45]

Each issue contained a supplement of the Jewish Teachers' Association in Bavaria, and a voluminous "books section" made the paper almost into a kind of literary review. The middle pages were reserved for the Jewish Kulturbund, established in Bavaria on February 15, 1934. As the situation faced by Jews deteriorated, more and more emphasis was placed on the topic of Palestine, from the Decree on Currency Regulations for Immigrants to Palestine"[46] to articles on Hebrew pronunciation,[47] the "Economic Bases of the Arab Problem"[48] and the "Report of the Royal Commission Headed by Earl Peel on the Partition of Palestine."[49]

A Commentary published in June 1933 on the census results reads like a dark vision: "While awaiting an uncertain fate, we are counted once again. We shall never be able to forget those huge questionnaires with their insistent questions. They belong to the aspects of recent distressing months that we will remember until the day we die."[50]

The symptoms of rapid decline left their stamp on the face of the paper in its final two years of publication. There were more and more announcements about the disbanding of small Gemeinden in Bavaria, events put on by the Kulturbund could no longer be held in the auditorium of the museum,[51] and on November 1, 1938, a week prior to the November pogroms, the Kulturbund was closed down completely. At that same time, the

Gemeinde administration was forced to vacate its house on Max-Herzog-Straße and to move to a rear building on Lindwurm-straße; a short time later, it went up in flames along with the syna-gogues.

## Frankfurt

The second largest Jewish community in Germany was in Frank-furt/Main. Its monthly publication, the *Frankfurter Israelitisches Gemeindeblatt*, had no political ambitions like those of the paper in Berlin, nor was its literary *niveau* a match for that of the *Gemeindezeitung* in Munich; nonetheless, the paper had special features distinguishing it from the large number of other Gemeinde papers.

Its supplement "Youth and Gemeinde" proved to be a bond between the generations and a forum for the frank and open dis-cussion of the problems and concerns of Jewish youth. The paper had another special characteristic: each issue contained a statisti-cal survey on births, deaths, causes of death, marriages, divorces, the number of Jews who had formally left or rejoined the Gemeinde, new members and those who had moved elsewhere – valuable source material for a sociological study of Frankfurt Jewry.

In 1933, the statistics indicated three times as many deaths as births (331:106, of which 7.2 percent were suicides); 73 persons declared their resignation from the Gemeinde, 37 rejoined, there were 58 new members, 656 moved to Frankfurt from other Jewish communities, and 2,068 departed.[52] Comparable statistics for 1936: more than four times as many deaths as births (346:83, including 22 suicides, 6.36 percent), 179 marriages, 10 divorces, 53 who formally left the Gemeinde, 11 who rejoined, 22 new members, 3,026 who had moved in from smaller communities, and 3,633 departures.[53]

The Jüdisches Lehrhaus, reopened in December 1933 by Martin Buber, played a special role in the cultural life of Jews in Frankfurt, as did the Kulturbund, which maintained its own sym-phony orchestra there.

A literary survey conducted by the Gemeinde paper among 16- to 20-year-old Jews in Frankfurt indicated that the ten most popu-lar authors were Jack London, Hermann Hesse, Martin Buber, Knut Hamsun, Jakob Wassermann, Stefan George, Thomas Mann, Rainer Maria Rilke, Rudolf Binding and Stefan Zweig. The ten most popular books, including three novels by Hesse, were: *Demian* (Hesse), *Buddenbrooks* (Mann), *Der Fall Mauritius* (Wassermann), *Ein kleiner Prophet* (E. Fleg), *Wanderer zwischen zwei Welten* (Walter Flex), *Cornet* (Rilke), *Brief an einen jungen Dichter* (Rilke), *Wallensteins Antlitz* (Flex), *Unterm Rad* (Hesse), and *Steppenwolf* (Hesse).[54]

An article entitled "On the History of Jewish Banking Houses in Frankfurt/Main" was accompanied by ads placed by eleven Jewish banking houses, several of which had founding dates in 1808, 1816, 1866 and 1873.[55] The volume of ads rose from five pages in 1932 (total length of paper: 26 pages; 19.2 percent ads) to 18 pages of advertisements in 1933 (total length: 42 pages; 42.8 percent ads).

## Breslau

The tendency toward harmony and compromise of the *Breslauer Jüdisches Gemeindeblatt* was typical of almost all Gemeinde papers at the time: in 1933, it averred its adherence to German culture, then allowed the Zionists to express their views and finally agreed on a compromise.

In Breslau, this development took no longer than three months. In May 1933, it carried an editorial asserting that it was imperative to keep alive German thinking and views among German Jews, and to encourage youth to engage in sports and fitness training, while promoting a sense of discipline and desire to serve the nation. In the next issue, the editors commented that certain groups of Gemeinde members were of the opinion that the positive ideas of Judaism had been pushed too much into the background. In order to make sure the paper maintained its distance from the internal disputes of partisan politics, an abridged version of the article "Say Yes to Judaism" was reprinted from the *Jüdische Rundschau* (May 16, 1933) – "for the sake of keeping a fair balance."[56]

In order to avoid such tensions in the future, people agreed on the following line: "We have always poked fun at the inordinate number of German associations and clubs, yet that same unworthy spectacle could be found in our own ranks. We did not only divide into Liberals, Orthodox, Zionists and Nationaldeutsch Jews; rather, each of these currents had its own subgroups. . . . Petty partisan disputes must be laid to rest in these times."[57] This indicated the direction future editorial policy would take.

## Cologne

There was a similar change in Cologne. On the eve of "Boycott Day" in 1933, the paper had commented: "In these days when the national revolution is pulsing through the fatherland . . . the Jewish community in Germany feels a sense of rejection, isolation and despair."[58] Two years later, the *Gemeindeblatt* reported with satisfaction on changes in the administration of the Gemeinde, whose board was now made up of 50 percent Zionists and 50 percent Liberals.[59] It noted that the Zionist idea was gaining in interest and importance. "Under the wise and sharp-tongued editorship of Fritz Neuländer of the *Gemeindeblatt,* a great deal within the intellectual and political currents among Jews in Cologne is being clarified in proper time and channeled in the right direction. Gradually, the gripping words of the Jewish poet Beer-Hofmann . . . are taking on a concrete shape: "Shore our being, deep in us courses the blood of past time – rushing onward toward what comes."[60]

Clarification was not an easy process. The Gemeinde was befallen in 1933 by an epidemic of suicides. The paper admonished: "Let there be no weakness in these trying times! Remain strong and steadfast!"[61] There is no doubt that the Jewish Kulturbund, which maintained one of its centers in Cologne, with its own stage and theater ensemble, proved itself to be a pillar of moral support. In an article entitled "Annual Balance Sheet in the New State," the first issue of the *Gemeindeblatt* for the year 1934 quoted remarks from the Christmas edition of the *Frankfurter Zeitung:* "Political journalism has not gotten any easier. What has been stated here about the daily press also holds true to an equal measure when it comes to the Jewish papers. The Jewish press has the task of speaking to a much afflicted readership virtually at the point of despair regarding its fate. That press cannot withhold material from that readership, content which must . . . be deeply offensive to Jewish sensibilities. . . . It has no reason to put a bright face on matters, yet it cannot – and should not – fill its readers with a new sense of pessimism."

# Notes

1. Max Gruenewald, "Critic of German Jewry. Ludwig Feuchtwanger and his Gemeindezeitung," *YLBI*, 18 (1972), p. 75.

2. *Frankfurter Israelitisches Gemeindeblatt,* July 1934.

3. Ibid., July 1934.

4. *Berliner Jüdisches Gemeindeblatt,* May 1933.

5. Ibid., October 1933.

6. Ibid., November 1933.

7. Ibid., February 2, 1934.

8. Leo Kreindler, main writer and representative on the list of the nonpartisan association.

9. Chairman of the ZVfD, elected on June 8, 1933 as an advisory member to the board of directors of the Gemeinde.

10. *Berliner Gemeindeblatt,* February 14, 1937.

11. Ibid., July 1933.

12. Ibid., December 8, 1934.

13. Ibid., October 6, 1934. The Jewish emigration from Berlin was compensated for to a certain extent by migration from the provinces to Berlin.

14. Ibid., February 7, 1934.

15. Ibid., February 14, 1934.

16. Ibid., May 12, 1934.

17. Ibid., May 26, 1934.

18. Ibid., June 9, 1934 (Dr. Alfred Klee).

19. Ibid., August 8, 1934.

20. The last elections for the representative council and the board of the Berlin Jewish Gemeinde had been held the end of 1930.

21. *Berliner Gemeindeblatt,* September 1, 1934.

22. Ibid., December 8, 1934.

23. Ibid., December 22, 1934.

24. Ibid., March 24, 1935.

25. *Israelitisches Familienblatt,* April 23, 1935.

26. *Berliner Gemeindeblatt,* May 5, 1935. Heinrich Stahl was present as a guest at festivities marking the tenth anniversary of the Hebrew University in Jerusalem.

27. The Jüdische Volkspartei was particularly active in the field of Zionist work in the diaspora. The "Zionist Faction" of the ZVfD was Palestine-centered.

28. *Berliner Gemeindeblatt,* May 26, 1935.

29. Ibid., May 12, 1935.

30. Ibid., November 17, 1935.

31. Ibid., September 15, 1935.

32. Ibid., September 22, 1935.

33. The program of the Reichsvertretung was published as a full page in the issue of September 29, 1935.

34. *Berliner Gemeindeblatt,* September 29, 1935.

35. Ibid., October 20, 1935.

36. Ibid., July 28, 1935.

37. Ibid., May 30, 1937.

38. Ibid., September 29, 1935.

39. Ibid., March 29, 1936.

40. Ibid., September 17, 1937.

41. Ibid., December 26, 1937.

42. Max Gruenewald, *YLBI,* 18 (1972), pp. 75f. The chief editor was Dr. Ludwig Feuchtwanger (1885-1947), "superbly equipped for this task. . . . His articles cover a wide range and reveal a solid training in history, law, economics and linguistics . . .

the eldest brother was Lion Feuchtwanger," ibid.

43. *Bayerische Israelitische Gemeindezeitung*, June 1, 1933.
44. Ibid., February 1933.
45. Cf. Joseph Walk (ed.), *Als Jude in Breslau 1941*, Gerlingen 1985.
46. *Bayerische Israelitische Gemeindezeitung*, March 1936.
47. Ibid., November 1936.
48. Ibid., June 1936.
49. Ibid., September 1937.
50. Ibid., June 15, 1933.
51. From February 1, 1937.
52. *Frankfurter Israelitisches Gemeindeblatt*, March 1934.
53. Ibid., May 1937.
54. Ibid., May 1936.
55. Ibid., October 1935.
56. *Breslauer Jüdische Gemeindeblatt*, March 31, 1933.
57. Ibid., July 1933.
58. *Kölner Jüdisches Gemeindeblatt*, March 31, 1933.
59. Asaria, 1959, p. 319.
60. Ibid., pp. 286f.
61. *Kölner Jüdisches Gemeindeblatt*, May 26, 1933.

# 7

## Religion and Politics

Jewish Orthodoxy in Germany had two long-established papers, *Der Israelit* (1864) and *Die Laubhütte* (1884). *The Israelit*, published in Frankfurt/Main, was the weekly of independent Orthodoxy, the Agudat Yisroel, and during the period under scrutiny here, the paper appeared in a modern format. The *Deutsch-Israelitische Zeitung Die Laubhütte* of the Orthodox community, subtitled *Israelitisches Familienblatt*, came out twice a month in Hamburg.

How did the Orthodox press react to the great test of German Jewry with the passage of the Nuremberg Laws in September 1935? "We do not want to admit that God has spoken, that the events . . . contain a call and appeal from God. We were like someone inebriated, we filled ourselves to bursting with the philosophy of the day then in vogue. . . . In the midst of this daze, the harsh language of the present has struck us in our stupor," wrote Rabbi Joseph Carlebach in *Die Laubhütte*. "World history is the blast of the ram's horn of heaven, the voice of God, not the senseless voice of chance."[1]

The *Israelit* did not think the Law on Protection of Blood had nothing but negative aspects. Whoever had turned his back on the faith and law of his people as a result of mixed marriage could no longer be considered as a member of the Jewish people in the sense of the Torah.[2] Jewish Orthodoxy, the paper argued, had always struggled against mixed marriage as constituting a complete break with Judaism, and, in particular, had waged a war against any extramarital sexual intercourse between Jews and non-Jews.[3] An appeal by the Association of Orthodox Rabbis in Germany stated that anyone who violated the laws of moral purity

117

desecrated the name of God, thereby endangering the Jewish people. Immorality, whether with Jews or non-Jews, had always been a crime in our religion.[4]

The *Israelit* thought it was especially interesting that there was explicit permission for the showing of the "Jewish colors," which were guaranteed the protection of state law. The paper commented that there was still no Jewish flag recognized by the Jewish people and based on historical tradition. The blue-and-white flag of the Zionists was a modern invention, the paper contended, and, since it was a party-political symbol, could never become a general Jewish flag. The paper believed the most significant element in connection with the new legislation was the declaration that "possibilities for a völkisch-national life of their own in all fields of endeavor had been opened up for Jews in Germany." It expressed the hope that the interests and institutions that were specifically religious would be enhanced and strengthened as a result. In this connection, the paper referred to comments by the chief editor of the DNB, Alfred Ingemar-Berndt, who asserted that the Jewish minority was being granted its own independent cultural life and an autonomous völkisch life.[5] The *Israelit* picked up this idea and elaborated: "With this Jewish legislation . . . the necessary Lebensraum is to be created for us in which to build our own Jewish house. . . . Some may feel that this plunge from full political law and rights into legislation specific for Jews is calamitous. But repentance and self-examination [can] transform calamity into a blessing."[6]

It is thus not surprising that the paper "warmly welcomed" the decree of the Reich Ministry of Education of April 1, 1936, which ordered the separation and removal of non-Aryans from public elementary schools and their simultaneous admission to special elementary schools for Jews and non-Aryans – "from the standpoint of Orthodox Judaism." Orthodoxy for years had been advocating special schools for philosophical reasons, and, often bearing the associated financial burdens, had indeed established and maintained such schools itself, the paper noted.[7]

A declaration by the Independent Jewish Orthodoxy, signed by Rabbis Drs. Ezra Munk and Isaac Breuer, took issue with the proclamation of the Reichsvertretung published shortly after the passage of the Nuremberg Laws. In their declaration, they rejected the claim of the Reichsvertretung to absolute leadership of all of German Jewry and the attempt to establish a single and obligatory, state-recognized organization for all Jews in Germany. For Independent Orthodoxy, it was an intolerable pressure of conscience to be incorporated into a community that did not recognize the laws of the Torah as its supreme norm. Moreover, proponents of diametrically opposed religious views could not be forced into a unitary organization without seriously threatening their freedom of conscience.[8]

Like so often when calamity befell the Jewish people, they engaged in self-examination, asking where they had gone astray.

> We ourselves are to blame that we have any problems. When the ghetto gates fell . . . it was our duty to demonstrate that Jews remain aware of their special character even when they are granted the opportunity to pursue the development of their external circumstances of life unimpeded – that they do not abandon the way of life based on the teachings and precepts of the Torah. Jews could have shown the entire world that it is certainly possible to acquire the treasures of culture such as art and science without abandoning the Jewish way of life. We have missed that opportunity of attaining a synthesis between Judaism and its eternal forms on the one hand, and the cultural assets of the surrounding world on the other.[9]

The question as to one's own guilt was also raised in the journal *Zion*, a monthly of Mizrahi, the religious-Zionist movement. The great guilt of German Jewry was its inability or unwillingness to believe that Am Yisrael (the people), Torat Yisrael (the teaching) and Eretz Yisrael (the land) had always been a unity.[10] Our guilt was taking its revenge in the lack of warmth and sincerity in marriage, in the mounting absence of mutual respect between marriage partners and on the part of children toward their parents, stated the executive boards of the traditional, Torah-faithful rabbis.[11]

The perspective from which the *Israelit* viewed the Nuremberg Laws is reflected a few years later in its evaluation of the annexation of Austria in March 1938: "There, in the city with the strongest assimilation [referring to Vienna], in the city where national Judaism was proclaimed a "private religion," Divine Providence apparently wishes to put something right."[12] Yet the paper noted that there was also a Jewish Orthodox community in Vienna, organized in Agudat Yisroel, and by pooling forces to some extent, the religious life of Jews in Germany could only profit from this development.[13]

The Jewish Orthodox press in Germany waged a struggle on

two fronts: against the assimilationism of the Religious-Liberals and against the nationalism of the Zionists. Liberalism and Zionism, the paper expounded, belonged together in respect to world outlook, just like individual and national assimilation. Both were a form of rebellion against a Jewish history that had been shaped and determined by religion. The *Jüdische Rundschau* failed to recognize or had closed its mind to the fact that among the Liberals there were nonetheless some for whom the Zionist project of the destruction of religion was a source of trepidation and disgust; and there were others who, no matter where the confusion of the age of emancipation had led them, were nonetheless filled with longing and desire for the holiness of the land of Yisrael – which Zionism, given its mentality, had neither the ability nor any intention to bring into being.[14] The paper conceded that to a certain extent what Zionism claimed was true: it had foreseen the present situation and predicted its coming many decades before. Yet to recognize and properly diagnose the sickness did not mean to cure it. If there was *one* current in Judaism that had not been blinded by the dazzling sun of emancipation, that was Orthodoxy. And now a situation had really developed where, in the wake of the collapse of so many illusions, Jews were once again seeking the path leading back to the house of their fathers.[15]

In response to an article in the *Jüdische-Allgemeine Zeitung*[16] arguing that Orthodoxy harbored a tendency toward the Middle Ages, and that religious Liberalism had to counter this "Judaism of the Wailing Wall" by a religion of the living spirit, the *Israelit* commented: "Does Orthodoxy wish to return to the Middle Ages? No, we want to go back much further, back to distant antiquity, namely to Sinai." At the same time, the paper protested against the Zionists and the arrogance of the ZVfD claim that they had the clearest understanding of what was necessary for the entire Jewish community. Moreover, Orthodoxy could not accept the monopoly of the Zionists.[17] However, it did not necessarily reject the idea of a Jewish state. One of its intellectual leaders, Dr. Isaac Breuer, noted:

> It's a strange thing when it comes to history. It certainly does not exclude the possibility of bold human action. . . . An action is non-historical, or even contrary to history, only if it attempts to put itself in the place of history, if it wishes to create entities whose ability to survive depends on conditions which only history itself can generate as

part of a gradual process. . . . Who can deny that the main parts of Palestine that have been settled already today bear all the features of Jewish statehood? Why shouldn't the Jews be a people capable of having a state?[18]

S. Schachnowitz, the veteran chief editor of the *Israelit*, was well aware of the significance of the press.[19] An organization without a press was a body without a mouth, although not without a soul, Schachnowitz noted in a speech to a group of Agudat Yisroel journalists. Referring to the Zionists, whose most effective weapon had always been their press, he observed ironically: "Zionism enjoys a form of protection, you might say, in editorial offices. After all, it was a book by a journalist that created it.[20] It's been propagated by writers and journalists."[21] Schachnowitz gave his paper a modern format comparable to that of Jewish papers with a far larger circulation. It had a substantial section on Palestine with reports from its own reporters on economic, political and cultural affairs. The paper featured a section "Literary Standpoint," a monthly supplement on education entitled "Education and Teaching" of the Association of Orthodox Jewish Teachers, and sections that published serialized stories about religious and historical themes, Jewish topics from the East European milieu, and cultural commentary and reports. A column "The Small Israelite" dealt with Jewish children at school and in the home. What is topicality, "current relevance"? "Today's events are topical, but even more so for us . . . are the great events of our beginning."[22]

The paper had a critical view of Martin Buber. One might imagine, it argued, that the masses dancing ecstatically around the idol were filled with "religiosity" in the Buberian sense, and thought they were able to rise up inwardly to the heights of divine creative power. But the type of religious exaltation in Buber's conception was, by its very nature, unable to bring about the decision expected of it. The element of enjoyment, even if sublimated to the highest level of the enjoyment of the divine, had too much in common with sensual pleasure for it to serve as an avenue for the overcoming of sensuality.[23] Although *Die Laubhütte* had nothing against the "purity and the seriousness of Buber's intentions," it also denied him any right to lead the community. Only those men could lead the Jewish people whose life and teachings were one. The Jewish leader, in all phases of his life, had to be an example for others, and Buber did not live up to this ideal.[24]

In contrast with the *Laubhütte*, which gave activities of the Kulturbund detailed coverage, the *Israelit* ignored the work of the cultural league and limited any mention of it solely to official announcements of an organizational nature. There was a reason for this. "Just as state law does not require us to recognize any particular non-Aryan as a Jew, we are likewise not obliged to accord the appellation 'Jewish' to an emergency organization of artists[25] whose members and spirit are non-Aryan." Dramatic arts had no roots whatsoever in genuine Jewish, Orthodox, Torah-true Judaism, and most of the other arts had but few such roots.[26] "Is it [to be considered] a Jewish act . . . when something that is frowned upon and forbidden by Jewish law is specifically designated as 'Jewish culture'?"[27]

The paper *Die Laubhütte* can be best characterized by its name ("tabernacle," "bower"), although the association between it and a Jewish *Gartenlaube*[28] is not completely accurate. More accurate is the designation "German-Jewish paper," with emphasis on the word "German" and the additional descriptor "*Familienblatt*" (family paper) in its subtitle. There was reportedly a portrait of Hindenburg hanging in its Hamburg editorial offices,[29] and as late as 1935, it published a poem whose last verse went: "We shall die for the fatherland / With quiet courage, remaining in the land. By our blood, we have consecrated you / Practice silently what duty and law command / Then once again, together with us, you shall attempt to win the trust / Of the German land, the German fatherland."[30]

Only in early 1935 was a column introduced entitled "News from Palestine"; up until that point, the foreign news had been dominated by a section "Foreign Survey" and reports on overseas countries, such as India and Cyprus. "It would be tantamount to putting on blinders were we to deny the profound influence that Palestine and pioneer work there is exercising on Jews in Western Europe. . . . But what do we see there? . . . A nationalism which, in all its forms, has been taken straight from the armory of Europe, and that means assimilation as much as does any amalgamation of elements that are alien one to the other."[31]

The paper had a copious entertainment section, published family news, but carried only few ads, and sufficed with a list of Jewish artisans and tradesmen. Its contributors occasionally included Jewish scholars and prominent authors. It took the term "full Jew" (*Volljude*), that had a derogatory racial meaning, and tried to give it a new reevaluative twist: there were cases in world history where groups had been branded by their environment with a name for the purpose of differentiating them, and then who had taken this name and ennobled it. "They have coined the name 'full Jew' for us as a racial designation – in the realm of religion, let it become for us the expression of our own striving and goal."[32]

The answer of the monthly *Zion*, whose regular contributors included names like Oskar Wolfberg, Jeschaja Leibowitz, Josef Burg and Mosche Unna, to the cataclysmic changes at the beginning of 1933 was in the form of a special issue on Palestine. It expressed the skepticism rife among religious Zionists regarding the future of Jews in Germany and their faith in the future of Palestine. The only way out that might restore inner balance to the Jews was "once again to create a Jewish material and intellectual center . . . in the homeland of the genius of our people."[33]

The paper rejected the claim of the *Israelit*[34] that Orthodoxy had the sole prerogative in assuming the intellectual and spiritual leadership of the community, and questioned the constructive actions that would supposedly give legitimacy to such a claim for leadership. It noted that the concept of the paramount position of Eretz Yisrael in Jewish religious life had also gradually penetrated into Aguda circles; however, such ideas had long been advocated by the religious-Zionist youth leagues, although the youth program of the Aguda made no reference to the proponents of these concepts, who had originally been considered enemies.[35]

On the other side of the religious spectrum was the *Jüdisch-Liberale Zeitung*, Berlin.[36] Up to October 30, 1933, it was a biweekly, and then came out twice a week until early November 1934. Starting November 7, 1934, it bore a new name: *Jüdische Allgemeine Zeitung – neue Folge der Jüdisch-Liberalen Zeitung*. The editors assured their readership that the spirit, outlook and attitude of the paper remained unchanged, and that the new title *Jüdische Allgemeine* (Jewish General Paper) was meant to underscore the paper's comprehensiveness: nothing Jewish should be alien to its pages.[37] Previous issues had normally been 6–8 pages long; it was now expanded to 12–16 pages, but soon shrank back to its earlier size due to a lack of advertisements. The paper was somewhere halfway between the *CV-Zeitung* and *Der Schild*, and although as the official organ of the Association for Religious-Liberal Judaism, it should be included within the category of political-religious journalism, its interests were more political than religious.

"Now when you say Germany, or hear the word from others, it rips like a painful rupture through one's very soul . . . ! Because the word Germany requires one to explain: which Germany? And if someone means the Germany of free intellect and humanism, he has to note that extra and specifically."[38] The paper, "proud to be a part of the German cultural heritage,"[39] was optimistic. It felt there was no reason for the pessimism that only a short while before had been the predominant mood.[40] The old Jewish saying when fate strikes – "there's some good in this too" – had proved its truth once more. "Millions of Germans who only a short time before had had scant regard for Judaism and Jews, find cause today to engage in a serious study of these things . . . in Judaism, they shall discover the religion of humanity, in the Jews, their brothers – and in the German Jew, despite his different faith, the religious *Volksgenosse*." To this supposed "gain," the paper added another: the return by innumerable persons of Jewish extraction to the eternal values of the Jewish religion. "Isn't all this . . . a blessing?"[41]

Heinrich Stern, chairman of the Religious-Liberal Association, rejected the arguments advanced by the *Israelit*, which was concerned about the future survival of Judaism under the Liberals and feared that their youth would be driven into the arms of nationalist Judaism. One did not have to be a nationalist Jew to profess Judaism, and it certainly was erroneous to maintain that Religious-Liberal Judaism had forfeited its justification for existence.[42] "The Zionist should not claim that the 'assimilationist' is betraying Judaism, nor should the latter accuse Zionists of betrayal."[43]

The *Jüdische Allgemeine* published a vehement response to the series by Robert Weltsch entitled "Saying Yes to Judaism" that appeared in the *Jüdische Rundschau* from April 1933 on into the summer. "Saying yes to Judaism? That's the big phrase in fashion now. . . . But the yeah-sayers and head-nodders usually are not counted among the heroic personalities. Generally speaking, it takes more courage to say no. . . . If those who wish to anyway, and those who are compelled, now express their affirmation of Judaism, this act can hardly awaken any special admiration. Maybe it would be more admirable if they wanted to say 'No' to so many of the things today that are happening to Jews."[44]

Criticism was also directed against the Kulturbund – not so

much its program, but rather the simple fact of its existence. The paper admitted quite openly that the Kulturbund would not have come into being if external factors had not urged its creation. German Jews had had a close and intimate bond with the German theater, as with all of German culture, for many generations, and they would have never conceived of the notion to put on a German play in a theater created exclusively for Jews, performed exclusively by Jewish actors before an exclusively Jewish audience.[45] "We know no such thing as 'Jewish art,' and we see that the term 'Jewish theater' can be meant to designate various genres of drama. We do not want to have any sort of 'Jewish theater.' Rather, what we desire, or perhaps are compelled by external circumstances to have, is: German theater for Jews."[46]

The paper expressed profound shock over the declarations of the 18th Zionist Congress in Prague. "With deep indignation," it rejected the press statement of Lord Melchett to the effect that there was only *one* solution to the Jewish question, namely the orderly emigration of Jewish youth to Palestine. It quoted the *Jüdische Rundschau* that "went so far" as to maintain that the true forces should not be sought where there were nice speeches and fancy rhetoric, but where the Jewish farmer was ploughing the fields and Jewish youth was marching through the newly gained homeland, Hebrew songs on their lips. "Well, we think you can find farmers and groups of singing youngsters everywhere. For that reason, it is our belief that the true essence of Judaism must consist of something other than that."[47] The editors appealed to German Jews to break free from "the spell that had been cast by Zionism."[48]

The journal *Der Vortrupp*, under the editorship of the religious philosopher Hans-Joachim Schoeps, should be discussed here in this category. Schoeps was a product of the free-German youth movement; he remained a Prussian Jew and based his actions on two principles: *Deutschtum* as an integral part of his existence, and efforts aimed at developing a systematic theology of German Judaism, under the influence of Karl Barth.[49]

On September 29, 1933, he wrote a letter to Reich Minister of the Interior Frick under the official letterhead "Der Deutsche Vortrupp, Gefolgschaft deutscher Juden" (The German Advance Guard, Retinue of German Jews) with a request that his paper be granted "the proper attention it deserves."

The Vortrupp regards it as its task to gather together Jews with a

German consciousness, and to be active in the vanguard of the struggle for their integration into the New Germany. . . . We believe that, based on our conservative-national ideology, certain prerequisites are now present that allow us to put forward concrete proposals to the government regarding an arrangement of the Jewish question that will be acceptable to both sides.

You can form some idea of the direction our proposals move in and our objectives from the enclosed sheet. They aim at guaranteeing the state a Jewish population which is reliable in a national sense, and which will no longer be a bastion of liberalism. Rather, that Jewish community will be given guidance and leadership and take on profile by dint of the youth-movement character [bündische Artung] and solidarity of the younger generation.[50]

As far as is known, he never received a reply, unless the banning of the journal after twelve months of existence can be considered a kind of official response. Nonetheless, Schoeps, who later became a professor for the history of religions and intellectual history in Erlangen after his return from exile in Sweden, remained an integral figure in Jewish journalism during that period.

"Initially, the first and most important thing is to survive and not be destroyed, all false prophets to the contrary, and to hold on as German Jews, even in the face of living conditions that are materially restricted. . . . German Jewry can only survive if it maintains itself as *Judaism*, no matter what its degree of willingness and preparedness when it comes to Germany." There should be a new understanding and appreciation of Jewish teachings, returning to the roots of the faith in order to find new ways of teaching and a new order for everyday life and festivals in accordance with today's philosophy of living.[51]

There was a mixed reaction in the Jewish press to Schoeps' articles and writings. *Der Morgen,* to which he occasionally himself contributed, commented on the anthology published by the Vortrupp Verlag publishing house, *Wille und Weg des deutschen Judentums,*[52] as follows: "For that reason, we must take even more emphatic issue with the claim by Hans-Joachim Schoeps that 'historical consciousness can be had only at the cost of freedom from purpose, a liberation from any purposive thinking' than with the conclusions he draws from that position. The latter are merely grotesque." He claims for himself no more or less than the security of prophetic vision. "A chiliastic perspective that flirts with itself does not gain any justification as a result."[53]

"Prophetic vision" indeed had its limits. Later on, Schoeps was haunted as though by a lingering nightmare by the thought that he had failed to advise his readers to flee at any cost.[54] His own parents died in Theresienstadt and Auschwitz.

Schoeps remained faithful to Judaism and repeatedly deepened his attachment by theological study and writing. "The fact that he borrowed from Protestant theology can still be integrated into the intellectual traditions of Judaism. . . . But Schoeps went so far in this regard that even as late as the 1960s, Günther Harder, a German theologian from the Confessional Church, called him a 'circumcised Lutheran'."[55]

Just how carefully the Jewish papers were observed by the authorities can be seen in an article published in the *Deutsche Zeitung* entitled "A Stroll through the Jewish Press." The author, apparently very well-informed about Jewish journalism at the time, sneered at the *Deutschtum* of the *Jüdische Allgemeine Zeitung*, which in its issue for September 1, 1933 had denied the Zionist Congress the right to speak in the name of German Jewry. The article noted that the polar opposite was represented by the stance of the *Israelit*, which had a loathing for all efforts aimed at assimilation, and regarded the defensive reaction of the German people as a divine punishment for the unfaithfulness of the "Jewish assimilationists."[56]

## Notes

1. Die Laubhütte, September 19, 1935.
2. *Der Israelit*, September 26, 1935.
3. Ibid.
4. *Die Laubhütte*, October 3, 1935.
5. *Der Israelit*, September 19, 1935.
6. Ibid., September 26, 1935.
7. Ibid., September 19, 1935.
8. Ibid., October 3, 1935.
9. *Die Laubhütte*, January 10, 1935.
10. *Zion*, May–June 1933.
11. *Die Laubhütte*, May 16, 1935.
12. *Der Israelit*, March 24, 1938.
13. Ibid., March 17, 1938.
14. Ibid., October 10, 1935.
15. Ibid., November 21, 1935.
16. *Jüdische Allgemeine Zeitung*, Berlin, January 12, 1936.
17. *Der Israelit*, January 16, 1936.
18. Ibid., May 7, 1937.
19. Author of *Flucht in die Heimat – ein Dokument der Zeit* (1924) and *Licht aus dem Westen – Erzählung aus der Zeit der Ghettodämmerung* (1926), Hermon Verlag, Frankfurt/Main.

20. The reference is to Herzl's *Der Judenstaat.*

21. *Der Israelit,* April 27, 1937.

22. Ibid., April 3, 1936. The monthly *Nachlat Z'wi – Monatsschrift für Judentum in Lehre und Tat* appeared in the same publishing house as *Der Israelit.* It was edited by the Rabbiner-Hirsch-Gesellschaft, Frankfurt/Main. Samson Raphael Hirsch (1808–1888) was the founder of neo-Orthodoxy and the Neuorthodoxe Israelitische Religionsgemeinschaft.

23. *Der Israelit,* February 10, 1938, on Martin Buber's 60th birthday.

24. *Die Laubhütte,* January 25, 1935.

25. The reference is to the Kulturbund.

26. *Der Israelit,* March 19, 1936.

27. Ibid., June 4, 1936.

28. The reference is to the highly popular illustrated weekly *Die Gartenlaube* [The Arbor], founded by E. Keil in Leipzig (1853). Probably the best example of a German middle-class family journal, it continued to be published until 1943 [trans. note].

29. Private archive, Schalom Ben Chorin.

30. Aron Wolff, Brieg, *Die Laubhütte,* March 7, 1935.

31. *Die Laubhütte,* January 10, 1935.

32. Ibid., November 8, 1935.

33. *Zion,* February–March 1933.

34. *Der Israelit,* vol. 74, no. 48.

35. *Zion,* January 1934.

36. Published by Hanns Loewenstein, chief editor George Goetz. Eugen Tannenbaum took over the editorship in the spring of 1934. After his sudden death in August 1936, Dr. Ernst G. Lowenthal was appointed editor.

37. *Jüdische Allgemeine Zeitung,* November 7, 1934.

38. *Jüdisch-Liberale Zeitung,* February 15, 1933.

39. Ibid., April 1, 1933.

40. Ibid., May 1, 1933.

41. Ibid., April 15, 1933.

42. Ibid.

43. Ibid., July 15, 1933.

44. Ibid., October 27, 1933.

45. Ibid., October 3, 1933; *Jüdische Rundschau,* April 4, May 12, May 16, May 30, 1933.

46. *Jüdisch-Liberale Zeitung,* March 6, 1934.

47. Ibid., September 15, 1933.

48. Ibid., December 22, 1933.

49. Private archive, Schalom Ben Chorin.

50. Archive, Leo Baeck Institute, Jerusalem.

51. *Jüdisch-Liberale Zeitung,* June 19, 1934. Excerpt from the book by Hans-Joachim Schoeps, *Wir deutschen Juden,* published in Berlin in 1934. The Orthodox monthly *Nachlat Z'wi* commented as follows: "Nonetheless, the book remains an interesting phenomenon among contemporary publications. And probably there has never been more vehement criticism expressed of the falsification of Jewish history which Zionism is guilty of" (1934–1935, p. 141).

52. (*The Will and Way of German Jewry*), ed. Hans-Joachim Schoeps, Berlin 1934.

53. *Der Morgen,* November 1934.

54. Dawidowicz, 1977, p. 222.

55. Schalom Ben Chorin, *Israel Nachrichten,* Tel Aviv, January 3, 1986.

56. *Deutsche Zeitung,* September 7, 1933, evening edition, quoted in *Jüdisch-Liberale Zeitung,* September 20, 1933.

# 8

## The Jewish State

In the wake of the Arab revolts that erupted in 1936, a royal commission was appointed, headed by Lord Peel, with the task of making proposals to the British government on a solution to the Arab-Jewish conflict.

The commission came to the conclusion that the mandate could not be maintained. It was impossible to bring about even a minimum of understanding between the Arab and Jewish populations in order to implement the transfer of state power to autonomous bodies as envisaged by the mandate charter. The commission examined various suggestions for a solution and then finally opted for that of partition. The country should be partitioned into a Jewish state, an Arab state, and a mandate zone that also included Jerusalem.[1]

The concrete realization of the idea of a Jewish state had a vital importance for German Jews, who were searching both for immigration options and for an affirmation of the dignity of Jewish existence. Naturally there were fears that a dwarf state in a partitioned Palestine would not be large enough to absorb enough immigrants. On the other hand, it was hoped that the creation of a sovereign Jewish state, no matter what its size, would provide protection in a moral sense.

The *Jüdische Rundschau* advocated an approach that put it in a particularly difficult position on this question. The paper's views in respect to Palestine policy and Jewish-Arab relations were highly controversial within the Zionist camp. It was attacked at Zionist congresses and its stance denounced as defeatist. The majority of Zionists believed their aim was full and total Jewish control of all of Palestine, while the *Jüdische Rundschau* recognized the presence of the Arabs, including it in political conceptions and searching for a solution that would take the legitimate claims of both populations into account.[2]

When Dr. Chaim Weizmann was empowered by the delegates at the 20th Zionist Congress held in Zurich in August 1937 to enter into negotiations on the basis of the Peel Commission Report, Robert Weltsch confessed: "We were always of the opinion that the sole possibility for realizing Zionism throughout *all* of Palestine lay in a Jewish-Arab agreement. . . . But we had to admit that that path is an illusion, and experience has confirmed this."[3] If even on the Jewish side, any and every psychological prerequisite was lacking, what could possibly be expected from the Arab side, Weltsch asked, since they quite naturally had far less interest in reaching such an understanding than did the Jews.

The solution of partition was not new and had been attempted in various countries over the previous fifteen years, the best-known examples being Ireland and Upper Silesia. Even if the results were far from perfect, the *Rundschau* argued that partition could serve to create a new arrangement that would, at the very least, last for some time to come.[4] The paper was in favor of including the territory of Transjordan in the area for partition,[5] and rejected the notion of introducing static concepts in the construction of the Jewish national home. After all, it noted, the "Jewish" areas had been Arab but a short time before, and if the partition plan had come up a few years earlier, the Jezreel Valley, the Hefer Valley and the bay of Haifa would have had to be included within the "Arab" areas. "Each area is potentially 'Jewish'."[6]

After publication of the Peel Report on July 8, 1937 and an appeal by the Executive of the Jewish Agency and the Zionist Organization to the Jewish people to retain its composure, the *Jüdische Rundschau* wrote that it would be very easy to react with violent emotion. The paper thought it quite conceivable that many would respond to the present document by terming it "unacceptable." On the other hand, the establishment of a Jewish state would probably be seen by many Jews as an exceptional step forward. Such feelings could be encountered specifically among persons who earlier on had not necessarily been proponents of the idea of a Jewish state. But a solution that withheld Jerusalem from the Jewish people was unacceptable, and a way had to be found to eliminate this source of dissatisfaction. "Now what is important is to demonstrate in the fullest sense the abilities of the Jewish people for engaging in state politics: that despite everything, we are now experiencing a unique moment in Jewish history – the beginnings of the first Jewish polity after more than 1,900 years."[7]

Aside from the principle of partition, other doubts and reservations surfaced: the problem of the specific borders of the proposed state, and the fact that even after its establishment, millions of Jews would still be living in other countries. The paper suggested that Zionists should make a clear and unambiguous declaration; namely that Jews in other countries would quite naturally remain citizens where they were just as before. Zionism had always wished that conflicts of this type should be avoided if at all possible.[8]

Dr. Siegfried Moses, then chairman of the ZVfD, regarded the characteristic feature of the Peel Report to be the fact that all the basic questions of the construction and development of Palestine were once again open for discussion and on the table. It is true that the commission maintained the mandate was impracticable, but it did nonetheless recognize the obligations incurred by Britain to create such political, administrative and economic conditions in Palestine that the establishment of a national home would be assured. Along with partition, there were basically two other options: continuing with the mandate and the possibility of cantonization. In principle, even two further eventualities were conceivable: that Jews and Arabs, under pressure from the proposal for partition, would come to an understanding on continuation of the mandate; the other option was to try to work out a new mandate under another mandatory power.[9]

Mizrahi, Ha-Shomer ha-Tzair, the Judenstaatspartei and a segment of Agudat Yisroel were against the partition plan. Weizmann's "conditional yes"[10] prompted Robert Weltsch to make two demands: first, a sufficient material basis for securing a Jewish culture, i.e., enough territorial space for a genuine Jewish life to be able to develop; second, at least a partial contribution to alleviating the material distress of Jews there. Weizmann spoke about the necessity for settling two million young Jews in Palestine over the coming several years.[11]

In September 1937, the League of Nations accepted the principle of partition to the extent that its practical implementation was in accordance with League views.[12] "All these statements . . .

indicate that there is sufficient understanding of the problem of the Jewish question within various circles in the League of Nations and that . . . the only type of partition that is desirable is one which attempts to do justice to Jewish needs to a certain degree."[13]

The gamut of reactions was reflected in the non-Zionist press in Germany. There was not a single Jewish paper that had not featured the drama taking place in Palestine and followed it in detail for weeks, even months. *Der Schild*, the organ of the Reichsbund jüdischer Frontsoldaten, arrived at a peculiar view, assessing the British plan from a specifically military perspective. "From a military point of view, the partition proposal clearly reveals Britain's military interests. England wishes to return the mandate to the League of Nations, but wants to preserve essential strategic advantages – Haifa, included in the Jewish state, is supposed to remain an important naval base under British control . . . and the area around Aqaba on the Red Sea is to retain an important strategic position."

The paper emphasized that it was small countries in particular that ought to be "imbued with the idea of defense" in order to develop their security. This is why, whenever *Der Schild* had spoken about Palestine, the concept of defense had been a primary consideration. A large settlement also required military self-defense. One need but look in strategic terms at the proposed borders of the new state – the plains and valleys, agriculturally undoubtedly of great potential wealth, allocated to the Jews – and, in contrast, the strategically far more favorable mountainous areas, set aside for the Arab state. A Jewish state in Palestine would have to have a strong defense, and a modern army was known to require substantial budget outlays. On the other hand, any Jewish state would find it necessary to utilize its material capabilities for economic development. "We Jewish combat soldiers of the Great War cannot imagine a Jewish state, if it is to become a reality, without general military conscription! Because we know, based on our own experience . . . what an enormous importance universal military conscription has for binding together a nation-state beyond all differences of party and class."[14]

It is interesting today to read this evaluation of a future Jewish state seen specifically from the perspective of an anti-Zionist paper at that time – an assessment that accurately characterized the necessities of present-day Israel decades in prescient advance.

The intellectual upheaval that occurred during those years within German Jewry was given its clearest and most pointed expression in the *CV-Zeitung*. That paper attempted to associate the now concrete possibility of a Jewish polity with the ideas of the uniqueness of Judaism. Its chief editor, Dr. Alfred Hirschberg, who attended the 20th Zionist Congress, stated:

> The Peel Report concerns all Jews, inside and outside Palestine, both Zionists and non-Zionists alike. Will it be included among those events that have had a destructive impact in our historical experience, or should it be regarded as one of the documents from which a renewed Jewish development might spring? . . . Shall a new Ezra rise, who, like that great innovator of the Jewish people almost 2,000 years ago, was able to awaken an impoverished, dwarfed land to new life and vigor because he chose to avoid making the Jews into a people just like any other? . . . Has Judaism now reached the end of its task of contributing to the effort to educate contemporary Jews to a life in the world imbued with Jewish values – because it must henceforth concentrate on the task of building a Jewish state and people within narrow boundaries? . . . By dint of its ideational content, the Peel Plan creates Jewish boundaries and delimitations even before that has become a political-geographical reality.[15]

The *CV-Zeitung* noted that the response the plan had evoked throughout the world was significant.

> The parties directly involved – Jews and Arabs – are dissatisfied, while the interested powers believe that there is a sensible proposal on the table. It is superfluous to engage in metaphysical speculation. No one disputes that relevant political solutions worked out on the basis of power can, at best, only be just in a relative sense. May the Peel Report create a Jewish state like any another state – yet no declaration can make the Jews into a people like any other people. The solution to the conflict, which all Jewish forces will have to work toward in coming weeks, will not yet be able to bring about a solution to the Jewish question.[16]

Alfred Hirschberg wished to make the moral imperative of Judaism the leitmotif of the Jewish state. The immediate conclusion drawn from this was that the Jewish state could not be like all others – since, as a rule, states were not constructed upon ethical and moral postulates, and the Jewish people in such a polity would have to be different from other peoples organized in nation-states. Nonetheless, he came to the conclusion: "There is no Jew who . . . can sense any satisfaction over the possible fiasco of political Zionism. Now it is no longer a question of whether one affirms or rejects Zionism . . . rather: a Jewish project visible for the whole world to see is in danger, and all necessary moral and material Jewish forces must be enlisted for its preservation."[17] In this way, the long road of opposition to Zionism among assimilationist circles within German Jewry came to its final end.

Hirschberg sent his editors a telegram from Zurich: "If anywhere, then one could sense at this moment in time just how party-oriented conceptions had turned into political thinking focused on [the goal of] a state. The consequences of a Jewish state for the many millions who never can nor will want to become its citizens are incalculable. . . . Yet aside from this, there is the hope that a Jewish state, no matter how large or small, will take its place among the states of the world in dignity and freedom."[18]

The *Morgen* called the Peel Report a "document of historical stature, equally remarkable for the maturity of its political vision, the brilliance of its literary form and the frank impartiality of its human stance . . . a work that can be studied in order to learn what politics really is and what it can accomplish."[19] Why take upon oneself the odium of saying "no" if with a "yes, but" one can certainly achieve the same success, and probably even a greater one? Ancient Israel, the paper noted, had gradually grown together into a whole from various different fragments; the new Israel would likewise not be the work of a single generation.[20]

The *Israelitisches Familienblatt,* then under the main editorship of Leo Kreindler, gave its pages over largely to the nay-sayers, including the Zionist rabbi Dr. Max Nussbaum, Berlin. Something whole which one had longed for, hoped for and dreamed of, could not be allotted in a partitioned form, accompanied by a gesture of generosity, he contended.[21]

In a special issue of the paper, Kreindler asked whether Jews could be satisfied with this solution. "The only Jewish answer can be No . . . Jews cannot give up Palestine and abandon Jerusalem. . . . There is great attractiveness inherent in the possibility that after so many long years we should have a concrete Jewish state; but far more compelling is the conviction that the way this Jewish state is to be constituted, it must necessarily act to impede development in Palestine."[22]

His dispatches from the Zionist Congress in Zurich indicated that he identified with the "impassioned resistance of the opposition" to any resolution that left open a possibility for accepting the Peel Plan. "Will the Congress listen to the entreaties of the opposition? . . . Those who want to say yes are not very happy about it, and those who wish to say no are also filled with a sense of apprehension. What will follow in the wake of the 'no,' once it has been uttered?" He concluded with a final reconciliatory, though not quite logically consistent sentence: "This Zionist Congress in Zurich can be regarded as the hour of birth of the Jewish state."[23]

The "no" of Agudat Yisroel was no surprise. In a public statement, the national board of the Aguda in Germany rejected the intention to separate Jerusalem from the other Jewish territories and was also opposed to the creation of a Jewish "dwarf state" if in return for statehood only a twelfth of the total land area, including Transjordan, was to be contained in its territory. The sovereignty of the Torah would have to be constitutionally guaranteed, because the absence of such a guarantee would endanger the holy shrines of the nation.[24]

The *Israelit* had a more differentiated position. It suggested that perhaps it was better to withhold Jerusalem from a secular Jewish state – rather than to expose it to desecration by an administration bereft of Torah. "The proposed separation of Jerusalem has plunged religious Jewry into a conflict. On the one hand, it appears inconceivable to naive Jewish sensibility that there could be a Jewish state without Jerusalem as its center; on the other hand, our sense of responsibility, all the wiser as a result of bitter experience, is resistant to the idea of delivering over Yerushalayim to a Jewish state devoid of Torah. Yet even the proponents of this second point of view would find it unacceptable unless at least a portion of Jerusalem remains in Jewish hands."[25]

The Orthodox journal *Nachlat Z'wi* termed the proclaimed establishment of a Jewish state to be the "paramount event of the Jewish present," though it would engender a number of questions and problems. There could be no doubt that Jewish teaching was fundamentally in favor of a Jewish state. But just as in earlier eras, today too there were two opposed views regarding the meaning of such a Jewish state. An eternal question ran like a thread through Jewish history: whose state – that of God, or of man?[26]

Like the Mizrahi faction in the Zionist Congress, the religious-Zionist movement in Germany also rejected the Peel Plan. Its monthly journal *Zion* considered the decisive factor to be that

Jews were not entitled to give up even an inch of Jewish soil and to surrender the historical right of the Jewish people and the claim of the Bible, to which there was no statutory limitation. Perhaps the knowledge that the dream of a Jewish state was to become a reality might delight certain "enthusiasts," but Zionism without Zion was an impossibility.[27]

Yet after the Zionist Congress had empowered Dr. Weizmann to negotiate, the tenor of debate changed. The proposed Jewish state was only the shadow of the envisioned Jewish state, but the fact that the British had made the proposal in the first place indicated that the movement's goal was not illusory and utopian. It was true that Eretz Yisrael had been promised to the Jewish people in the borders laid down in the Torah, and believing Jews had no right to agree to giving up any part of the land. However, after the Congress had accepted the resolution, Jewish leaders could feel they were instruments and tools of providence. "It is our task to support them in their efforts. For that reason . . . the demand of the hour . . . is that all who accept the proposal and all who say nay must stand resolutely together behind the newly-elected leadership," the journal urged.[28]

The *Jüdische Zeitung* in Breslau was only able to comment on the Peel Report before its official publication, since the paper had to close down operations in April 1937. "We Jews must emphatically reject any emergency compromise solution, such as the plan of a tripartite partition of the country, as being unacceptable. We are not striving for a national home or a Jewish state in order to be able to play the game of state – rather, what we require is a country that can provide space for a sufficiently large number of our people."[29]

## Notes

1. *Zionism*, 1973, pp. 107f.
2. Robert Weltsch, in Gärtner, Lamm, and Lowenthal, 1957, pp. 104ff.
3. *Jüdische Rundschau*, August 13, 1937.
4. Ibid., April 16, 1937.
5. Ibid., April 9, 1937.
6. Ibid., April 23, 1937.
7. Ibid., July 7, 1937.
8. Ibid., July 20, 1937.

9. Ibid., July 30, 1937.

10. Paragraphs 8 and 9 of the resolution of the 20th Zionist Congress read: "The Congress declares the partition plan proposed by the Royal Commission to be unacceptable. The Congress empowers the Executive to enter into negotiations in order to determine the exact conditions of the British government for the proposed creation of a Jewish state," quoted in *Jüdische Rundschau*, August 23, 1937.

11. *Jüdische Rundschau*, August 6, 1937.

12. Ibid., September 24, 1937.

13. Ibid., September 17, 1937.

14. *Der Schild*, July 16, 1937.

15. *CV-Zeitung*, July 15, 1937.

16. Ibid., A.H., July 22, 1937.

17. Ibid., A.H., July 29, 1937.

18. Ibid., A.H., August 12, 1937.

19. Hans Bach in *Der Morgen*, October 1937.

20. Werner Cahnmann, in *Der Morgen*, June 1937.

21. *Israelitisches Familienblatt*, July 15, 1937.

22. Ibid., July 9, 1937.

23. Ibid., August 12, 1937.

24. Ibid., quoted from *Israelitisches Familienblatt*, July 15, 1937.

25. *Der Israelit*, July 22, 1937.

26. Dr. Maximilian Landau, in *Nachlat Z'wi*, 1937–1938, pp. 100ff.

27. *Zion*, July 1937.

28. Ibid., September 1937.

29. *Jüdische Zeitung*, April 9, 1937: "As our readers have already learned in the meantime, the *Jüdische Zeitung* is to be prohibited from appearing beginning May 1st of this year. . . . It grew out of the paper founded by Dr. Louis Neustadt (1885), a former well-known figure in Breslau. . . . At the beginning of 1924, the paper was transferred to exclusive Zionist control as the *Jüdische Zeitung für Ostdeutschland* under the editorship of Joachim Prinz; he was succeeded by Dr. Rudolf Samuel. From 1926 on, it bore the present name of *Jüdische Zeitung*. . . . We regret that such an independent Jewish press, as was rightfully the pride of the founder of the paper, is today not represented even in a single paper. Signed Dr. Fritz Becker," ibid., April 30, 1937.

# 9

## Der Morgen

The principal reason for devoting a special chapter to the journal *Der Morgen* is that this monthly cannot readily be classified in terms of the categories applicable to the rest of the Jewish press. It developed "from a scientific journal into a lively review for the world of German-Jewish culture,"[1] a discussion forum for intellectual issues of direct relevance to German Jewry.

*Der Morgen*, founded in 1925 as a bimonthly in Darmstadt by the Jewish professor of philosophy Julius Goldstein, stated in its program that it intended to serve the "religious idea" as conceived in terms of religious liberalism. Its achievement consisted "mainly in [the publication of] outstanding philosophical essays . . . high-quality studies on topics in the history of ideas, and discussion of the so changeful German-Jewish problem – viewed from the still unshaken position 'that we are Jews when it comes to origin and religion, and Germans in respect to culture and fatherland'."[2]

The true strength of the journal, as Ludwig Feuchtwanger noted in a retrospective glance, lay in its lively observation of all phenomena and currents in European intellectual life as a whole, and German intellectual life in particular; it also kept a watchful eye on economic changes and their impact on German Jewry. Both non-Jewish and Jewish experts contributed articles, and bridges of understanding were often built through give and take between Jewish and Christian theologians.[3]

After the death of Julius Goldstein in June 1929, *Der Morgen* was directed by his widow and Rabbi Max Dienemann until it was taken over by the Berlin publishing house Philo-Verlag in April 1933. From November 1933 on, it appeared as a monthly under the editorship of Drs. Eva Reichmann-Jungmann and Hans Bach.

The journal, in a new format and under new editorial guidance, expressly intended to serve the needs of the "intellectual fate of German Jewry," offering an unembellished picture of Jewish matters not just to the outside world, "whose judgment shows strong fluctuations," but also for German Jews themselves. For that reason, it would not exclude any current in Jewish life. Programmatically, *Der Morgen* intended to "follow the [lights of the] purer life of the spirit, standing above all parties, and to point the way for German Jews to a position" that could function as a sphere for intellectual life – not a new ghetto, even if it did not attain the level of the elite of the nation which Nietzsche had prophesied and welcomed.[4]

The first statements under its new editorship in 1933 gave an indication of the fact that the journal had moved, and not just in terms of the location of its new publishing house, into the close proximity of the Centralverein: "We German Jews, faithful to our blood and belonging to German soil and spirit, shall share the German fate and someday, God willing, will also participate again in that fate."[5]

Heinz Kellermann remarked that external emancipation had come to an end, but not its inner variant. From the intellectual point of view, Zionism today was neither a profession of faith nor a meritorious deed, and it filled the heart of the "honest opponent" with sadness to see how a grand idealistic edifice had been remodeled into a kind of social welfare institution. The popular thesis advocating German-Jewish concentration as a national minority meant voluntary abandonment of any claim to belong to the German nation, thus surrendering one's allegiance to Germany – quite aside from the fact that its political realization was highly questionable. The Jewish question in Germany, the author argued, could only be solved inside Germany and within the German people, not shunted off to one side or outside its borders.[6]

In the same issue of the journal, Hanns Reissner noted that German bourgeois humanism had been supplanted by the Christian-völkisch claim to organic totality. For that reason, it was imperative now to profess adherence to the educational ideals of Jewish humanism that had developed from the German Wandervogel youth movement after the war among a circle of Jewish youth, and whose spiritual mentors were Plato, Shakespeare, Goethe, Hölderlin and Stefan George. "In these guiding spirits, they experienced their Jewishness. Martin Buber spoke to them from the Jewish shore: be the 'men who determine the choice' between outer world and inner."

After the first year of National Socialist rule, *Der Morgen* attempted to sum up and take stock of the basic developments. In the journal's view, all options for coping intellectually and psychologically were still open: from heroism to exodus, from solemn protest to swaggering declaration, from an egocentric "to the lifeboats!" to a committed devotion to serve the community. "Reactions that could have damaged the image of German Jews in the eyes of the German people – and the eyes of history – lay dangerously near as a distinct possibility." The fact that German Jews were no longer supposed to have any part in the artistic-creative, art-promoting life of the nation, charity activities or the world of active politics was leading to a situation where some, the journal observed, were doing a full about-face due to their bitterness and wounded pride: formerly indifferent and denying there was any Jewish problem, they had become adherents of radical nationalist-Jewish schemes. However, when it came to the majority, their ties with their homeland grew ever more palpable as the hour approached for deciding whether they would be able to go on living in Germany in the future. For many, even the experience of emigrating to Palestine had not been able to compensate for the loss of their old psychological homeland.[7]

In this labyrinth of theses and countertheses, *Der Morgen* proposed a discussion on the topic "diaspora as a challenge" and invited contributions, because a careful examination of the foundations of Jewish existence had to cast profound suspicions on the possibility of existence in the diaspora. "If it was possible for German Jewry to be hurled aside and aborted by the forces of history, then this now casts a condemning shadow on the diaspora itself as a Jewish possibility." The mere fact that there will have to continue to be Jewish life in the outside world because of the physical limitations of the territory of Palestine was not a sufficient basis for a meaningful integration of the diaspora into the course of Jewish history. "The diaspora . . . is in jeopardy – not only in the sense of actual physical danger, but in that its task for Jewish life is being devalued."[8]

Ignaz Maybaum commented on this thesis: "Our fate, for which we have been chosen, is to exist in this world without any basis of power. . . . Is that possible? Can such an existence be endured?

We say: yes. For 2,500 years already. The sociological space of Jewish electedness is exile. Exile is not a geographical concept. . . . Exile means existence without any basis of power. In this sense, Jews in Palestine are in the same situation as we are. Our fate is exile."[9]

Gregori Landau wrote: "Let's just imagine that the Jews had remained in Palestine, a small people in a tiny state. What would have become of them? Probably a fate similar to that of the tiny people of Assyrians. . . . Would we have become a kind of fellah? . . . The diaspora brought much calamity upon the Jews . . . yet at the same time, it saved them from the worst thing of all, the extinction of the spirit. The diaspora preserved Judaism, and what was insecure became . . . the most secure thing of all."[10]

Ernst Simon added: "Palestine and Germany today constitute the two poles of the recognizable Jewish world. . . . If the worker in Palestine has gained a new image because he once again is actively shaping Jewish history, that is also true of the man praying in the synagogues of Germany, once more filled to overflowing – because he bears a burden of fate."[11]

At the beginning of 1935, *Der Morgen* examined the crisis in education that had spilled over into the Jewish sphere. For that reason, admonitory voices were needed in order to determine what elements derived from developments in the surrounding ambience, and what was specific to the situation of German Jewry. How was their culture in future to identify itself as a German-Jewish culture? What should be preserved and continued, what new additions should be made? Where could the criteria for selection be found?[12]

Martin Buber observed: "We live . . . in an age when, in quick succession, the great dreams and hopes of mankind are becoming reality: as their own caricatures. What is the cause underlying this massive pretence? I can name no other than the power of fictive ideology. I call this power the uneducated ignorance of the age."[13]

Fritz Friedländer wrote: "In the field of education as well, we must regain the courage to face reality. In contrast with the monotonous phantom of an autonomous or 'self-contained' education – which, in its application to German Jewry today, bears only too clearly the stamp of resentment and defiance – we must reaffirm the polyphony of our tradition of education. . . . Thus, it is indispensable for us to preserve an 'ambidextrous vitality'

[*Beidlebigkeit*] – to borrow an apt expression from Jean Paul – in the polarity between German and Jewish life and culture."[14]

*Der Morgen* regarded the appointment of the managing director of the Reich Chamber of Culture, Hans Hinkel, to the post of Cultural Commissar for Jews in Germany as a "significant step in cultural respect . . . along with a great deal negative" which had taken place. The journal's stance should be interpreted against the backdrop of the anxieties and hopes of the time. Yet one can read with some astonishment: "We believe the most important aspect here is that here for the very first time in the sphere of culture, the *formal* boundary drawn by the state vis-à-vis the Jews living within its boundaries is now to have a concrete manifestation in terms of *content*. Not only what is *forbidden* is laid down. A great deal that is permitted . . . is to be spelled out in authoritative guidelines. . . . From now on, our activities in the cultural area will be clearly characterized as an achievement of Jews in the Jewish sector."[15]

A number of Jewish authors responded to a survey conducted by the journal on the present and future of Jewish literature:[16]

Max Brod : "A limitation to Jewish themes would be senseless – for the mere reason alone that poetic genius . . . does not permit itself to be set any limits."

Georg Hermann (Borchardt): "The way I look at the current situation in Jewish literature . . . well, you could dismiss it with a word, namely: no view at all! And then, you could write a book about the topic."

Else Lasker-Schüler: "Let verses speak! I always stick by poetry, because it's not of this world. So I can't and don't want to say anything more."

Ernst Lissauer: "I can assure you of one thing: the unspeakable distress and travail of present-day humanity echo within in me, unceasingly, and . . . everything that I write is a testimony to this and helps to clarify [it]."

Alfred Mombert: "Probably, the main thing today is what it always was: the need for the divinity to send down a few geniuses. Their reception down here will basically not be much different from what it was in earlier ages."

Soma Morgenstern: "If the most miserable sorry effort, hastily spliced together for the supposed cultural boom, is proffered to the reader as a veritable revelation of the Jewish spirit, he will probably stick with all those sorry artistic efforts that don't have to be clothed first in 'Jewish' garb; he does it out of old habit."

Jakob Picard: "A work will be Jewish because one had the good fortune to come from a Jewish world or from German Jewry, and was still able to experience that world consciously. And it would be a happy act of grace were one to be granted in this way the possibility of returning to the community something of what one effectively had obtained from it originally."

Kurt Pinthus: "I regard the . . . task of the present-day literary critic, and thus my own, as the following: To uncover . . . the conscious and unconscious connections with Judaism in every Jewish author. At the same time, to determine what connects him artistically and philosophically with the thinkers and poets of the country whose language he writes, as well as with world literature."

Alfred Wolfenstein: "I believe that Jewish art and literature . . . nowadays do not by any means have to despair. On the contrary, chaos can give birth to its own special achievements. . . . Not only those who are its bearers should be interested in the preservation of the substance of Jewish being . . . its element of a special inner freedom, which cannot be eradicated or even blurred, an inner freedom that forms the shared nature of the Jew and of every art: it is this which strengthens us in our faith that Jewish creativity shall overcome every affliction."

Otto Zarek: "I believe . . . the honest struggle to rescue what is Jewish in us imbues each creative work with so much power that everywhere one finds people whose minds are open to literature and can read without bias, new friends will be gained for the Jewish spirit."

Stefan Zweig: "I am convinced that the very pressure to which we are exposed morally must generate a greater sense of responsibility in Jewish artists. . . . And it is my hope that everything which we create, drawing on this consciousness of responsibility for our people in distress, can garner from the current state of tragedy and shock a higher meaning, and a passionate strength."

Over a number of years, there was a running discussion in the journal's pages regarding Zionism and the basic principles of Jewish politics. The Zionist diagnosis of the Jewish question first had to prove its ability by showing it could shape living reality in the light of its teachings, *Der Morgen* argued. They wished to present Jewry in Germany, cast out from the culture of its surroundings, as a definitive [negative] example, contrasted with the solution of the Jewish question in Palestine.

> Perhaps this could occur if the experiment . . . involved the course of certain physical or chemical processes. . . . The partial experiment . . . remains unconvincing. Even when there is apparent success here, the Jewish question flares up again there, in disguised form. A mass transplantation from Germany to Palestine . . . would take place at the expense of the Jewish world in Eastern Europe. . . . And that is how it must be everywhere, and at all times: there can be no solution to the Jewish question as long as there are Jews.[17]

Had anti-Zionism really always been nothing but a petty-bourgeois protest on the part of those who felt safe and secure in their status as citizens? Was it not, at least in its best representatives, a protest against a reshaping of authentic Judaism by means of politicization?[18] "From a Jewish perspective, politicized Judaism fails on two counts. It fails vis-à-vis the fate compelling it to be a unit despite its dispersion, and it also miscarries in that the individual who is guided by a Jewish political ideology is no longer an individual, but becomes an atomic particle in a social mass."[19]

Our brothers in Palestine view their fate with a feeling of creative joy, wrote Ignaz Maybaum, a creative joy that is described by Goethe in the sixth book of *Wilhelm Meister*: "all of the universe lying there before us, like an enormous quarry at the feet of the master"; and with the pride "that man can determine circumstances as much as possible." In contrast, German Jewry would have to *bear* its fate. "Wilhelm Meister's ideal of 'shaping life as a work of art' was, for a long period, also possible as the ideal of German Jewry. All that is finished now. Now, we must *live* our life."[20]

The *Jüdische Rundschau* commented: "The storms of the time have left their mark as well on a journal that was known to have espoused the line, in the sense of its founder, of extreme assimilation. Already . . . it is clear that it has shifted to a direction that is more positive in its Jewish orientation. . . . Seen from a Zionist perspective, one can undoubtedly object to the attitude expressed in many articles. But unlike before, a basis has now been created for a possible discussion."[21]

Nonetheless, *Der Morgen* never succeeded in exerting an intellectual influence on German Jewry beyond the confines of a limited readership. Despite its intellectual ambitions, and perhaps specifically because of them, it remained a marginal phenomenon. "True, many German Jews have lived beyond their intellectual means," Max Gruenewald wrote several generations later, but "the total number of readers did not keep up with the enormous book production."[22]

What are the criteria for judging a journal? Are they the structure of its readership, its content or the volume of circulation? Margarete Edelheim investigated this problem, coming to the conclusion that circulation figures were dependent on content, and the structure of readership in turn on the reading material it contained. Hence, none of these factors could be the sole criterion.

It could be said of some periodicals that they would be less good if they tried to aim at a mass audience. "That is roughly how it was back in those early years when *Der Morgen*, then still a bimonthly, was founded by Professor Julius Goldstein in Darmstadt as a journal for discriminating intellectuals. After 1933, *Der Morgen* descended somewhat from its Olympian heights. It still retained a very distinctive character as a monthly, yet adopted forms of expression that made it accessible to broader segments as well." However, Edelheim observed, reputations are a curious thing. "It's not always just a bad reputation that can prove to be an impediment in life; the reputation of excessive refinement can stick to a person – and a periodical – so indelibly that it eventually becomes a hindrance." For years, *Der Morgen* had tried to provide a varied "menu": "still served up on fine porcelain," yet no longer in such an "absolutely aristocratic form as before." Nonetheless, there were only few who dared to sample what it had to offer.[23]

## Notes

1. *Der Morgen*, "In eigener Sache," December 1933.
2. Ibid., Ludwig Feuchtwanger, "Der Morgen im zehnten Jahr," March 1934.
3. Ibid. Cf. also *Israelitisches Familienblatt*: "The journal *Der Morgen* remains as the only example of all the attempts, outside the realm of purely scientific periodicals and that of the weeklies, to create a forum for intellectual confrontation with the questions and issues that are on the minds of all of us. For that reason alone, it deserves special recognition" (January 14, 1937).
4. *Der Morgen*, October 1933.
5. Ibid., Hans Bach, August 1933.
6. Ibid., Heinz Kellermann, August 1933.
7. Ibid., E. R.-J. (Eva Reichmann-Jungmann), April 1934.
8. Ibid., E. R.-J., June 1934.
9. Ibid., June 1934.
10. Ibid.

11. Ibid.
12. Ibid., E. R.-J., February 1935.
13. Ibid., February 1935.
14. Ibid.
15. Ibid., August 1935.
16. Ibid., September 1936.
17. Ibid., E. R.-J., February 1936.
18. Ibid., Ignaz Maybaum, June 1936.
19. Ibid., Ignaz Maybaum, October 1936.
20. Ibid., August 1934.
21. *Jüdische Rundschau*, December 5, 1933.
22. Max Gruenewald, in *YLBI*, 17 (1972), p. 80.
23. Margarete Edelheim, in *Blätter des Jüdischen Frauenbundes*, November 1937.

# 10

# The Image of Women in the Jewish Press

If we categorize women according to the criteria of the theater – a not quite correct, although practical approach – into the naive and sentimental, elegant socialites, heroines, character actresses, mothers, and comical old ladies, and then extend this schema to the various Jewish literatures, we find that the naive types are conspicuous by their virtually complete absence. . . . Could it be that perhaps there are no naive Jewish women, since we Jews are such a clever people to begin with anyhow?" queried Leo Hirsch.[1]

It was a justified question, because the psychological quality of naiveté, according to his own definition, presupposed a "harmonious, idyllic state of all other conditions in life," and the Jewish situation at that time was far removed from any such blissfulness.

The fact that a portion of the Jewish press devoted special columns to the problems of women during the period 1933–1938[2] can serve as an indication that such problems differed in many respects from those faced by males – when it came to possibilities and prospects for emigration, choice of profession, work in education, and the female ability to muster internal resistance to external discrimination.

The surplus of females in the Jewish population in Germany, that had increased from a ratio in 1933 of 105.69 women per 100 males to 109.29 per 100 males by 1936 (a 3.4 percent rise), was attributed by the *Israelitisches Familienblatt* to the fact that more young males than females were emigrating.[3] In a press release of the Hilfsverein der deutschen Juden (Aid Society for German Jews), it was pointed out that the heavy surplus of emigrating males was leading to serious defects and problems. "The marriage prospects for those girls remaining on in Germany must necessarily decline to the same degree that emigration by men of marriageable age exceeds that of women." Of course, there were certainly cases where it was justified for an adult daughter to stay at the side of her parents and assist them. Nonetheless, the paper observed, it was desirable if parents would desist from trying to keep their daughters from emigrating for "egoistic reasons of their own." However, girls wishing to emigrate should receive occupational training suitable for such emigration.[4]

In the pages of the *Blätter des Jüdischen Frauenbundes*, the topic of female emigration became a kind of leitmotif. The paper felt that the special situation of women within the overall complex of emigration had been overlooked or not properly recognized.[5] "That girls stay on here is still not explained by the quite plain fact that those who are in demand abroad – girls with domestic skills, various commercial trades and professions in education and social work – are also needed in Germany." Another factor was that a large number of women now had to provide financially for the family. But that still did not completely account for the situation. Female youth may perhaps have felt closer bonds than the sons with the older generation in the family, which was not always able to decide on the step of emigration; this, the author suggested, was due to female psychology.

In 1933, there had been a substantial number of single, unmarried, widowed and divorced working women, but three years had been wasted in failing to promote the emigration of these valuable workers. It would thus appear that the most important precondition for increased emigration by women was, the author argued, the loosening up of a rigid and antiquated view: overcoming resistance to the idea of independent emigration by single women.[6]

The *Familienblatt* noted that there were instances where married women envied the type of modern girl who, despite the difficulties Jews were facing, had gone her own way in a freely chosen career and had found a new way of life for women. Such girls had missed out on a certain aspect of life, but in place of that had attained something denied to married women. "When God closes a door, he opens a window."[7]

While in the case of the single woman one could presuppose a certain degree of preparation for the new country of destination, it could be assumed that married women often took no active part in the decision to emigrate; rather, under constraint of necessity, they decided to accompany their husbands to the country they had chosen. Despite the familiar promise that one was willing to take on any job, a large percentage of male emigrants proved unable to put that intention into practice; women, in contrast, were generally better able to accommodate to the new circumstances of living by dint of their ability to adjust, the *Blätter* observed.[8]

"If things continue on this way, the young men who emigrate may enter into mixed marriages in massive numbers . . . while the girls, on the other hand, just stay on in Germany with no prospects for marriage."[9]

A recurrent topic was the choice of profession among Jewish girls. A survey was conducted in December 1936 in the interest of planning while there was still time.

> It is remarkable that only a bit more than ten percent of the girls desire further general education . . . the number of those who would like to enter commerce (13.1%) has declined considerably in comparison with earlier years. The circumstance that only a tiny number are considering the teaching profession (1.75%) may be connected with reluctance to embark on a long period of training. The profession of kindergarten teacher is listed comparatively often (11.72%). The reason for the fact that only a small number of girls wish to dedicate themselves to professions in social work and the care of the sick is that there are no institutions now for such training. A total of 5.82% opted in favor of agriculture.[10]

A survey conducted in Frankfurt yielded similar findings, though it stressed that it was no longer possible to speak about a choice of profession in the narrower sense, since the number of occupations open to Jewish females was very small. Influenced by the circumstances, the notion that a school education was worthless had gained broader acceptance; this was manifested in the "evil of bad marks." Of 77 girls – 40 Orthodox and 37 from a religious-liberal background – 46 had attended the nine-grade comprehensive main school (*Volksschule*), but only eight had finished with a leaving certificate; 30 had gone to academic high school (with seven graduating), and one had completed a ten-grade secondary school (*Mittelschule*).[11]

The problem of domestic help was illuminated from both sides – from the standpoint of the housewife, who needed help at home, and that of the girls seeking employment and training opportunities. The *Israelitisches Familienblatt* observed that you could also "discuss certain questions to death."[12] Both the employer and her employee had to be repeatedly reminded that nothing should be concealed: neither the demands one made nor the knowledge and skills one did not possess.

"By now, it is probably generally accepted in broad circles of the population that the work of a domestic is looked upon today as a profession – one that can be learned like any other, and which makes certain intellectual demands." Training as a domestic should be done in a planned, orderly fashion, and every private household would have to become a place for apprenticeship.[13] No words were minced in criticizing the situation: although the home and family had always been the focus for the Jewish woman, there was no tradition of domestic work in a professional sense among Jewish women and girls. Mothers still frequently thought that domestic employment was not "good enough" for their daughters.[14]

For the benefit of the religious structure of the house, *Der Israelit* called for an attitude that would regard the Jewish domestic servant as a member of the religious community in the home; she should be actively included in religious practices. This would enhance her feeling of responsibility for the ritual aspects of duties in the kitchen.[15]

The Jüdischer Frauenbund suggested that there be an exchange of daughters between families with the express purpose of learning domestic tasks, say for the duration of six months. "We are of the opinion that this approach is very important . . . both for the psychological attitude of the girls and the housewife."[16]

Associated with occupational training was the need felt by Jewish women for more education, the strong desire "to gain an understanding of our changed circumstances by mastering new areas of knowledge." First on the list was an interest in Jewish history, a subject in which those factors became visible "which have shaped us and made us what we are"; this was seen as "access to the past, which in our case has never completely 'passed', but rather . . . remains an element determining our present." Were the existing institutions enough, or did women need special additional opportunities for women's education?[17] To deal with such needs, the Jüdischer Frauenbund organized a special seminar "Lernzeit" in Bad Nauheim in October 1934, with Martin Buber and Ernst Simon among its lecturers.[18]

The entire women's movement, correctly conceived, wished to be regarded as a movement for education. "In our generation, we have, to an alarming degree, lost the courage to educate. What can we give our youth, what can we demand of it – we who have given birth and brought them into such a chaos, we who ourselves have so little understanding of how to set our own lives in order?" Mothers should know that they were part of a course of history that could not be measured using the yardstick of guilt and expiation. "Have we left a field of ruins for our youth? All right, then let's teach them how to build."[19]

But were Jewish mothers ready and able to break with forms of life that had become empty vessels, and to allow their children to go down the path they had chosen with a sense of self-responsibility – when they themselves had been unable to tread that path? There was a danger that many of them were unable to free themselves from the legacy of the past – values and practices that had become useless. "The tempo of our age is inexorable . . . whoever does not keep up with the pace, is left behind, alone. Alone like Lot's wife, who loses her children when she glances back."[20]

Again and again, one can note the motif of not looking back. Jewish women should draw the line and forget what was in the past. "Now bereft of the old, arrogant pomp . . . only she can give who does not turn to look backward. Only those who are resolved . . . to make a decision without glossing things over, without foolish hopes, has understood what is being demanded today of the Jewish woman."[21] People should stop preaching the "romanticism of suffering," and cease making a philosophy out of every act of washing the dishes.[22]

Jewish mothers now knew the experience of standing in a station watching a train pull out with their children on it. They also knew what it was like to have to give up an apartment or take leave of a city where one has lived a long time. "Let's stop, let's finish now with all the whining and tears. We've gazed long enough now into the mirror of our pain. Now we will stop looking back on what used to be. . . . Let's not take ourselves so seriously. . . . Everybody has something to do. . . . So: eyes straight ahead, and hands ready for action."[23]

In actual fact, observed the *Familienblatt*, Jewish women for a long time had done nothing but clean up. Moving from a big apartment to a smaller place, from a small apartment to an unfurnished room as a boarder in the house of other Jews – they were always busy rummaging about, vacating, packing. "One of these days, we also have to jettison the ballast of our memories. We shouldn't cry so much any more . . . mustn't be so sad. Every doctor claims that his optimistic patients recover more quickly."[24]

"Keep your sense of humor" became a kind of slogan. "Who knows better than a mother what a wonderful educational tool friendly, warm-hearted poking fun can be. Aunt Molly who sits on the sofa and takes matters amiss will soon be complaining about the fact that she has to be alone so much. . . . Humor is as far removed from self-overestimation as it is from moral cowardice . . . 'my daughter doesn't need to do work like that', hauling coal, cleaning the back stairs. . . . Look, she needs to do everything! And if, later on, it turns out that she really doesn't 'need to' – well then, all the better for her!"[25]

Of particular importance was the question of women's involvement in the various official bodies of the Gemeinde. The Gemeinde had changed from an administrative bureaucracy into a life community, and its social and cultural tasks lay in areas that were the primal and particular preserve of women. Only if women could gain insight into Gemeinde affairs as representatives could they apply their abilities in the proper and effective way. "For that reason, we must reject the question that repeatedly is raised regarding what special achievements women who had been active in Gemeinde bodies in the past could point to. . . .Just as the achievements and merits of the individual male representative are not weighed upon a scale, so women should not be judged according to other yardsticks. What is it that they want? – To put female thinking and feeling right alongside that of the men." A special challenge in this connection was to reconcile existing differences. A useful goal should be the injection of "motherly spirit into the offices of the Gemeinde." For that reason, there could be no question that women were allegedly trying to provoke an electoral struggle. "Women in their demands are not concerned with winning seats on the council, but in adding their energy to Gemeinde activities." One repeatedly could observe, the author noted, that it was precisely those men who were most adamantly opposed to women working in Gemeinde administration, based on equal rights, who later on were the most demanding when it came to the level of female achievement on the job.[26]

There were numerous references to the therapeutic "stabilizing effect" of the Jewish woman in public life. "Her voice is that of evening things out, of balance. And such an effect is necessary. Our Jewish press is replete with reports about differences and friction. . . . Everywhere there seems to be fratricidal struggle and disunity. . . . Undoubtedly, we need a lively confrontation. . . . However, the role of women is: 'I'm there to help love, not hate' . . . it is a truly Jewish challenge not to allow one's own feeling of being shoved aside to decline into a kind of malice toward others."[27]

This politics of reconciliation by the Jewish woman was called for beyond the confines of Germany's borders – "reconciliation turned inward, in one's intellectual and psychological attitude." The *Israelitisches Familienblatt* recounted the story of a woman in Jerusalem who had watched on as a small Jewish boy, his face filled with hatred, threw a stone at an Arab girl. When his mother scolded him, the boy gazed at her with large, uncomprehending eyes and said in Yiddish: "Why? In Poland they persecuted us – here, we're at home."[28]

The paper noted that Jewish women were experiencing the changing times in a more powerful way than the average Jewish male. Like the non-Jewish woman, she had been granted emancipation as a result of the war and its consequences – quickly and unexpectedly. Capable and hungry for new experience, Jews had placed themselves at the forefront of those women who were streaming into the newly opened professions. Jewish women more often chose free professions than their non-Jewish counterparts, and they frequently broke free from the control of their homes and families by their choice of occupation. Hounded out of the professions, they were now reoccupying their primal sphere, that of the home, but it had in the meantime become an alien place to them. Jewish children, accustomed to mingling with non-Jewish peers at school, in sports clubs and other associations, now were without friends and clung more closely to the parental home – unless they lived in larger metropolitan areas where they could participate in Jewish youth leagues. "Now, in this hour of distress, the Jewish woman should dedicate her concentrated energies to the family."[29]

Wherever the woman was not occupied with working life, wherever she was active in the "bosom of the family," she should find her way back to the "fount of Judah," to the religious and cultural wellsprings from whence she had sprung and evolved over the course of millennia. "We have no intention to turn back the wheel of progress. On the contrary: more than ever, we demand today of the Jewish woman that she should protect and preserve the intellectual interests of her people." Nowadays, it was noted, Jewish women could no longer hold demanding positions in the bourgeois world. In place of that, the Jewish woman would have to carry a greater burden of responsibility within her own work community. "She will require a great deal of tact and sensitivity in order not to make notice of herself in the bourgeois world – while at the same time preserving with dignity the position befitting her in her own community."[30]

Viewed historically, the "*lady* of the house had become its *servant.*" Her most important task was the education of her children; here, it was not so much a matter of her fund of knowledge, but her adherence to and avowal of Jewish values. The school could not lead the way alone – mothers would have to learn to be leaders. "In accordance with the symbol in *Faust,* mothers carried the key to the realm of ideas in their hands.[31]

The *Israelitisches Familienblatt* observed that the year 1933 had caught the Jewish woman in Germany just as much unawares as had emancipation when it first took women by surprise with its advent. First of all, she should take stock of herself. Once, she had stood together side by side with German women in the struggle for job and educational opportunities. Now all that was past history.[32]

In June 1934, the Jüdischer Frauenbund sent the following message to the national umbrella organization, the Federation of German Women's Associations: "Thus, although we are leaving the organization which up until now has embodied the German women's movement, we nonetheless continue to remain inwardly attached to the women's movement, which is also a foundation of our own league. In this connection, it should not be forgotten that there were also a number of Jewish women who were not only members of the German women's movement from its inception, but who had a creative impact on its development. . . .Those women live on in our ranks as bearers of the idea that paved the way for us to education and a profession. . . . Signed Bertha Pappenheim, Bettina Brenner, Paula Ollendorff, Dr. Margaret Brenner, Hannah Kaminski."[33]

The relationship women had with their husbands also had to be readjusted; many men, "without giving it any thought," still thought in terms of the domestic situation as it used to be. To help an overburdened woman at home and in the kitchen – is that something "unmasculine"? Naturally, the man was also burdened down with more worries and stress and strain, but, at the very least, he ought to make sure that the children in the family helped their mother around the house.[34] Another piece of upper-class tradition crumbled when it was noted that the changing times no longer allowed for the woman to be addressed by the academic title of her husband. "Many women took their doctorate down at city hall when they registered their marriage. Just leave the title of doctor for those who have honestly earned it by years of study, an academic dissertation and exam."[35]

In any event, Jewish women should avoid being conspicuous, and refrain from adopting every new and modish trend. "Well-groomed and well-dressed, certainly; but to be in fashion at any cost – that is something she should have given up long ago."[36]

The *Familienblatt* commented that the Biblical figure of Ruth could serve the German-Jewish woman as a model. She did not just say "I would do any job," but rather had gone out into the sun between the furrows of the wheat fields and had bent down until her back ached, her fingers burned and the soles of her feet stung with pain. And why? Because of the old woman Naomi, with whom she went out into the field, so that she would not be left alone. "It is a promising sign that nowadays among Jewish girls in Germany the name of Ruth is the one most in vogue."[37]

The paper pointed to a social phenomenon that demanded the assistance of women – namely the rise in the number of illegitimate births among Jews in Germany. It attributed this to the political situation, which acted to dissuade people from getting married, but also to the fact that Jews were cut off from an outside world that might otherwise have exercised a stabilizing influence. It was not just a question of welfare services for the unmarried mother, of providing her with employment – not merely a matter of material problems. "Her distress must not become an anguish of the heart . . . we must adopt the attitude toward mother and child that we normally take toward the widow and orphan, and which is demanded of us by Jewish law."[38]

The *Familienblatt* observed that the first three decades of the 20th century had witnessed a strong dedication, particularly by the Jewish woman, to all intellectual and artistic values. The German-Jewish woman had also been affected by the basically

155

spiritual orientation of German Jewry; earlier, as a consequence of "male arrogance," she had been excluded from the realm of matters of the mind. The new Jewish society would, the paper contended, no doubt differ considerably from that of the bourgeois-capitalist age – simpler, with fewer needs, poorer – but it would not be more impoverished in a genuine cultural sense.[39]

# Notes

1. *Blätter des Jüdischen Frauenbundes – für Frauenarbeit und Frauenbewegung*, February 1938. The Jüdischer Frauenbund (Jewish Women's League) encompassed 430 associations, with a total membership of over 50,000.
2. *Israelitisches Familienblatt*, "Aus der Welt der Frau," edited by Martha Wertheimer; *Frankfurter Israelitisches Gemeindeblatt*, "Für die Frau," edited by Stephanie Forchheimer.
3. *Israelitisches Familienblatt*, February 27, 1936.
4. *Jüdische Rundschau*, January 21, 1938.
5. *Blätter des Jüdischen Frauenbundes*, December 1936.
6. Ibid., Arthur Prinz, December 1936.
7. *Israelitisches Familienblatt*, February 27, 1936.
8. *Blätter des Jüdischen Frauenbundes*, December 1936.
9. Ibid., February 1937.
10. Ibid.
11. *Frankfurter Israelitisches Gemeindeblatt*, February 1935.
12. *Israelitisches Familienblatt*, April 21, 1938.
13. *Frankfurter Israelitisches Gemeindeblatt*, January 1935.
14. Ibid., September 1935.
15. *Der Israelit*, October 3, 1935.
16. *Israelitisches Familienblatt*, March 19, 1936.
17. *Frankfurter Israelitisches Gemeindeblatt*, October 1934.
18. Ibid., November 1934.
19. Ottilie Schönfeld, in *Blätter des Jüdischen Frauenbundes*, February 1934.
20. *Frankfurter Israelitisches Gemeindeblatt*, January 1935.
21. *Israelitisches Familienblatt*, July 16, 1936.
22. Ibid., January 21, 1937.
23. Ibid., October 29, 1936.
24. Ibid., July 7, 1938.
25. Ibid., February 17, 1938.
26. *Blätter des Jüdischen Frauenbundes*, November 1936.
27. *Israelitisches Familienblatt*, April 19, 1934.
28. Ibid., June 25, 1936.
29. Ibid., February 1, 1934.
30. Ibid., January 15, 1935.
31. Ibid., May 17, 1934. The reference is to Goethe's *Faust*, pt. II, v. 6258 ff.
32. Ibid., July 19, 1934.
33. Ibid., June 15, 1934.
34. Ibid., May 30, 1935.

35. Ibid., March 7, 1935. The reference is to the German practice of addressing the wives of male doctorate-holders as "Frau Dr."
36. Ibid., February 14, 1935.
37. Ibid., June 2, 1938.
38. Ibid., November 11, 1937.
39. Ibid., June 14, 1934.

# 11

## The Final Station

J ewish life within the borders of the *Altreich* was jolted anew in March 1938 in the wake of the annexation of Austria into the territory of the Reich and the "instantaneous" initiation of persecution of Jews there. Journalistic commentary, interpretation – which had still been a possibility but two-and-a-half years earlier after the issuance of the Nuremberg Laws – was now no longer a realistic option. The fetters had been tightened, and new regulations further circumscribed the permissible manner of expression in the press; the attitude of the authorities had become more brutal. For that reason, it was extremely risky to comment on the events taking place in Austria. In retrospect, what was in fact written can be viewed as the final statement by the Jewish press on a political act of the government.

The *Jüdische Rundschau* attempted to overcome the difficulties by arguing that Jews should not look at "great events" only from a Jewish point of view, but should evaluate them objectively, although the impact of those events on Jews would have to be integrated into the context of Jewish history. It had taken a long time before Germany's Jews had comprehended the profound changes taking place in all spheres of political, intellectual and cultural thought.

> In Austria, this change is even more powerful, because it involves a new sovereignty, a completely new restructuring of the constitutional situation in the country . . . and when a new ordering of affairs is initiated, the Jews have a . . . special position. . . . At such moments, only the conscious affirmation of Jewish *Volkstum* can provide individuals with psychological support. . . . Complaints have been voiced in Vienna that there is a lack of Jewish initiative. . . . But the hour for Jewish activity shall arrive.[1]

Commentary in *Der Schild* sufficed by pointing out that the principle of making special exceptions in the case of men who were veteran combat soldiers had also been introduced in Austria, for example, in regard to Jewish attorneys and patent lawyers.[2]

The *Israelitisches Familienblatt* admonished that Jews, if they wished to comprehend history, had to be aware that in great historical moments, the rule of fate became manifest. In the previous century, Theodor Herzl had come forward out of the midst of Austria's Jewish community to interpret Jewish history in his particular way. The paper then alluded to the contrasts and disputes within Austrian Jewry. "There will probably be far greater difficulties in connection with the creation of a unified working community of all Jewish segments in Vienna, where the Jewish population is so diverse in its groupings, than was the case here in Germany." One could expect that the work to be done in the area of social welfare and the necessity to adopt a new and serious approach to problems of emigration would serve to promote the sense of solidarity and cohesion amongst the various different groups.[3]

The *CV-Zeitung* felt it was premature, "caught up in the midst of the historical events now taking place," to say any more to Austria's Jews "than that we intend to be there if they need us, and when permitted, shall assist them with advice and action." It noted that the composition of Austrian Jewry, and thus its inner attitude, differed considerably from that of Jews in the former borders of the Reich.

> The goal and direction of work will accordingly have to differ from those we have tried and tested over the past five years, and which are now in effective use. For that reason, our assistance will initially . . . have to consist in the example of the attitude with which we have approached the mastering of our fate: that combination of Jewish consciousness and cosmopolitanism, objective work and activity aimed at the future, consciousness of community and formation of personality – traits that have stamped the character of our people at home and abroad.

But Austrian Jews should also learn from the mistakes Jews had committed in the *Altreich* – mistakes that were made because there had been far too much ideological and historical theorizing, instead of practical action.[4]

It did not take long before the storm over Austria also reached the Jews back in the old territory of the Reich. On November 10, 1938, for example, a group of some dozen civilians were ordered to Berlin police headquarters. They were greeted there by a guard dressed in a black uniform with a skull insignia on his cap. One of those summoned reported:

> These men and women, editors of the Jewish papers published in Berlin, had no clear idea of what awaited them. The small group had appeared promptly, all of their number present, at the appointed hour in the building that had rightfully been feared since 1933. They were locked up in a broad corridor, flanked by high iron-bar doors. The SS man there, who walked back and forth for hours, declined to speak with them. You only heard the click of his boots. It was possible to look down into the courtyard through the large windows of the unadorned, bare hallway. People were being loaded onto trucks there, undoubtedly Jews. Eight hours passed. Nothing happened. Finally they were sent home with the order that they should appear the next morning again at 8 a.m.[5]

On November 7, 1938, a young Polish Jew, Herschel Gryn-szpan, whose parents had been deported from Hannover to the Polish border, had shot the legation secretary of the German Embassy in Paris, Ernst vom Rath, mortally wounding him. On the evening of November 9th, the top echelon of the "old veterans" [*Alte Kämpfer*] of the Nazi movement had met, as always, for their annual reunion at the Old Town Hall in Munich. During the festive meal, Hitler was informed of the news that vom Rath had died that afternoon. Shortly thereafter, he left the hall. A few minutes later, Goebbels rose to give a speech and spoke about the hour of revenge that had arrived.[6]

That same night, between 11 p.m. and 4 a.m., the "soul of the people, unbridled, discharged its rage," as official reports the next day stated. Jewish businesses, factories, homes, offices and clinics suffered damage, 280 synagogues were set on fire and many more demolished in other ways. On November 10th, all Jewish institutions and organizations, associations, clubs, leagues and federations were closed and banned, except for the local Gemeinden, the Reichsvertretung, and the Reich Federation of Jewish Kulturbünde.

> Early the morning of November 11th, the ten, twelve or fourteen editors reappeared at the "familiar" spot. Once again, after waiting for hours, the SS man asked us to line up. We were brought into an office, where we could note the presence of unpleasantly familiar

faces, namely of Gestapo agents who were by no means strangers to the editors of the Jewish press in Berlin. One after the other, we were asked to sign our names to short, carefully prepared statements: they said no more or less than that we agreed to the immediate and irrevocable cessation of the appearance of the papers and periodicals which we had directed up until that point. Then we were released. Only after we were several kilometers away from Alexanderplatz did we dare to speak to one another once again.[7]

From the *CV-Zeitung* staff, Dr. Alfred Hirschberg, Dr. Eva Reichmann-Jungmann and Dr. Ernst G. Lowenthal were among those summoned. "While we were waiting in Dr. Hirschberg's apartment for his return, the detective squad arrived. We were still negotiating with them when Dr. Hirschberg walked in. He explained that he had just been dismissed from his post, and in response to his objections, the police officers phoned headquarters. However, it proved to be in vain. Dr. Hirschberg was arrested."[8] He later was able to emigrate, going to Brazil via Paris and London, where he died in Sao Paulo in 1971.

After the banning of the Jewish press, the Jewish community and the authorities were faced with a problem: how to continue to inform the Jewish population in Germany about the new official changes and ordinances that were being issued virtually on a daily basis. As a result of discussions with Jewish functionaries, the Propaganda Ministry decided to launch a new publication, a *Jüdisches Nachrichtenblatt* [Jewish News Bulletin].[9] Its offices were set up in the former rooms of the *Jüdische Rundschau*, at Meinekestraße 10; editorship and distribution were assigned to the Kulturbund, which, effective January 1, 1939, was divided into four departments; theater and music; lectures; films; publications (printing house for books and periodicals, as well as distribution). All Jewish papers that had been published up until then and had been subsequently dissolved were instructed to put their subscriber lists at the disposal of the *Jüdisches Nachrichtenblatt* in order to require of all Jews in Germany that they subscribe to the new paper. The postal authorities were informed they should limit the period for submitting subscriber lists to a minimum so that delivery of the paper could begin without any delays.[10]

Erich Liepmann was appointed director of the printing house; previously, he had been publishing manager of the *Jüdische Rundschau*. Right after the *Reichskristallnacht* pogroms, he had been ordered over the telephone by SS Major Owens of the

Propaganda Ministry to liquidate the *Jüdische Rundschau* immediately. Several days later he was instructed to appear at once at Goebbels' office.

> I wanted to take a taxi, but the driver refused to let me get in – the reason he gave was that he didn't transport Jews. Only when I demanded to be driven directly to Goebbels because I had been summoned was I able to get a car. I was conducted in to him without delay. Hinkel, the director of the Jewish Section of the Ministry, was sitting there too. Goebbels greeted me by shouting: "Is the Jew here?" He was sitting at his desk, I had to stand about eight meters out in front of him. Goebbels bellowed: "A news bulletin has to appear within two days. Each issue will be presented to me. You'll curse the day if even one article should appear that I have not seen. That's all!" I passed the order on immediately to Kurt Löwenstein and Walter Gross.[11]

This directive by Goebbels to submit all material for approval before going to press constituted a change in procedures.

Kurt Löwenstein had joined the staff of the *Jüdische Rundschau* in 1933 as second editor, and after Robert Weltsch left Germany in September 1938, he took over the paper, directing it until its closing on November 10th. Dr. Walter Gross had been a member of the editorial staff since the spring of 1938.

Right after the decision to publish a *Jüdisches Nachrichtenblatt*, Kurt Löwenstein was considered for its editorship. Yet when the first issue was ready to go to press and was presented for approval, the Propaganda Ministry rejected it in the form submitted. There are only two or three copies of this banned issue in existence, one of which is in the National Library in Jerusalem. "It was not all too surprising that the issue was confiscated, since we had tried to a certain extent to continue on with the *Jüdische Rundschau* in terms of content."[12] Löwenstein was fired and replaced by Leo Kreindler, until then editor of the *Gemeindeblatt* in Berlin.

The banned first issue carries the date November 22, 1938, and consists of two pages. The publisher listed is the "Jüdische Rundschau GmbH." Its banner headline on the first page, which has three columns, reads in bold letters: "Efforts to Emigrate." "Efforts to promote Jewish emigration from Germany are being intensively pursued in numerous countries. The initiative is especially strong in England, the United States and Palestine. A number of measures have already been decided upon; in the main, these are meant to assist in preparations for the emigration of children and youth. One can only hope that further measures will take on a concrete shape in the near future – in particular, a substantial expansion of immigration possibilities in Palestine for Jews from Germany."[13]

News items from Jerusalem, London, New York, Warsaw, Budapest and Oslo reflect the Jewish political scene around the world. Of six columns, only one deals with communications and notices from Jewish organizations and bodies in Germany. A frame box containing some words of encouragement by Leo Baeck had been included: "A word to all Jews in Germany in these fateful times: hold on to one another, tread the path of uprightness, believe in your future, and place your trust in the Eternal One, our God."

The *Jüdisches Nachrichtenblatt* was printed in the "Aryanized" printing house of the former *Israelitisches Familienblatt*. In the summer of 1939, the management was ordered to transfer printing of the paper to the Nazi publishing house Eher-Verlag. The publishing manager, however, insisted that he should never have any direct contact with Jews. No one Jewish was allowed into the premises of the printing house except the editor and his assistants – to check the makeup before going to press.[14]

As the only Jewish paper and the only periodical in which to place advertisements, the *Jüdisches Nachrichtenblatt* was a flourishing financial success. There were always a lot of people in its business offices at Meinekestraße 10. In order to cope with the extra work, the paper hired on all the former external sales representatives of the *Jüdische Rundschau*, and, upon official instruction, took on as many former staff of other Jewish papers as possible. Nobody with Polish citizenship was allowed to be employed, although the ministry finally made several exceptions, since they were interested in augmenting the income of the paper. However, the attempt to hire on the former Reichstag president Paul Löbe, a Social Democrat who was a typesetter by profession, proved unsuccessful.[15]

> During that period, only the Palestine Office was granted permission to operate out of the Meinekestraße address. But officials were dissatisfied with it because emigration was taking too long. We were constantly reminded of how decent it was of them to allow Jews to work at all following the murder of vom Rath. And they were furious that we were not doing more to promote illegal emigration to Palestine. Finally, we were told that they would no longer retain any interest in

this whole matter – unless emigration procedures were substantially speeded up. And they said that they would no longer tolerate the *Jüdisches Nachrichtenblatt* either, especially after it became known that there was a plan in Palestine to bring out a paper called *Jüdische Weltrundschau* [Jewish World Review]. Dr. Weltsch was in Palestine at that time. We had to ask Mr. Wallbach from the Palestine Office to go to Holland immediately, and from there to inform offices in Palestine that we would be seriously threatened should a *Weltrundschau* see the light of day.[16]

When it first appeared, the *Jüdisches Nachrichtenblatt* consisted of two pages, and contained nothing but regulations issued by the authorities and announcements of cultural events put on by the Kulturbund. Death notices were not permitted at that time, though the prohibition was later rescinded. The ads section consisted of small ads for rooms for rent, employment wanted ads and family notices. Since ordinances and regulations pertaining to Jews were proliferating and the ads section was growing at a rapid rate, the paper was soon appearing twice a week: a Tuesday edition of four pages, and a Friday issue with six pages. After a short time, even that was no longer sufficient, and the Tuesday edition was expanded to eight pages, the Friday edition to 16. The publication of articles was also permitted, in particular reviews of theater performances in the Kulturbund, and critical evaluations of its musical events; the paper also published a series of instructional letters to help readers learn English.

An edition for Vienna was also initiated. Dr. Werner Levie, director of the Jewish Kulturbund, Heinrich Stahl, chairman of the Jewish Gemeinde in Berlin and Erich Liepmann were ordered to Vienna and brought by SS Major Owens to Eichmann.

Since Heinrich Stahl was dressed somewhat casually, he was immediately shouted at, called "old slob" and forced to stand at attention for two hours. Eichmann informed them that a news bulletin patterned on the Berlin model was also planned for Austria.[17]

The regulations for Austria were the same as for the *Altreich*. There too, the practical operations for the paper were made the responsibility of the Jewish Kulturbund, though the Kulturbund worked together with the staff of the Palestine Office. The plates were prepared in Berlin and sent to Vienna, so that only those ordinances and advertisements that were meant for Austria were printed and censored in Vienna. The censor was not under the

Propaganda Ministry as in Berlin, but was subject to the authority of the Gestapo.[18]

Since every Jew living in Germany and Austria was required by law to be informed about the new orders and instructions that were constantly being issued, the number of subscribers was quite large. Income from the paper was put to use in accordance with official directives. Almost all the money was channeled to the theater department of the Jewish Kulturbund after deducting costs for production and distribution; an additional sum was transferred monthly to the Reichsvereinigung der Juden in Deutschland, the successor organization to the Reichsvertretung, presumably for purposes of assisting emigration. Erich Liepmann left Germany in April 1939, and the management of the paper was taken over by Hanna Marcus.

She was obliged to make a daily appearance at the ministry, together with a representative of the Kulturbund, in order to be given instructions. Later on, the liaison to the ministry was Dr. Martin Brasch of the Berlin Jewish Gemeinde, and Hanna Marcus was not permitted to appear unless accompanied by him. Kreindler was only asked to come to the ministry twice a week. Jews were not allowed to use the main entrance on Wilhelmplatz, but had to enter through a back door on Mauerstraße. Hanna Marcus and her escort Dr. Brasch had to appear at 10:30 a.m., and often were kept waiting, without chairs, until 2:30. Most of that time they spent out in the corridor, which had a special clothes stand marked "for Jews only." As a rule, the meetings would last for hardly more than ten minutes. Hanna Marcus was given a chair, the men had to stand.

In the daily conferences, they were required to account for all business transactions, such as mail received, orders and payments. After the report on the daily situation of the cashdesk and postal checking accounts, the official then decided on how the funds were to be used. Originally, Hanna Marcus was supposed to ask the ministry's approval for every decision on expenditures. But since it became obvious that the paper could not be managed in that way, she was given permission to spend a daily amount of up to 50 reichsmarks. For larger sums, she had to have the counter-signature of the Reichsvereinigung.[19] After Dr. Werner Levie emigrated in November 1939, Dr. Brasch was appointed to the post of general director of the Jewish Kulturbund in Germany.

165

A shorthand text written by Hanna Marcus describes such a "visit" by her to the ministry:

> Dr. Brasch and I had special permission to use taxis, something which otherwise was forbidden for Jews. Once he was riding in a small taxi, in a very cramped position, since he was very tall, and when the taxi came to a sudden stop, he broke a collar-bone. He then lay sick at home running a high fever, and I went to the ministry alone.
> "Where's Brasch?"
> "He's at home. He broke his collar-bone during a trip by taxi."
> "This is what happens when Jews take taxis. He has to be here tomorrow."
> "But he's running a high temperature."
> "He will have to appear. It's possible to walk when you have a broken collar-bone." The next day Brasch came, his shoulder and arm heavily bandaged. He was carrying a briefcase in his other hand. I wanted to give him my chair. "Just remain sitting. Brasch can stand."
> Then Dr. Brasch was asked for some papers in his briefcase. However, he couldn't manage to get at them with his free hand. I wanted to assist him. Dr. Lock[20] forbade me to do so. "We want to have the papers from Brasch, not from you."
> Finally he allowed him to place the briefcase on my knees, and in that way he was able, with great difficulty, to remove the papers. Dr. Brasch was later shot.[21]

During the months up to the outbreak of the war, the *Jüdisches Nachrichtenblatt* had a brief period in which it flourished, both in the want ads section and other parts of the paper. In some areas, it reached a remarkable level, and also provided freelancers – journalists, historians and writers – with a chance to augment their shrinking income. Its pages reflected events taking place in Palestine and the political struggle in London; a speech by Chaim Weizmann in London, for example, covered a full page. The second Evian Conference figured prominently, as did the preparations for, debates and results of the 21st Zionist Congress. Quite naturally, the problem of emigration headed the list. There were news stories and articles on America, England, Argentina, Rhodesia, Shanghai, British Guinea and the Dominican Republic, along with items on the situation in Poland, Romania, Bulgaria and Czechoslovakia.

The cultural section consisted of articles on literary and historical subjects. Bialik's childhood memories, the history of the Jewish folksong and Sholem Aleichem's place in Yiddish literature were published in series form; Dr. Abraham Heschel authored a series entitled "Personalities in Jewish History."

There were reports with titles such as "Music in Palestine," "Religious Life in Eretz Israel," "A Sabbath in the Kibbutz," "The Yishuv Works," "Cultural Questions in Palestine," "Transit Camps in England," "As a Domestic Servant in England," "Jews at the Lathe" (on the Berlin ORT school), "Jewish Women in the United States," "A Day in a Settlement," and "Labor Law in America." One article was entitled "Emigration as the Final Solution," before that word took on its ominous meaning. The editorials, generally from the pen of L.I.K. (Leo Kreindler), bore titles such as "Criticism of the White Paper," "Jews in Palestine," "Clay in the Potter's Hand," "Education for Being a Jew," "Proposals for Occupational Training," "New Perspectives" (after the 2nd Evian Conference), "The Time of the Shekel" (before the Zionist Congress) and "In Europe and Abroad."

News from the local scene was dominated by the Jewish Kulturbund, with its announcements, detailed reviews and the many photos from its diverse functions. Occasionally there were commentaries assessing the work of the Reichsvereinigung. When it came to the activity of the Gemeinden, there were nothing but notices of various kinds.

Shortly after his arrival in the United States, Rabbi Max Nussbaum summed up the situation: "In the first few years of the Third Reich, the German authorities were in agreement with the idea of intensive emigration by Jewish youth to Palestine. For a short time, it even seemed as though the Third Reich looked with especial favor, due to national reasons, on emigration by Jews to Eretz Israel. . . . A change in this attitude appeared during the beginning months of the war. We were no longer allowed . . . to propagate the idea of Palestine – in fact, it was forbidden . . . even to publish the word 'Palestine'."[22]

Yet it was not only the word "Palestine" that was prohibited. In the first issue of the *Nachrichtenblatt* after the beginning of the war, neither the word "war" nor the event as such are mentioned. The only report indicating a fundamental change in the situation is the announcement that all Kulturbund functions had been cancelled until further notice, and the following appeal to the readers:

> In the current situation, it is of course the duty of every Jewish man and woman in the territory of the Reich to adhere scrupulously to the existing and newly introduced official orders as well as the guidelines

of the various authorities. Complying with this warning is in the interest of the entire Jewish population in Germany. There will be very unpleasant consequences should individuals fail to show the requisite attention. The *Jüdisches Nachrichtenblatt* will, from now on, regularly publish all official laws and orders as well as the guidelines of various offices. Our paper regards it as its task, now more than ever, to create a close bond with its readership and to inform those readers about everything of importance for the Jewish population in Germany. However, this means that every person must read the paper and pay subscription fees promptly. Only in this way can we guarantee that there will be no interruption or delay in delivery. Today, the Jewish community and each individual within it has higher duties. Every individual, of course, bears responsibility should he violate that duty by ignorance of official orders and announcements. [Signed,] The editors and publishers of the *Jüdisches Nachrichtenblatt*.[23]

The issue of September 8, 1939 contained notices about ration coupons and economic decrees. "The Poland campaign was launched, and a short time thereafter the first anti-Jewish measures were introduced. Everyone is familiar with them – the prohibition on Jews going out after 8 p.m. and the order to hand in one's radio were only the beginning. The strange thing was that these new regulations were not published anywhere. The only Jewish paper in Germany, the *Jüdisches Nachrichtenblatt*, had been explicitly enjoined from announcing these two measures."[24]

The edition of September 17 published the basic elements of a statistical survey on the Jewish population which, as it later turned out, served as an aid in implementing the deportations. The same issue announced various activities of the Kulturbund, which had resumed operations on September 24, though without any mention that (and when) the ban on it had been lifted.

> The authorities go so far as to force the editor to accept certain sentences or even entire articles – all these are aimed at demonstrating that Jews no longer placed any hopes in England, that England had never done a thing for the Jews and would, given the new world order, never be able to do anything. This is intended to awaken the impression that German Jewry, along with so many other small nations that were asking Hitler to solve their problems . . . was likewise on its knees, beseeching Hitler to remedy their specific situation as part of Europe's new order.[25]

Almost every headline now on page one was identical: "New Ordinances." The editorials, still signed by L.I.K. (Leo Kreindler), continued to appear: "The Jewish Kulturbund –

Yesterday and Now," one of the first editorials after the outbreak of the war, "Prospects in Argentina," "Jewish Winter Relief Begins," "Results of the Statistical Survey," "The Jewish Gemeinde," and "How to Retrain." The number for November 24, 1939 contained a half-page article on "Jewish Cabaret Theater – Life's Jesting and Serious Side."

The paper could not be obtained outside Germany. Many Jews from Germany in Palestine had tried to order it, but in vain. Finally a copy managed to make its way there and gave rise to the following commentary in the Tel Aviv-based *MB* newsletter:

> Approximately one third of the paper is devoted to the Jewish Kulturbund. That is the saddest and most frightening part of the whole publication. The headline alone is quite revealing in this regard: "Intensified Activity in the Kulturbund." At a time when most Jews do not even know what they are going to have to eat the next day and no one has a proper income of any kind, the impression is being created that Jews have recently developed a special interest in the theater. . . . It is quite likely that a large proportion of Kulturbund members are in no position to attend the performances – even if one might assume that these tormented and harried individuals would certainly like to do so.[26]

The first issue for the year 1940 (price 15 pfennig) also carried an article on the Kulturbund, "Word and Sound," announcement of a film starring Zarah Leander, "Song of the Desert," and artistic performances in Hamburg and Breslau. A report from Shanghai and a lesson in Spanish (instead of English) completed the main section. The advertising section included the following headings: education and instruction, hotels and guest houses, marriage and death notices, rooms for rent and apartment wanted notices, employment wanted ads, ads for Jewish health services (doctors), dental practitioners and legal counsels (lawyers).[27] The first page of the issue for January 6, 1940 was dedicated to the memory of Franz Rosenzweig; the May 31st issue featured an article "Wanderer, Where To?" Further first-page articles in 1940 included "Prospects in Bolivia," "The Florida Peninsula," "Hints for Emigrants," "As an ICA Settler in Argentina, "Life in Brazil," "Facts from Chile" and "Life in the USA."

The *Jüdisches Nachrichtenblatt* had been approved as a channel for publication of the decrees on Jews issued by the various authorities. However, one can search its pages in vain for the ordinances that pulled the veritable noose around Jewish life:

decrees that terrorized Jews, drove them from their homes, left them without sufficient food rations, commanded them to forced labor under humiliating conditions, isolated and degraded them – and finally deported them to the East.

There continued to be detailed reporting on the activities of the Kulturbund. Yet one announcement is absent: its banning on September 11, 1941, an act based on a law issued by Hindenburg on February 28, 1933 "in the interest of protecting the state and the people." The property of the Kulturbund was confiscated and its staff arrested.[28] On the eve of its prohibition, the long-standing "patron" of the Kulturbund, Hans Hinkel, threw a party in the Hall of Friendship of the German Artists to mark his 20th anniversary as a member of the NSDAP. The invitation stated: "Food will be served without ration coupons at about 7 p.m." This closing down of the Kulturbund was simultaneous with the new police ordinance introducing a distinctive badge for Jews, namely the Jewish star, to be affixed "approx. over the region of the heart on the left side of the chest, sewn to the outermost garment."[29] The *Jüdisches Nachrichtenblatt* and the book sales section were transformed into a division of the Reichsvereinigung der Juden in Deutschland.[30]

In 1942, the *Nachrichtenblatt* was published only once a week; its offices were no longer on Meinekestraße, but in the building of the Jewish Gemeinde on Oranienburgerstraße. A subscription cost 76 pfennig a month, 2.28 reichsmarks for a quarter-year. The paper contained few articles now – only announcements, ordinances and excerpts from traditional Jewish Midrashic literature, along with assorted advertisements. In all issues from July 3 to November 6, the main headline stereotypically read "New Ordinances," with sub-captions like "Distribution of Food in Berlin" or "Handing In of Bicycles, Typewriters and Optical Instruments."

On June 12, Leo Baeck published an appeal for the fund drive "Jüdische Pflicht" [Jewish Duty]: "Today, more than ever before, Jewish community means one thing: a community of those who help. Help given with one's whole heart, soul and might is a Jewish duty." Another series of articles began in September 1942, this time on Jewish archaeology.

The issue for November 27, 1942 (the last one available to the author) contains an announcement by the Reichsvereinigung on a statistical census of all Jews in Berlin, information on the relocation of offices for ration cards, a schedule of times for turning out all lights and an article on the question "Can Charcoal be Stored out on Balconies?" An appeal by Winter Relief urges: "Give again and again – be happy to give! Door-to-door collection on November 29. Your contribution also helps." A serialized legend from Yiddish appears for the first time (author not given). Thoughts from the Midrash are scattered through the editorial sections of the paper: "Wisdom which shuts itself off is like a myrtle in the desert that brings delight to none"; "Small students sharpen the wit of adult students in the same way as thin pieces of wood aid thicker ones in starting a good fire"; "Pride is a mask for one's own mistakes." In the announcement section, there are notices of engagements, expressions of gratitude for good wishes on the occasion of marriage, wedding and death notices, job wanted ads, apartments for rent and apartments wanted, and notices about health care and legal services. The issue also contains an ad from a publisher on various books in their current list: A. Abeles, *Das Buch für das jüdische Kind* [Book for the Jewish Child], Frieda Mehler, *Feiertagsmärchen* [Traditional Tales for Holidays], L. Wagner-Tauber, *Jüdische Märchen und Sagen* [Jewish Folktales and Legends], L. Perez, *Chassidische Erzählungen* [Chassidic Tales], Franz Rosenzweig, *Stern der Erlösung* [The Star of Redemption], and *Die Heilige Schrift* [The Holy Scriptures], edited by Harry Torczyner.

"In the autumn of 1942, when the Gestapo went about 'sifting out' the staff of the Berlin Gemeinde, the employees of the welfare division headed by Leo Kreindler were also summoned to appear before the notorious Gestapo officer Günther. For Leo Kreindler, the excitement of the previous weeks and months proved too much, and he was stricken with a heart attack. It was fatal. On December 2, he was laid to rest in the Jewish cemetery in Berlin-Weißensee. His grave in the row of honor at the cemetery bears the number 110221."[31] It is probable that the November 27 issue cited above was the last one that he edited. Hans Hirschfeld succeeded him as editor.

The last issue in Vienna available in the archives is dated December 3, 1942 and lists the address Seitenstättengasse 4. Like its counterpart in Berlin, the paper at that time had two pages and was published on a weekly basis. There were virtually no individual death notices; instead, there was a general announcement: "In the period from November 20 to November 30, the following burials were carried out at the central cemetery by the Jewish Kultusgemeinde of Vienna," along with a list of the names of the deceased. Most of the content consists of ordinances regarding food coupons, use of public transportation, news from the Gemeinde and a few passages from Jewish literature. There are only a few scattered want ads.

Letters written by a former employee on the staff of the Jewish *Gemeindeblatt* in Berlin, who was hired on in early 1939 by the *Jüdisches Nachrichtenblatt*, gave a picture of developments during that period: "November 12, 1940: we're living in the premises of the former *Jüdische Rundschau* . . . there are about 40 persons working in our office. July 2, 1941: Our little paper is only coming out now once a week, with four pages. Despite that, I still haven't been laid off." On November 30, 1941, he hinted that his job with the paper was serving to protect him from being deported. "December 9, 1942: I'm still working at the paper. 'Paper' may be somewhat exaggerated . . . it consists of 1/4 page of text and 3/4 of a page of ads, mainly for rooms, plus some death notices.[32] It's a miracle though that I'm still here, if you consider how many have been laid off in recent years. If I didn't have the job, I'd probably no longer be in Berlin."

On February 7, 1943, he wrote: "As I mentioned to you over the phone, I'm no longer with the paper. The middle of December, our paper was forbidden to publish ads and announcements, and at the same time the Gestapo decided that I should be 'let go' (i.e., deportation to the East)." After this date, nothing more was heard from him.[33]

The so-called "yellow certificate" [*Gelber Schein*] was distributed to employees of the Gemeinde and the Reichsvereinigung; though it did not grant lasting protection, it did serve as a means to postpone deportation. This certificate contained the following data: employee's name, names of family members living together with him, and the age and place of work of all persons listed. The chairman of the Gemeinde, Moritz (Israel) Henschel – who was also simultaneously a member of the board of the Reichsvereinigung – vouched for the correctness of the data. This "yellow certificate" had to be affixed in a visible spot in one's place of residence. Those who occupied furnished rooms were supposed to put it up on the door. "A few skeptics carried the 'yellow certificate' around with them in their pocket, and the future showed that this thinking hadn't been wrong."[34]

On June 1, 1943, the *Jüdisches Nachrichtenblatt* was closed down. "The idea to continue on with it at least in the form of a paper reporting on ordinances for the Jews still living in Berlin was thwarted by Dr. Lustig, who was in charge of managing the liquidation of the assets of the Reichsvereinigung."[35]

Shortly before his death in 1964, Hans Reichmann, cofounder of the Leo Baeck Institute, wrote:

> On August 17, 1938, Jews were compelled to take the first names of Israel and Sara; these were meant to mark them in a visible manner and, at the same time, to hold them up to ridicule. The following September 1, the *CV-Zeitung*, organ of the Central Association of German Citizens of the Jewish Faith (called at that time Jewish Central Association), printed a terse response, explaining the origin of the names "Sara" and "Israel" without any further commentary: " . . . Thy name shall be called no more Jacob but Israel (He who striveth with God); for thou hast striven with God and with men, and hast prevailed victorious." However, victory was not granted to German Jewry in its strife.[36]

# Notes

1. *Jüdische Rundschau*, March 25, 1938.
2. *Der Schild*, April 8, 1938. On "exceptions" for former combat veterans, see Barkai, 1989, p. 26.
3. *Israelitisches Familienblatt*, March 17, 1938
4. *CV-Zeitung*, March 17, 1938.
5. E.G. Lowenthal, *Allgemeine Wochenzeitung der Juden in Deutschland*, October 30, 1953.
6. Kochan, 1957, pp. 50f; see also Pehle, 1991, pp. 8, 76.
7. E.G. Lowenthal, op. cit.
8. Erich Cohn, Yad Vashem Archives, doc. 02/546, November 22, 1938.
9. "The Nazis, for their own purposes, maintained several Jewish weeklies. The 'Gazeta Zydowska' in Cracow, the 'Informations Juives' in Paris, the 'Jüdisches Nachrichtenblatt-Zidowska Listy' in Prague ... and the 'Joodsche Weekblad' in Amsterdam were such papers," Fraenkel, 1967, p. 14.
10. Hanna Marcus, Archives, Yad Vashem, doc. 01/26, July 16, 1947. Mrs. Marcus was employed until November 1938 in the management of the *Jüdische Rundschau* and the offices at Meinekestraße 10.
11. Erich Liepmann, Archives, Yad Vashem, doc. 01/135.
12. Kurt Löwenstein, Archives, Yad Vashem, doc. 01/133.
13. National Library, Jerusalem.
14. Hanna Marcus, loc. cit. See also Oschilewski, 1975, p. 210: "General Director of the NS [National Socialist] publishing house Eher-Verlag, Max Amann ... whose income of 108,000 reichsmarks in 1934, as reported to the tax

authorities, rose to 3.2 million reichsmarks in 1942 through extortion, intimidation, harassment and purchases of property far below market value."

15. Erich Liepmann, loc. cit.

16. Ibid.

17. Ibid.

18. Hanna Marcus, loc. cit.

19. Ibid.

20. Dr. Gerhard Lock was one of the experts on Hebrew at the ministry. He controlled the language and knew the literature.

21. Hanna Marcus, loc. cit. According to information given by Max Plaut, "Die Juden in Deutschland von 1934–1941" (Archives, Yad Vashem, doc. 01/53, 1945), Dr. Brasch died of serious injuries inflicted on him while an inmate in the concentration camp Oranienburg-Sachsenhausen, "only because he was the director of the Kulturbünde." See also Freeden, 1964, p. 165. The volume *Juden unterm Hakenkreuz*, Frankfurt/Main 1973 follows the version of Hanna Marcus, including the incorrect spelling "Basch" instead of "Brasch" in her shorthand notes (p. 233f.). Mrs. Marcus emigrated on October 16, 1939.

22. Max Nussbaum, Archives, Yad Vashem, memorandum, doc. II, 01/232; written in August 1940 for Stephen Wise.

23. *Jüdisches Nachrichtenblatt*, September 5, 1939.

24. Max Nussbaum, loc. cit., doc. III.

25. Ibid., doc. I.

26. *Mitteilungsblatt der Hitachduth Olej Germania*, Tel Aviv, Nr. 6 (1938).

27. Under the Fourth and Fifth Ordinances of the Reich Citizenship Law, promulgated in July and September 1938, the licenses of all Jewish doctors, dentists and lawyers were rescinded. The interior minister was authorized to grant special permission for such professionals to deal with Jewish clientele exclusively, but they had to use the professional title of *Krankenbehandler* ("practitioner for the sick"), *Zahnbehandler* ("dental practitioner") and *Rechtskonsulent* ("counsel for legal advice"). See Walk, 1981, II, 510, 547 and Barkai, op. cit., pp. 121f., 171.

28. Freeden, 1964, p. 163.

29. *Jüdisches Nachrichtenblatt*, October 24, 1941.

30. Freeden, 1964, p. 164.

31. Lowenthal, 1957, p. 107.

32. From August 1–6, 1942: 44 deaths.

33. Hermann Samter, Wiener Library London, Archives, Yad Vashem, doc. 02/30.

34. Hildegard Henschel, Archives, Yad Vashem, doc. 01/52, 1947.

35. Else Harnack, Archives, Yad Vashem, doc. 01/58. On the disbanding of the Reichsvereinigung in 1943, see Barkai, op. cit., pp. 184f.

36. E.G. Lowenthal, *Bewährung im Untergang*, Dusseldorf, 1957, p. 8. The biblical reference is to Genesis 32:29.

# Appendices

# Glossary

AGUDAT YISROEL  World Jewish movement and political party of Orthodox Jews, founded in Poland in 1912; also known as Agudas Yisroel, Agudas Jisroel or simply the Aguda.

ALTREICH  The German Reich in its 1937 borders. A term often used after the annexation of Austria in 1938.

C.V.  Centralverein deutscher Staatsbürger jüdischen Glaubens (Central Association of German Citizens of the Jewish Faith). Large assimilationist organization; its official organ was the *CV-Zeitung*.

DEUTSCHNATIONAL  German-National, associated with the conservative, right-wing Deutschnationale Volkspartei.

DEUTSCHTUM  "Germanism," German national culture and traditions, a key conservative/nationalist/chauvinist term and value complex (cf. also Volkstum).

DNB  Deutsches Nachrichtenbüro (German News Agency). Principal German press service in Nazi Germany.

ERETZ YISRAEL  The Land of Israel, the traditional Jewish name for the Holy Land or Palestine.

EVIAN CONFERENCE  An international conference on the refugee problem which initially met in January 1938 at Evian on Lake Geneva. Attended by delegates from 31 countries, it established an Intergovernmental Committee on Refugees.

GEMEINDE  Autonomous, incorporated Jewish local community, to which every Jew who did not officially declare his withdrawal automatically belonged and paid taxes (*Gemeindesteuer*). Related variants are the terms *Kultusgemeinde, Synagogengemeinde,* or *Religionsgemeinde.*

HA-SHOMER HA-TZAIR  A pioneering, left-wing, Labor Zionist movement.

JTA  Jüdische Telegraphen-Agentur (Jewish News Service). The major international Jewish wire service in the 1930s.

JUDENPRESSE  A derogatory term used by anti-Semites to refer to German newspapers supposedly dominated and controlled by Jews. A related anti-Semitic epithet was the expression "Judenblatt" for an individual paper.

JÜDISCHER FRAUENBUND  Jewish Women's League, cofounded by Bertha Pappenheim in 1904.

JÜDISCHER KULTURBUND  Jewish Cultural League, established in March

1933 in various cities, and active until September 11, 1941 [plural: Kulturbünde]. They were associated nationally in a Reichsverband der Jüdischen Kulturbünde (Reich Federation of Jewish Cultural Leagues).

JÜDISCHE WINTERHILFE (Jewish Winter Relief Fund). A special fund set up to aid needy Jews during the winter months.

LANDSMANNSCHAFT Cultural and welfare association for Jews stemming from a particular area in Europe.

MIDRASH A category of Jewish post-Biblical homiletic and wisdom literature, replete with legends, stories and sayings.

MIZRAHI Religious Zionist movement, founded in 1902 as a religious faction in the Zionist Organization. Also spelled Mizrachi.

NSDAP Nationalsozialistische Deutsche Arbeiterpartei (National Socialist German Workers' Party). The full official name of the Nazi party from its founding in 1919.

REICHSVEREINIGUNG Reichsvereinigung der Juden in Deutschland (Reich Association of Jews in Germany). Compulsory organization of all "Jews by race" (*Rassejuden*), established in February 1939 as successor to the Reichsvertretung (q.v.) and supervised by the Gestapo. It was disbanded by the authorities in June 1943.

REICHSVERTRETUNG Reichsvertretung der Juden in Deutschland (Reich Representation of German Jews). Organization officially representing all Jews in Germany, established in the autumn of 1933.

RGBl Reichsgesetzblatt (Reich Legal Gazette). It contained the official text of all decrees and ordinances.

RJF Reichsbund jüdischer Frontsoldaten (National League of Jewish Combat Veterans). Conservative organization of Jewish veterans from World War I; its paper was *Der Schild.*

VÖLKISCH Folk-oriented, conservative-nationalistic, with especial emphasis on elements of race. The adjective was also used on occasion in the Jewish press in reference to Jewish national life.

VOLKSGEMEINSCHAFT Organic folk community, a Nazi and right-wing racial term for the "nation," from which Jews were excluded by definition.

VOLKSGENOSSE Member of the German Volk, a Nazi racial term for "citizen."

VOLKSTUM Ethnic national folk culture and mores, a key term among conservative nationalists and in National Socialist ideology. It was also sometimes used in the Jewish press in reference to Jewish national-ethnic culture.

YAD VASHEM Israel official authority for commemorating the Holocaust in the Nazi era and Jewish resistance at that time.

ZVfD Zionistische Vereinigung für Deutschland (German Zionist Association). The major Zionist organization in Germany; its paper was the *Jüdische Rundschau*.

## A Note on the Names of Jewish Periodicals in Germany

The most commonly encountered term is Blatt ("sheet," "paper," plural Blätter), often in a compound: Gemeindeblatt, Familienblatt, Informationsblatt, Mitteilungsblatt, Monatsblätter (monthly), and Nachrichtenblatt (newsletter). Second in frequency is Zeitung, the general word for newspaper, also found in compounds such as Gemeindezeitung, Wochenzeitung (weekly) and CV-Zeitung. Mitteilung (announcement, news, plural Mitteilungen) is occasionally used, especially for a newsletter. The name Rundschau (review) was most closely associated with the large-circulation Zionist paper *Jüdische Rundschau* published in Berlin. Zeitschrift is the general term for "journal."

A standard official preferred adjective of self-reference among German Jews – especially in the sense of "religious affiliation" – was "israelitisch" instead of "jüdisch," primarily in combination with Gemeinde ("Jewish [religious] community"), and popular in the names of Gemeinde papers established during the Weimar Republic, as well as in several general (*Israelitisches Familienblatt*) and religious papers (*Deutsche Israelitische Zeitung*) founded in the nineteenth century. Unlike the similar adjective and substantive in English, the German "israelitisch/Israelit" can be used to denote both the ancient Israelites and modern Jewry. The use of the noun was rare and more "old-fashioned"; one example among papers was the *Verordnungsblatt des Oberrats badischer Israeliten* (Official Bulletin of the Regional Council of Jews in Baden), founded in 1884 and published in Karlsruhe. The long-established (1860) weekly of Independent Orthodoxy bore the title *Der Israelit*. Adjectival use was more common, though generally restricted to the formal name of the Gemeinde.

# Official Ordinances

## Import and Sale of Foreign Jewish Papers

August 16, 1933: Prohibition on import and sale of foreign Jewish papers – Joseph Walk (ed.), *Das Sonderrecht für die Juden im NS-Staat*, Karlsruhe 1981.

## Law on Editors

On October 4, 1933, the Reich government issued a law (RGBl I, p. 713) classifying the profession of editor as an activity with public responsibilities. In the sense of this law, an editor is defined as a person who, as his main profession or on the basis of appointment as chief editor, is actively engaged, via the medium of word, news report and photography, in shaping the intellectual content of newpapers and political periodicals published in the territory of the Reich.

Active engagement in shaping the intellectual content of German papers is likewise present in cases where this activity does not take place in the production offices of the paper, but rather in an enterprise whose task is to provide papers with a serious content (words, news reports, photos) (para. 4). No one may designate himself as editor who is not entitled to do so in accordance with the provisions of this law.

Formal admission to the profession of editor is effective concomitant with registration in the professional list of editors (para. 8). That registration is subject to certain preconditions. Thus, only those persons can be editors who are German citizens, and have not forfeited their civil rights or their eligibility to occupy public office; they must be of Aryan origin and must not be married to a person of non-Aryan extraction; they must be at least 21 years of age, legally competent and with relevant expertise; they must possess the qualities requisite for exercising an intellectual influence on the public (para. 5). The director of the Reich Federation of the German Press, with the permission of the Minister for Popular Enlightenment and Propaganda, is empowered to grant exceptions in respect to the preconditions of German citizenship, Aryan descent and Aryan marriage, as well as the prerequisite of expertise. The granting of an exception may be limited to specific branches of the activity of an editor (para. 9).

Editors are legally organized in the Reich Federation of the German Press. By virtue of this law, the Reich Federation is regarded as a body of public law (para. 23).

The Reich Minister for Popular Enlightenment and Propaganda shall determine the date when this law becomes valid.

(*Informationsblätter des Zentralausschusses der deutschenJuden für Hilfe und Aufbau*, No. 13, October 20, 1933)

## Editors

The date of December 15, 1933, by which applications for admission to the various chambers of the cultural professions must be submitted, is not binding in the case of editors, for whom it is likely that a special regulation will be issued, since inclusion in the Reich Chamber of the Press cannot occur until the Law on Editors takes effect; a date for that has not as yet been set. In addition, special conditions arise in connection with editors due to the fact that the Law on Editors contains a paragraph on Aryan race, while the Law on the Reich Chamber of Culture does not include any restrictions pertaining to non-Aryans. Details about the final legal registration for the profession of editor can only be announced after issuance of regulations for implementation and the transition period.

(*Informationsblätter des Zentralausschusses*, no. 1, December 8, 1933)

## Editors

The Law on Editors of October 4, 1933 (RGBl I, p. 713) became valid law on January 1, 1934 in accordance with the regulation on implementation of December 19, 1933 (RGBl I, p. 1085).

The implementation regulation contains the specific regulations on implementing the paragraph on Aryan race which is, as is known, a part of the Law on Editors (para. 5, sec. 3 of the law). In accordance with para. 16 of the implementation ordinance, the following persons may be exempted from the requirement of Aryan descent:

1. Persons who fought at the front in the service of the German Reich or its allies during the World War, or whose fathers or sons were killed in battle during that war. The regulations of the implementation ordinance on the Law for the Reestablishment of the Professional Civil Service shall be correspondingly applied.

2. Persons wishing to practice the profession of editor on the staff of a Jewish paper; such individuals will be exempted, however, with restriction to their activity on the staff of such papers only.

In accordance with the ordinance on implementation, directors of the state associations of the Reich Federation of the German Press shall approve applications for an exemption from the requirement of Aryan descent only in special cases, and only for special branches of the activity of an editor.

(*Informationsblätter des Zentralausschusses*, no. 2, January 12, 1934)

## Editors

*Registration in the Professional List*

January 31, 1934 marked the deadline for registration in the professional list of editors as set by the Reich Federation of the German Press. While up until that date, registrations until otherwise determined were admissable . . . registration in the professional list can, effective from February 1, 1934, only take place in strict compliance with the regulations of the Law on Editors.

## Appeal Boards of the Press

The Law on Editors of October 4, 1933 (RGBl I, p. 713) provides for the creation of special professional appeal boards for the protection of the profession of editor (para. 27 of the law). . . . Professional appeal boards can be convened within a period of four weeks if the director of a state federation rejects the registration of an applicant for the professional list of editors, or has ordered the removal of a name from the list (para. 10, 11 of the law).

## Exceptions to the Law on Editors

In connection with the implementation ordinance on the Law on Editors of December 19, 1933 (RGBl I, p. 1085), the Reich Ministry for Popular Enlightenment and Propaganda has determined that the following shall be exempted from application of the Law on Editors: federation announcements limited to short communications of a practical nature in fulfillment of federation functions, sent solely to the members of the federation, appearing only when necessary at irregular intervals, containing no notices other than family notices and association announcements, and with no indication of price when included in the postal listing of papers.

For persons on the staff of such periodicals, there is therefore no obligation to register in accordance with regulations of the Law on Editors.
(*Informationsblätter des Zentralausschusses*, no. 2, February 9, 1934)

## Prohibition on Establishment of New Papers

By order of the president of the Reich Chamber of the Press, dated August 6, 1934, the ban on establishment of new papers and periodicals in effect since December 13, 1933 has been extended until March 31, 1935. The following actions are viewed as equivalent to the establishment of a new periodical: the expansion of the content of a periodical (however, it is not considered an expansion if a small number of pages are added in an issue for dealing with the same content material), an increase in the regular frequency of publication of a periodical, the extension to new districts of a periodical limited to certain districts, a change in the title of a periodical, and the renewed publication of a periodical that had ceased publication. Measures of the type mentioned are thus permissible only if the president of the Reich Chamber of the Press has approved an exception in an individual specific case.
(*Informationsblätter des Zentralausschusses*, no. 7/8, November 16, 1934)

## Restructuring of the Jewish Press

The Reich Minister for Popular Enlightenment and Propaganda, in an order dated July 15, 1937, has stipulated fundamental guidelines for the Jewish press.

All persons and enterprises of the Jewish press within the territory of the German Reich have been placed under the jurisdiction of the special officer of the minister, Reich Superintendent of Culture Hinkel. Those persons employed in the publishing houses and firms of the Jewish press, such as publishers, editors, staff writers, reporters, publishing house staff, circulation personnel, press officers and employees of press offices in Jewish organizations, associations and Gemeinden, shall be registered in official lists, and will receive approval of their admission in the form of a certificate or identification card.

After October 1, 1937, persons without such a certificate or identification card can no longer be employed in the Jewish press. Applications for registration in the official lists and all other applications relating to matters of the Jewish press should be submitted without exception to the Reich Ministry for Popular Enlightenment and Propaganda, Special Section Superintendent of Culture Hinkel, Wilhelmplatz 8/9, Berlin W 8. (*Informationsblätter der Reichsvertretung der Juden in Deutschland*, vol. 5, June–July 1937, No. 6/7)

## Registration in the Jewish Press

The Reich Minister for Popular Enlightenment and Propaganda has forwarded the following notice to the press section of the Reichsvertretung der Juden in Deutschland, to be passed on the the Jewish press:

"The Reich Minister for Popular Enlightenment and Propaganda hereby announces that due to the numerous applications for registration as editors or staff members in the Jewish press, it will require additional time to process the applications submitted. For that reason, the period for issuance of identification cards and certificates shall extend until January 1, 1938. Until that final date, all applicants can continue to be employed in the Jewish press without any special document of registration."

(*Informationsblätter der Reichsvertretung*, vol. 5, June–July 1937, no. 6/7)

## Provision of Periodicals by Associations

With effect from April 1, 1938, in accordance with an announcement by the president of the Reich Chamber of the Press, organizations and other associations are no longer permitted to engage in the provision of periodicals. The Reich Commissar for Pricing Policy has dealt with questions arising from this in connection with the ordinance on freezing of prices in circular no. 31/38, dated March 25, 1938. In this circular, the

183

Reich Commissar for Pricing Policy points out the following in particular: to the extent that organizations, etc. have previously made it compulsory for their members to subscribe to a periodical, and the price of that periodical has been included in the membership dues, those dues must now be correspondingly reduced in consideration of the elimination of provision of the periodical. The circular contains detailed regulations regarding the magnitude of the reduction. The organizations affected are required to inform the price surveillance office responsible for their district of the reduction in membership dues by May 15, 1938.

(*Informationsblätter der Reichsvertretung*, vol. 6, May–June 1938, no. 5/6)

## Prohibition on the Provision of Newpapers, Periodicals and Law Gazettes to Jews by Publishers and Dealers

July 10, 1942: The prohibition on provision of papers, etc. to Jews dated February 17, 1942 affects all those persons who are required to wear the Jewish star and, in cases of mixed marriages, the non-Jewish spouse as well. Exceptions are possible only in the case of individuals whose mixed marriage is classified as privileged.

(Joseph Walk, op. cit., p. 389)

# Sources

## Newspapers and Periodicals

Jüdische Rundschau, Berlin
CV-Zeitung, Berlin
Israelitisches Familienblatt, Hamburg-Berlin
Der Schild, Berlin
Jüdische Zeitung, Breslau
Der Staatszionist, Berlin
Der Vortrupp, Frankfurt/Main
Der Nationaldeutsche Jude, Berlin
Jüdisches Nachrichtenblatt, Berlin
Der Israelit, Frankfurt/Main
Die Laubhütte, Hamburg
Jüdisch-Liberale Zeitung, Berlin
Jüdische Allgemeine Zeitung, Berlin
Zion, Berlin
Nachlat Z'wi, Frankfurt/Main

Der Morgen, Berlin
Monatsblätter des Jüdischen Kulturbundes, Berlin
Monatsblätter des Jüdischen Kulturbundes, Hamburg
Mitteilungen des Reichsverbandes der Jüdischen Kulturbünde, Berlin
Blätter des Jüdischen Frauenbundes, Berlin

Berliner Jüdisches Gemeindeblatt
Bayerische Israelitische Gemeindezeitung, Munich
Frankfurter Israelitisches Gemeindeblatt
Breslauer Jüdisches Gemeindeblatt
Kölner Jüdisches Gemeindeblatt

Allgemeine Wochenzeitung der Juden in Deutschland, Düsseldorf-
  Bonn
MB, Mitteilungsblatt des Irgun Olej Merkas Europa, Tel Aviv
Israel Nachrichten, Tel Aviv

Sulamith, Dessau
Der Orient, Leipzig
Der Jude, Altona
Allgemeine Zeitung des Judenthums, Leipzig-Berlin
Die Menorah, Hamburg

## Archives

Leo Baeck Institute, Jerusalem
Central Zionist Archives, Jerusalem
National Library, Jerusalem
Yad Vashem, Jerusalem
Central Archives for the History of the Jewish People, Jerusalem
Wiener Library, London (now Tel Aviv University)
Zeitungs-Archiv, Aachen

Private archive, Robert Weltsch
Private archive, Max Bodenheimer
Private archive, Alfred Klee
Private archive, Schalom Ben Chorin

# Bibliography

Arbrecht, R., W. Brandt and R. Giordano (eds.). *Widerstand und Exil 1933–1945*. Bonn, 1985.

Asaria, Zvi. *Die Juden in Köln*. Cologne, 1959.

Ball-Kadouri, Hugo. *Das Leben der Juden in Deutschland 1933*. Frankfurt/Main, 1963.

Barkai, Avraham. *From Boycott to Annihilation. The Economic Struggle of German Jews 1933–1943*. Hanover, N.H., 1989.

Bodenheimer, Max. "Die jüdische Presse." In *Presse. Kulturschau am Rhein*. Berlin, 1928.

Bodenheimer, Max. *So wurde Israel*. Cologne, 1958.

Boehm, Max Hildeberg. *Das eigenständige Volk*. Göttingen, 1932.

Dahm, Volker. *Das jüdische Buch im Dritten Reich*. 2 Vols. Frankfurt/Main, 1979, 1982.

Davidowicz, Lucy. *The War against the Jews 1933–1945*. Harmondsworth, 1977.

Dovifat, Emil. "Neue Aufgaben der deutschen Publizistik." In Karl-Dietrich Abel (ed.), *Presselenkung im NS-Staat*. Berlin, 1968.

Dunker, Ulrich. *Reichsbund jüdischer Frontsoldaten 1919–1938*. Düsseldorf, 1977.

Focka, Harald and Uwe Reimer. *Alltag der Entrechteten*. Hamburg, 1980.

Fraenkel, Josef. *The Jewish Press of the World*. London, 1967.

Freeden, Herbert. *Vom geistigen Widerstand der deutschen Juden*. Jerusalem, 1963.

Freeden, Herbert. *Jüdisches Theater in Nazideutschland*. Tübingen, 1964.

Gärtner, Marcel W., Hans Lamm and E.G. Lowenthal (eds.). *Vom Schicksal geprägt*. Düsseldorf, 1957.

Hale, Oron J. *The Captive Press in the Third Reich*. Princeton, New Jersey, 1964.

Hegemann, Walter. *Publizistik im Dritten Reich*. Hamburg, 1948.

Hinkel, Hans. *Einer unter Hunderttausend*. Munich, 1938.

Hinkel, Hans (ed.). *Handbuch der Reichskulturkammer*. Berlin, 1937.

Huber, Walter. *Theater im Exil*. (Schriftenreihe der Akademie der Künste, 12). Berlin, 1979.

*Jüdische Presse im 19. Jahrhundert*. Zeitungsmuseum Achen, 1967.

Katz, Jacob (ed.). *Toward Modernity. The European Jewish Model*. New Brunswick, 1986.

*In den Katakomben*. Ed. I. Belte, Marbach, 1983.

# Bibliography

Kochan, Lionel. *Pogrom*. London, 1957.

Lamm, Hans. *Von Juden in München*. Munich, 1958.

Leo Baeck Institute. *Yearbook Leo Baeck Institute*. Vols. 1 (1956), 5 (1960), 10 (1965), 17 (1972), 18 (1973), 25 (1980), 27 (1982).

Lowenthal, E.G. *Bewährung im Untergang*. Düsseldorf, 1957.

Lowenthal, E.G., (ed.). *Philo-Lexikon*.

*Monumenta Judaica. 2000 Years of History and Culture of the Jews in Rhineland*. Ed. Konrad Schilling for the City of Cologne. Cologne, 1963.

Oschilewski, Walther J. *Zeitungen in Berlin*. Berlin, 1975.

Paucker, Arnold (ed.). *Die Juden im Nationalsozialistischen Deutschland 1933–1943*. Tübingen, 1986.

Pechel, Rudolf. *Zwischen den Zeilen*. Weisenheid, 1948

Pehle, Walter H. (ed.). *November 1938: From "Reichskristallnacht" to Genocide*. Translated by W. Templer. Oxford, 1991.

Philippson, Phöbus. *Biographische Notizen*. Leipzig, 1864.

Sänger, Fritz. *Politik der Täuschungen*. Vienna, 1975.

Schmidt, Hans-Dieter, Gerhard Schneider and Wilhelm Sommer (eds.). *Juden unterm Hakenkreuz*. Frankfurt/Main, 1973.

Shirer, William. *The Rise and Fall of the Third Reich*. Greenwich, Conn., 1968.

Simon, Ernst. *Aufbau im Untergang*. Tübingen, 1959.

Strauss, Leo. *Persecution and the Art of Writing*. Glencoe, 1952.

Tramer, Hans (ed.). *In zwei Welten*. Tel Aviv, 1962.

Tramer, H. and K. Löwenstein. *Robert Weltsch zum 70. Geburtstag, von seinen Freunden*. Tel Aviv, 1961.

Walk, Joseph. *Das Sonderrecht für die Juden im NS-Staat*. Karlsruhe, 1981.

Walk, Joseph (ed.). *Als Jude in Breslau*. Gerlingen, 1985.

Weltsch, Robert (ed.). *Deutsches Judentum, Aufstieg und Krise*. Stuttgart, 1963.

Weltman, Lutz. *Pult und Bühne*. Berlin, 1937.

Wolff, Theodor. *Der Marsch durch zwei Jahrzehnte*. Amsterdam, 1936.

World Federation of Jewish Journalists (ed.). *The Jewish Press that Was*. Tel Aviv, 1980.

Wulf, Joseph. *Presse und Funk im Dritten Reich*. Gütersloh, 1964.

Zeller, B. (ed.). *Klassiker in finsteren Zeiten 1933–1934, Marbacher Kataloge 38*. Marbach, 1983.

*Zionism*. (Compiled from *Enclyclopaedia Judaica*), Keter Publishing House, Jerusalem, 1973.

# Index